普华永道

普华永道国际财务报告准则实务指引系列（第十二册）
PricewaterhouseCoopers IFRS MOA Series (Volume Twelve)

Manual of Accounting — IFRS 2013

Chapter 14 – Earnings per share

国际财务报告准则实务指引

第十四章——每股收益

中英文对照

U0823491

翻译组主要成员：沈　洁　黄翠燕　梁少宝　阮慧瑶　符文娟
马　骏　王　洁　徐　娟

中国财政经济出版社

This book has been prepared for general guidance on matters of interest only, and does not constitute professional advice. You should not act upon the information contained in this book without obtaining specific professional advice. No representation or warranty (express or implied) is given as to the accuracy or completeness of the information contained in this book, and, to the extent permitted by law, PricewaterhouseCoopers does not accept or assume any liability, responsibility or duty of care for any consequences of you or anyone else acting, or refraining to act, in reliance on the information contained in this book or for any decision based on it.

This book covers one of the chapters of the English version and its Chinese translation, which the English version remains the definitive source of guidance. The publishers and the authors cannot accept any responsibility for any errors or misunderstandings arising from the English version and its Chinese translation. Neither can the publishers and the authors accept any responsibility for loss occasioned to any person acting or refraining from action as a result of the material in this book.

编写本书之目的是对感兴趣的事项给予一般性的指导，而非提供专业建议。未征得具体专业意见之前，不应依据本书所述内容采取任何行动。我们不对书中所述信息是否准确或完整作出任何明示或暗示的承诺或保证。除非法律另有明文规定，普华永道不对任何个人或单位因为阅读了本书而采取或未采取某项行动的后果、或基于本书所作出的任何决定承担任何责任。

本书内容为英文本中的一个章节及其中文译文，指导概以英文为准。出版社和编译者不对英文原文及中文译文的偏差或误解承担任何责任，也不对任何个人或单位因为阅读了本书而采取或未采取某项行动所发生损失承担任何责任。

Preface

Recent years have seen major changes in financial reporting worldwide with the single most important change being convergence around IFRS. There has also been a keen focus to improve the long term development of the CPA profession within China. As the Ministry of Finance and other regulatory bodies continue to promulgate legislation to promote the development of the Chinese CPA profession, we hope the release of our IFRS Manual of Accounting with Chinese Translation will also contribute to this effort.

The Ministry of Finance issued the Accounting Standards for Business Enterprises (hereafter referred to as "China Accounting Standards" or "CAS") in 2006. CAS incorporates all of the principles of IFRS and there has been a continued focus on convergence over the last few years. Additionally, IFRS is becoming increasingly important for many companies in China, including domestic companies seeking to raise capital overseas, as well as for foreign companies that have operations in China. With the continued convergence of CAS and IFRS, the release of our IFRS Manual of Accounting with Chinese Translation brings to China the extensive collective experience of the PwC's global network of firms in applying IFRS.

We hope this Manual will play a part in promoting consistent, comparable, relevant and reliable IFRS financial information and will serve as a reference tool for accounting students, academics, practitioners and users of financial statements in better understanding and implementing IFRS. More importantly, we hope the advice given in this text will assist those dealing with the many issues faced in preparing IFRS financial statements and provide helpful insight to users of such statements.

Raymund Chao
Asia Pacific Assurance Leader
PwC

前言

近年来，全球财务报告领域发生了重大变化，其中最为重要的一项变化是与国际财务报告准则的趋同。同时人们也热切地关注着中国境内注册会计师行业的长期发展。财政部及其他监管机构不断完善法规，推动中国注册会计师行业的发展，我们希望这本中英文对照的国际财务报告准则实务指引能够对此作出贡献。

财政部于2006年颁布了《企业会计准则》（以下称为中国会计准则，或CAS）。CAS包含了IFRS中的所有原则，且在过去的几年里持续趋同。此外，IFRS对于中国的许多公司来说越来越重要，包括寻求筹集海外资本的国内公司，以及在中国境内运营的外国公司。随着CAS与IFRS的持续趋同，本书的发行将给中国读者带来普华永道全球成员机构网络在应用IFRS方面积累的丰富的经验。

我们希望本书能够在推广一致的、可比的、相关的以及可靠的IFRS财务信息方面起到作用，并且可以作为会计领域的学生、学者、从业人员及财务报表使用者更好地理解及运用IFRS的参考工具。更为重要的是，我们希望本指引中提出的建议能够帮助其处理在编制IFRS财务报表时遇到的问题，并向此类财务报表使用者提供有用的观点。

赵柏基
普华永道亚太区审计部主管合伙人

Overview/Introduction

The IFRS Manual of Accounting is a practical guide to International Financial Reporting Standards. With close to 70 countries that have converged their local accounting standards with IFRS as at the time of writing, the application of IFRS has attracted significant attention in the world stage. At the same time, as more and more countries adopt IFRS (or its equivalent local standard), views continue to develop or evolve as to how particular aspects of a standard should be interpreted and applied. The views expressed in this Manual are based on years of experience from PricewaterhouseCoopers' Global Accounting Consulting Services team. The views expressed are a guide to applying IFRS rather than a set of definitive interpretations. The application of IFRS to a specific company is a matter of judgement given its particular facts and circumstances. Moreover, the application of IFRS might be influenced by the views of regulators.

The Manual covers diverse areas of accounting from the recognition and measurement of financial instruments to accounting for deferred taxation, business combinations and share-based payments. It explains in detail the rules that apply to preparing consolidated financial statements and considers the other statements that appear in annual reports such as cash flow statements as well as disclosures required by each specific standard.

Due to the continued convergence of China Accounting Standards and IFRS, PwC China has undertaken a significant project to translate our Global IFRS Manual of Accounting into Chinese. We sincerely hope that our IFRS Manual of Accounting with Chinese Translation provides practical insights to transactions commonly-seen in China and can help preparers, auditors, analysts and other users of financial statements to bridge the gap between accounting principles and their applications.

Yvonne Kam
Accounting Consulting Service Lead Partner
PwC China and Hong Kong

概述/引言

《国际财务报告准则实务指引》是应用国际财务报告准则的实务指南。于撰稿之时，已有近70个国家将其本国的会计准则与国际财务报告准则趋同，在世界范围内，国际财务报告准则的应用已广受重视。与此同时，随着越来越多的国家采用国际财务报告准则（或其等同的本地准则），关于某条准则特定方面应如何解释及应用的各种观点在持续发展或演变。本实务指引中所表达的观点是基于普华永道全球会计咨询服务团队以往多年的经验得出。我们所传达的观点是应用国际财务报告专业准则的指南，而非一系列确定的解释。一家特定的企业在应用国际财务报告准则时需根据特定的事实和环境作出判断。此外，国际财务报告准则的应用也可能受到监管机构观点的影响。

本实务指引涵盖从金融工具的确认和计量到递延税项、业务合并和以股份为基础的支付的核算等不同的会计领域。它详细解释了编制合并财务报表所应用的原则，并考虑了年报中出现的其他报表，如现金流量表以及每条特定准则所要求的披露。

鉴于中国会计准则与国际财务报告准则的持续趋同，普华永道中国启动了一项具有重大意义的项目，即将《国际财务报告准则实务指引》译成中文。我们诚挚地希望这套中英文对照的《国际财务报告准则实务指引》能够为中国常见的交易提供实用的见解，为编制者、审计人员、分析人员以及其他财务报表使用者们在会计原则与其具体应用之间架起一座桥梁。

金以文
会计专业咨询服务首席合伙人
普华永道中国及香港

How to use this publication

Given the increasing importance of IFRS in China and the continued convergence of CAS and IFRS, the Accounting Consulting Services team of PwC China and Hong Kong have undertaken a significant project to translate the IFRS Manual of Accounting into Chinese.

The Manual is a practical guide in applying IFRS and the views are based on the extensive experience of the PwC's global network of firms. However, IFRS is not static and is continuously developing. The views on its interpretation and application will adapt and evolve. The views expressed in this Manual are a guide to applying IFRS rather than a set of definitive interpretations. The application of IFRS requires significant judgement and specific facts and circumstances should be carefully considered.

IFRS Manual of Accounting with Chinese Translation will be released in different volumes. Depending on the topic, each release may be a chapter or a combination of a number of chapters from the Manual.

Because of the interdependencies between individual IFRS, there are many cross references between different chapters of the Manual. Although the IFRS Manual of Accounting with Chinese Translation will be released in different volumes, the cross references have been maintained. Users are encouraged to refer to those cross references in other translated chapters or to the English version of the Manual if it helps in their understanding.

This book is the twelfth volume of IFRS Manual of Accounting Series with Chinese Translation. The content covers Chapter 14 – Earnings per share of the English version and its translation. While every effort has been made to ensure an accurate translation, reference should be made to the English version in the event there are any differences between the Chinese and English versions.

使用说明

鉴于 IFRS 在中国愈发重要以及 CAS 和 IFRS 的持续趋同，普华永道中国及香港的会计专业咨询服务小组已着手开始了一项具有重大意义的项目，即将《国际财务报告准则实务指引》译成中文。

《国际财务报告准则实务指引》是对应用 IFRS 的实务指引，其中的观点是基于普华永道全球成员机构网络丰富的经验。然而，IFRS 不是静止的，而是持续发展的；因此，对 IFRS 的解释和适用会有所改变和发展。本指引表达的观点是对应用 IFRS 的一种指引，而非一套具有决定性的解释。IFRS 的应用需要大量的判断，还应当谨慎考虑特定的事实及所处的环境。

IFRS 实务指引及其中文翻译版将分成多册发行。根据主题，每一册可能是本指引的某一章节或是包含某几个章节。

由于各个 IFRS 准则之间的相互依存，因此本指引中不同的章节会相互参照索引。尽管 IFRS 实务指引及其中文翻译版将分成多册发行，但仍保留此类相互参照索引。如果有助于理解，我们鼓励读者阅读此类相互参照索引时参考其他已翻译的章节或指引的英文版。

本书为普华永道国际财务报告准则实务指引系列（中英文对照）的第十二册。内容为英文原版的《国际财务报告准则实务指引》中的《第十四章——每股收益》。我们已尽最大的努力来确保翻译的准确，但中文翻译版与英文版出现不一致时，应参考英文版。

The chapters of our IFRS Manual of Accounting have been restructured in 2013 and changes have been marked as follow:

IFRS Manual of Accounting (MoA)

Accounting rules and principles

01 – Introduction

02 – Accounting principles and applicability of IFRS (combined with chapter 1 in MoA 2013)

03 – First-time adoption of IFRS

04 – Presentation of financial statements

05 – Accounting policies, accounting estimates and errors (chapter 3 in MoA 2013)

06 – Hyper-inflation (chapter 31 in MoA 2013)

07 – Foreign currencies

08 – Insurance contracts

Income statement and related notes

09 – Revenue and construction contracts

10 – Segment reporting

11 – Employee benefits

11A – Employee benefits (IAS 19 revised)

12 – Share-based payment

13 – Taxation

14 – Earnings per share

Balance sheet and related notes

15 – Intangible assets

16 – Property, plant and equipment

17 – Investment property

18 – Impairment of assets

19 – Lease accounting

20 – Inventories

英文原版《国际财务报告准则实务指引》的章节已在2013年再版时重新排列，变动已列示如下：

国际财务报告准则实务指引

会计规则和原则

01 – 引言

02 – 会计原则和国际财务报告准则的适用性（在2013版中与第一章合并）

03 – 首次采用国际财务报告准则

04 – 财务报表的列报

05 – 会计政策、会计估计和差错（在2013版中为第三章）

06 – 恶性通货膨胀（在2013版中为第三十一章）

07 – 外币

08 – 保险合同

利润表及相关附注

09 – 收入与建造合同

10 – 分部报告

11 – 职工福利

11A – 职工福利（IAS 19 修订版）

12 – 以股份为基础的支付（“股份支付”）

13 – 所得税会计

14 – 每股收益

资产负债表及相关附注

15 – 无形资产

16 – 不动产、工厂和设备

17 – 投资性房地产

18 – 资产减值

19 – 租赁会计

20 – 存货

Consolidated financial statements

Other subjects

IFRS Manual of Accounting—Financial Instruments (chapter 6 in MoA 2013)

合并财务报表

其他主题

国际财务报告准则实务指引——金融工具（在2013版中为第六章）

06 – Classification of financial instruments (chapter 6.4 in MoA 2013)

07 – Financial liabilities and equity (chapter 6.5 in MoA 2013)

08 – Recognition and derecognition (chapter 6.6 in MoA 2013)

09 – Measurement of financial assets and liabilities (chapter 6.7 in MoA 2013)

10 – Hedge accounting (chapter 6.8 in MoA 2013)

11 – Presentation and disclosure (chapter 6.9 in MoA 2013)

12 – IFRS 9, "Financial Instruments" (chapter 6.10 in MoA 2013)

06 – 金融工具的分类（在 2013 版中为第 6. 4 章）

07 – 金融负债和权益（在 2013 版中为第 6. 5 章）

08 – 确认和终止确认（在 2013 版中为第 6. 6 章）

09 – 金融资产和金融负债的计量（在 2013 版中为第 6. 7 章）

10 – 套期会计（在 2013 版中为第 6. 8 章）

11 – 列报和披露（在 2013 版中为第 6. 9 章）

12 – 国际财务报告准则第 9 号——金融工具（在 2013 版中为第 6. 10 章）

International standards and interpretations

International standards

IFRS 1	First-time adoption of International Financial Reporting Standards
IFRS 2	Share-based payment
IFRS 3	Business combinations
IFRS 4	Insurance contracts
IFRS 5	Non-current assets held for sale and discontinued operations
IFRS 6	Exploration for and evaluation of mineral resources
IFRS 7	Financial instruments: Disclosures
IFRS 8	Operating segments
IFRS 9	Financial instruments
IFRS 10	Consolidated financial statements
IFRS 11	Joint arrangements
IFRS 12	Disclosure of interests in other entities
IFRS 13	Fair value measurement
IAS 1	Presentation of financial statements
IAS 2	Inventories
IAS 7	Cash flow statements
IAS 8	Accounting policies, changes in accounting estimates and errors
IAS 10	Events after the balance sheet date
IAS 11	Construction contracts
IAS 12	Income taxes
IAS 16	Property, plant and equipment
IAS 17	Leases
IAS 18	Revenue
IAS 19	Employee benefits
IAS 20	Accounting for government grants and disclosure of government assistance
IAS 21	The effects of changes in foreign exchange rates
IAS 23	Borrowing costs

国际财务报告准则及解释公告

国际财务报告准则

国际财务报告准则第 1 号	首次采用国际财务报告准则
国际财务报告准则第 2 号	以股份为基础的支付
国际财务报告准则第 3 号	企业合并
国际财务报告准则第 4 号	保险合同
国际财务报告准则第 5 号	持有待售的非流动资产和终止经营
国际财务报告准则第 6 号	矿产资源的勘探和评价
国际财务报告准则第 7 号	金融工具：披露
国际财务报告准则第 8 号	经营分部
国际财务报告准则第 9 号	金融工具
国际财务报告准则第 10 号	合并财务报表
国际财务报告准则第 11 号	合营安排
国际财务报告准则第 12 号	对其他主体中权益的披露
国际财务报告准则第 13 号	公允价值计量
国际会计准则第 1 号	财务报表的列报
国际会计准则第 2 号	存货
国际会计准则第 7 号	现金流量表
国际会计准则第 8 号	会计政策、会计估计变更和差错
国际会计准则第 10 号	报告期后事项
国际会计准则第 11 号	建造合同
国际会计准则第 12 号	所得税
国际会计准则第 16 号	不动产、工厂和设备
国际会计准则第 17 号	租赁
国际会计准则第 18 号	收入
国际会计准则第 19 号	职工福利
国际会计准则第 20 号	政府补助的会计和政府援助的披露
国际会计准则第 21 号	汇率变动的影响
国际会计准则第 23 号	借款费用

IAS 24	Related-party disclosures
IAS 26	Accounting and reporting by retirement benefit plans
IAS 27	Consolidated and separate financial statements
IAS 28	Investments in associates
IAS 29	Financial reporting in hyper-inflationary economies
IAS 31	Interests in joint ventures
IAS 32	Financial instruments: Presentation
IAS 33	Earnings per share
IAS 34	Interim financial reporting
IAS 36	Impairment of assets
IAS 37	Provisions, contingent liabilities and contingent assets
IAS 38	Intangible assets
IAS 39	Financial instruments: Recognition and measurement
IAS 40	Investment property
IAS 41	Agriculture

Interpretations

IFRIC 1	Changes in existing decommissioning, restoration and similar liabilities
IFRIC 2	Members' shares in co-operative entities and similar Instruments
IFRIC 4	Determining whether an arrangement contains a lease
IFRIC 5	Rights to interests arising from decommissioning, restoration and environmental rehabilitation funds
IFRIC 6	Liabilities arising from participating in a specific market – Waste electrical and electronic equipment
IFRIC 7	Applying the restatement approach under IAS 29 Financial reporting in hyper-inflationary economies
IFRIC 8	Scope of IFRS 2
IFRIC 9	Re-assessment of embedded derivatives
IFRIC 10	Interim financial reporting and impairment
IFRIC 11	IFRS 2 – Group and treasury share transactions
IFRIC 12	Service concession arrangements

国际会计准则第 24 号	关联方披露
国际会计准则第 26 号	退休福利计划的会计和报告
国际会计准则第 27 号	合并财务报表和单独财务报表
国际会计准则第 28 号	联营中的投资
国际会计准则第 29 号	恶性通货膨胀经济中的财务报告
国际会计准则第 31 号	合营中的权益
国际会计准则第 32 号	金融工具：列报
国际会计准则第 33 号	每股收益
国际会计准则第 34 号	中期财务报告
国际会计准则第 36 号	资产减值
国际会计准则第 37 号	准备、或有负债和或有资产
国际会计准则第 38 号	无形资产
国际会计准则第 39 号	金融工具：确认和计量
国际会计准则第 40 号	投资性房地产
国际会计准则第 41 号	农业

解释公告

国际财务报告解释公告第 1 号	现有退役、复原和类似负债的变动
国际财务报告解释公告第 2 号	成员在合作主体中的股份和类似工具
国际财务报告解释公告第 4 号	确定一项协议是否包含租赁
国际财务报告解释公告第 5 号	退役、复原和环境恢复基金产生的权益
国际财务报告解释公告第 6 号	参与废弃电器和电子设备特定市场产生的负债
国际财务报告解释公告第 7 号	应用《国际会计准则第 29 号——恶性通货膨胀经济中的财务报告》中的重述法
国际财务报告解释公告第 8 号	《国际财务报告准则第 2 号》的范围
国际财务报告解释公告第 9 号	嵌入衍生工具的重估
国际财务报告解释公告第 10 号	中期财务报告和减值
国际财务报告解释公告第 11 号	《国际财务报告准则第 2 号》：集团和库藏股交易
国际财务报告解释公告第 12 号	特许服务权安排

IFRIC 13	Customer loyalty programmes
IFRIC 14	IAS 19 – The limit on a defined benefit asset, minimum funding requirements and their interaction
IFRIC 15	Agreements for the construction of real estate
IFRIC 16	Hedges of a net investment in a foreign operation
IFRIC 17	Distributions of non-cash assets to owners
IFRIC 18	Transfers of assets from customers
IFRIC 19	Extinguishing financial liabilities with equity instruments
IFRIC 20	Stripping costs in the production phase of a surface mine
SIC 7	Introduction of the euro
SIC 10	Government Assistance – No specific relation to operating activities
SIC 12	Consolidation – Special purpose entities
SIC 13	Jointly controlled entities – Non-Monetary contributions by venturers
SIC 15	Operating leases – Incentives
SIC 21	Income taxes – Recovery of revalued non-depreciable assets
SIC 25	Income taxes – Changes in the tax status of an entity or its shareholders
SIC 27	Evaluating the substance of transactions in the legal form of a lease
SIC 29	Service Concession Arrangements: Disclosures
SIC 31	Revenue – Barter transactions involving advertising services
SIC 32	Intangible assets – Web site costs

国际财务报告解释公告第 13 号	客户忠诚度计划
国际财务报告解释公告第 14 号	《国际会计准则第 19 号》：对设定受益资产的限制、最低资金要求及其相互作用
国际财务报告解释公告第 15 号	房地产建造合同
国际财务报告解释公告第 16 号	对境外经营净投资的套期
国际财务报告解释公告第 17 号	以非现金资产对所有者进行分配
国际财务报告解释公告第 18 号	从客户处转移资产
国际财务报告解释公告第 19 号	以权益工具解除金融负债
国际财务报告解释公告第 20 号	露天矿生产阶段的剥离成本
国际会计准则解释公告第 7 号	引入欧元
国际会计准则解释公告第 10 号	政府援助：与经营活动没有特定联系的政府援助
国际会计准则解释公告第 12 号	合并：特殊目的主体
国际会计准则解释公告第 13 号	共同控制主体：合营者的非货币性投入
国际会计准则解释公告第 15 号	经营租赁：激励措施
国际会计准则解释公告第 21 号	所得税：已重估非折旧资产的收回
国际会计准则解释公告第 25 号	所得税：主体或其股东纳税状况的改变
国际会计准则解释公告第 27 号	评价涉及租赁法律形式的交易实质
国际会计准则解释公告第 29 号	特许服务权安排：披露
国际会计准则解释公告第 31 号	收入：涉及广告服务的易货交易
国际会计准则解释公告第 32 号	无形资产：网站成本

Abbreviations and terms used

Accounts	financial statements
AG	Application Guidance
App	Appendix
ARC	Accounting Regulatory Committee
BC	Basis for Conclusions (to an accounting standard)
C	currency unit
Chp	Chapter
chapter (1)	'PricewaterhouseCoopers' Manual of accounting' – chapter (1)
CESR	Committee of European Securities Regulators
CPP	current purchasing power
DP	discussion paper
EBIT	earnings before interest and tax
EBITDA	earnings before interest, tax, depreciation and amortisation
ED	exposure draft
EFRAG	European Financial Reporting Advisory Group
EPS	earnings per share
EU	European Union
FASB	Financial Accounting Standards Board (US)
Framework	Framework for the preparation and presentation of financial statements
GAAP	generally accepted accounting principles (and practices)
IAS	International Accounting Standard (see also IFRS)
IASB	International Accounting Standards Board
IFRIC	International Financial Reporting Interpretations Committee
IFRS	International Financial Reporting Standard (see also IAS)
IG	Implementation Guidance (to an accounting standard)

缩写及词汇对照

财务报表
实施指南
附录
会计监管委员会
（某一准则的）结论基础
货币单位
章
第一章（普华永道《国际财务报告准则实务指引》——第一章）

欧洲证券监管委员会
现行购买力
讨论稿
息税前收益
扣除利息、所得税、折旧和摊销之前的收益
征求意见稿
欧洲财务报告咨询组
每股收益
欧盟
（美国）财务会计准则委员会
编报财务报表的框架

公认会计原则
国际会计准则（亦请参见 IFRS）
国际会计准则理事会
国际财务报告解释委员会
国际财务报告准则（亦请参见 IAS）
（某一准则的）应用指南

para(s)	paragraph(s) of Schedules to the Companies Acts, or IFRSs or IASs or FRSs, or SSAPs, or FREDs, or EDs, or DPs, or text
PPE	property, plant and equipment
US SEC	US Securities and Exchange Commission
SIC	Standing Interpretation Committee of the IASC (see IFRIC)
SPE	special purpose entity
UK	United Kingdom
US	United States of America

段落（公司法、国际财务报告准则、国际会计准则、财务报告准则、会计实务准则、财务报告征求意见稿、征求意见稿、讨论稿或文章中的段落）

不动产、工厂和设备
美国证券交易委员会
国际会计准则委员会的常设解释委员会（参见 IFRIC）

特殊目的主体
英国
美国

Chapter 14 Earnings per share

Contents

第十四章　每股收益

目　录

Introduction

14.1 Earnings per share (EPS) is a ratio that is widely used by financial analysts, investors and others to gauge a company's profitability and to value its shares. Its purpose is to indicate how effective a company has been in using the resources provided by the ordinary shareholders (described as ordinary equity holders in IAS 33). The allocation of earnings accruing to other providers of finance, such as preference shareholders is a prior charge and is often fixed. Therefore, the income remaining after making allocations to those parties is attributable to ordinary shareholders. This amount, when presented on the face of the profit and loss account on a C per share basis, assists the ordinary shareholders to gauge the company's current net earnings and changes in its net earnings from period to period. It can, therefore, be relevant as a measure of company performance and in evaluating management's effectiveness. Another reason for the popularity of EPS is that it forms the basis for calculating the 'price-earnings ratio', which is a standard stock market indicator. Price-earnings ratios relating to both past and prospective profits are widely used by investors and analysts in valuing shares.

14.2 EPS is simply a ratio of the numerator – earnings measured in terms of profits available to ordinary shareholders – to the denominator – the number of ordinary shares. Therefore, it is very simple in concept, but it is the determination of the numerator and, in particular, the denominator that can make the calculation of this ratio rather complex in practice. Also if the ratio is to be meaningful it must be calculated on a similar basis for every entity so as to facilitate comparisons between different accounting periods for the same entity and between different entities in the same period.

[The next paragraph is 14.40.]

引言

14.1 每股收益（以下简称“EPS”）是金融分析师、投资者及其他方广泛用于衡量一家公司的盈利能力及对其股份进行估值的一项比率。该比率旨在表明公司在使用普通股股东（在 IAS 33 中被描述为普通股权益持有者“ordinary equity holders”）所提供的各类资源方面的成效如何。对赋予诸如优先股股东等其他融资提供者的收益分配是一项优先承付款项，并且通常是固定的。因此，向这些融资提供者进行分配后剩余的收益归属于普通股股东。当这一金额在利润表主表中按元/每股为基础列示时，能帮助普通股股东衡量这家公司的当期净收益以及在各期之间净收益的变动。因此，该比率作为公司业绩的衡量指标以及在用于评价管理层的效率时是有重要意义的。EPS 广受欢迎的另一原因是其构成了计算一项标准的股票市场指标“市盈率”的基础。与以往和预期利润有关的市盈率被投资者和分析师广泛地使用于股份估值。

14.2 EPS 仅仅是一个简单的比率，分子——按普通股股东可获得的利润计量的收益，除以分母——普通股股数。因此，其在概念上极为简单，但分子特别是分母的确定能够使这一比率的计算在实务中变得相当复杂。而且，如果为了使这一比率变得有意义，每个主体必须以一个类似的基础进行计算，以便于在同一主体的不同会计期间之间以及在同一期间的不同主体之间进行比较。

[下一段为第 14.40 段。]

Objectives and scope of IAS 33

Objectives

14.40 IAS 33 specifies the way in which earnings per share data should be calculated, presented and disclosed in the financial statements of entities. In doing so, it focuses primarily on determining the number of shares to be included in the denominator of the earnings per share calculation. [IAS 33 para 1].

14.41 Although it is accepted that earnings per share data may have limitations because of the different accounting policies used for determining 'earnings', a consistently calculated denominator will improve the comparison of the performance of different entities in the same period and of the same entity in different accounting periods. Furthermore, a denominator calculated in accordance with international consensus will go a long way in enhancing global comparison of earnings per share data in spite of different national methods for determining 'earnings'.

Scope

14.42 The standard applies to entities whose ordinary shares or potential ordinary shares (for example, convertible debt, warrants etc) are publicly traded. [IAS 33 para 2]. Therefore, entities whose securities are listed on a recognised stock exchange (for example, London Stock Exchange, Luxembourg Stock Exchange, NASDAQ) or are otherwise publicly traded, will have to calculate earnings per share data in accordance with the standard. Furthermore, entities that file or are in the process of filing financial statements with a securities commission or other regulatory body for purposes of issuing ordinary shares (that is, not private placements) are also required to comply with the standard. [IAS 33 para 2].

14.43 When both the parent's separate and consolidated financial statements are presented, the disclosures are required only on the basis of consolidated information. Users of the financial statements of a parent are normally concerned with, and need information on, the results of operations of the group as a whole.

IAS 33 的目的和范围

目的

14.40　IAS 33 明确说明了每股收益数据应当在主体财务报表中进行计算、列报及披露的方式。因此，其主要着重于确定应纳入计算每股收益的分母中的股数。[IAS 33 第 1 段]。

14.41　虽然人们公认由于用于确定“收益”的会计政策各不相同，每股收益数据可能存在局限性，计算一致的分母将提高不同主体在同一期间的业绩以及同一主体在不同会计期间的业绩的可比性。此外，尽管各国确定“收益”的方法各有不同，根据国际上一致的分母计算方法将对增进每股收益数据的全球可比性大有帮助。

范围

14.42　该准则适用于其普通股或潜在普通股（例如，可转换债务、认股权证等）被公开交易的主体。[IAS 33 第 2 段]。因此，其证券在认可的证券交易所（例如，伦敦证券交易所、卢森堡证券交易所、纳斯达克）上市或以其他方式被公开交易的主体，将必须根据该准则计算每股收益数据。此外，为了发行普通股（即，非私募配售）向证券委员会或其他监管机构提交财务报表或处于提交过程中的主体也必须遵循该准则。[IAS 33 第 2 段]。

14.43　当母公司的单独财务报表和合并财务报表同时被列报时，仅要求以合并信息为基础进行披露。母公司财务报表使用者通常关注并且需要关于集团整体经营成果的信息。在某一主体自愿选择列报基于其个体财务报表的每股收益以及基于合并财务报表的每股收益的情况下，个体的每股收益数值可能

Where an entity chooses voluntarily to present earnings per share based on its entity financial statements as well as earnings per share based on the consolidated financial statements, the entity earnings per share figures may be shown only on the face of the entity statement of comprehensive income (or income statement, if presented). They must not be shown in the consolidated financial statements. [IAS 33 para 4, 4A].

14.44 Entities whose securities are not publicly traded are not required to disclose earnings per share data because, generally, they have a smaller number of ordinary shareholders. However, where such entities choose to disclose earnings per share data, to maintain comparability in financial reporting, they should comply with the standard's provisions. [IAS 33 para 3]. Such entities are likely to be those that intend to establish a track record before seeking entry to the public market at a future date.

[The next paragraph is 14.46.]

Basic earnings per share

Measurement

14.46 Entities that fall within the standard's scope must calculate basic (and diluted) EPS for the profit or loss attributable to the parent entity's ordinary equity holders. Basic (and diluted) EPS should also be calculated for profit or loss from continuing operations if this is presented. [IAS 33 para 9]. Where an entity has no operations that qualify as discontinued under IFRS 5 the profit or loss for the year will all be attributable to continuing operations and so calculation of an additional EPS figure for continuing operations will be unnecessary. Where an entity has operations that qualify as discontinued under IFRS 5, however, it has to give separate disclosure of the results of such operations. IAS 33 then requires the basic (and diluted) EPS for profit or loss attributable to continuing operations to be calculated. The standard requires disclosure of basic and diluted EPS for profit or loss from continuing operations and profit or loss for the year, for each class of

仅列示于该主体个体的综合收益表（或利润表，如有列报）主表中，而不得列示于合并财务报表中。[IAS 33 第4段4A]。

14.44　无公开交易证券的主体无需披露每股收益数据，因为在一般情况下，其拥有数量较少的普通股股东。然而，在此类主体选择披露每股收益数据以保持财务报告可比性的情况下，则其应当遵循该准则的规定。[IAS 33 第3段]。此类主体很可能是打算在未来某一日期寻求进入公开市场之前建立业绩记录的主体。

[下一段为第14.46段。]

基本每股收益

计量

14.46　列入该准则范围内的主体必须对归属于母公司普通股股东的损益计算基本EPS（及稀释EPS）。如果列报了持续经营损益，还应当对持续经营损益计算基本EPS（及稀释EPS）。[IAS 33 第9段]。在主体的经营没有符合IFRS 5中终止经营条件的情况下，年度损益将全部归属于持续经营，因此计算一项额外的持续经营的EPS数值将是没有必要的。然而，在主体的经营有符合IFRS 5中终止经营条件的情况下，其必须单独披露此类经营成果。IAS 33因此要求计算归属于持续经营损益的基本EPS（及稀释EPS）。该准则要求对在当期利润中具有不同分享权的各类别普通股，披露持续经营损益以及年度损益的基本EPS和稀释EPS——参见下文第14.173段“列报和披露”。下列段落描述了归属于普通股股东的当期损益的EPS计算，但是计算持续经营损益和终止经营损益的EPS的原则是相同的。

ordinary shares that has a different right to share in profit for the period—see 'Presentation and disclosure' from paragraph 14.173 below. The following paragraphs describe the EPS calculation for profit or loss for the period attributable to ordinary equity holders, but the principles are the same for calculating EPS for profit or loss from continuing and discontinued operations.

14.47 Basic EPS should be calculated by dividing the profit or loss for the period attributable to the parent entity's ordinary equity holders by the weighted average number of ordinary shares outstanding during the period. [IAS 33 para 10].

14.48 The term 'ordinary share' is defined as an equity instrument that is subordinate to all other classes of equity instrument. An equity instrument is any contract that evidences a residual interest in the assets of an entity after deducting all of its liabilities. [IAS 33 para 5; IAS 32 para 11].

14.49 Ordinary shares participate in profit only after other types of shares such as preference shares have participated. [IAS 33 para 6]. Indeed preference shares that provide for mandatory redemption by the issuer for a fixed or determinable amount at a fixed or determinable future date or that give the holder the right to require such redemption are treated as liabilities under IAS 32. [IAS 32 para 18 (a)]. An entity may have more than one class of ordinary share (see further para 14.59 below). Ordinary shares of the same class will have the same rights to receive dividends. [IAS 33 para 6].

14.50 The computation of the EPS figure requires a calculation of the earnings as the numerator and the relevant number of ordinary shares as the denominator. If no adjustments are required to the numerator or the denominator, the profit or loss attributable to the ordinary equity holders and the relevant number of ordinary shares can be obtained directly from the financial statements and the figure computed. However, in practice the numerator or to the denominator or both may need to be adjusted for the reasons discussed in the paragraphs that follow. The circumstances in which such adjustments should be made are considered in the paragraphs that follow.

Computation of earnings

14.51 For the purposes of calculating basic EPS, the profit or loss from

14.47　基本 EPS 应当通过归属于母公司普通股股东的当期损益除以当期发行在外普通股的加权平均数进行计算。[IAS 33 第 10 段]。

14.48　“普通股”一词被定义为次于所有其他类别权益工具的一种权益工具。一项权益工具是指能证明拥有某一主体在扣除所有负债后的资产中的剩余权益的任何合同。[IAS 33 第 5 段；IAS 32 第 11 段]。

14.49　只有在其他类型股份诸如优先股已参与利润分配后，普通股才分享利润。[IAS 33 第 6 段]。根据 IAS 32，实际上规定发行者在未来某一固定或可确定的日期以某一固定或可确定的金额强制性赎回或者赋予持有者要求作出此类赎回的权利的优先股，被视为负债。[IAS 32 第 18（a）段]。一个主体可能拥有不止一种类别的普通股（参见下文第 14.59 段）。同一类别的普通股将具有同等收取股利的权利。[IAS 33 第 6 段]。

14.50　EPS 数值要求计算作为分子的收益和作为分母的相关普通股股数。如果分子或分母无需进行调整，则归属于普通股股东的损益以及相关普通股股数能够直接从财务报表和经计算得出的数值中获得。然而，在实务中，由于下文所讨论的原因，分子或分母或两者均有可能需要作出调整。在下文中对于应当作出此类调整的情况进行了讨论。

收益计算

14.51　出于计算基本 EPS 的目的，归属于母公司普通股股东的持续经营损益

continuing operations and the profit or loss for the period attributable to the parent entity's ordinary equity holders are the profit or loss after tax and non-controlling interest and after adjusting for the after tax effects of preference dividends, differences arising on settlement of preference shares and other similar effects of preference shares classified as equity under IAS 32. [IAS 33 paras 12, A1]. In the absence of any preference shares, it is relatively simple to calculate the earnings figure for EPS purposes. However, where the entity has preference shares in issue, some further adjustments as stated above may be necessary. The ways in which such adjustments are likely to affect earnings for the purposes of calculating basic EPS are considered below. There is no requirement to compute 'Comprehensive earnings per share', but this information could be provided as supplementary information (see para 14.187).

Preference dividends

14.52 Where an entity has preference shares in issue, those shares will be classified as financial liabilities or equity under IAS 32, depending on the terms of the shares. Where preference shares are classified as liabilities in accordance with IAS 32 (see para 14.49 above) any dividends or other appropriations in respect of such preference shares (for example, a premium payable on redemption) will be treated as finance costs in arriving at profit or loss for the period. [IAS 32 paras 35, 36]. However, where preference shares are classified as equity, any dividends and other appropriations would be debited directly to equity and an adjustment is, therefore, needed to deduct it from the profit for the period to arrive at the profit attributable to ordinary equity holders for the purpose of calculating EPS. [IAS 33 para 12]. Whether the preference shares are treated as liabilities or as equity, the calculation of amounts of dividend and other appropriations and adjustments attributable to such shares is the same, and in both cases the amounts are deducted to arrive at the profit attributable to ordinary equity holders for the purpose of calculating basic EPS.

14.53 Where preference shares carry the right to a fixed dividend, then those dividends can either be cumulative or non-cumulative. If the preference dividends are cumulative, the dividend for the period should be taken into account, whether

和当期损益是扣除所得税和非控制性权益后，并且对优先股股利的税后影响额、优先股结算所产生的差额以及根据 IAS 32 被分类为权益的优先股的其他类似影响进行调整后的损益。[IAS 33 第 12 段 A1]。在不存在任何优先股的情况下，计算用于 EPS 的收益数值是相对简单的。然而，在主体拥有已发行优先股的情况下，上文所述的某些进一步调整可能是有必要的。下文将讨论此类调整很可能影响用于计算基本 EPS 收益的方式。虽然不要求计算“每股综合收益”，但是该信息可以作为补充信息予以提供（参见第 14.187 段）。

优先股股利

14.52 在主体拥有已发行优先股的情况下，根据 IAS 32，这些优先股将被分类为金融负债或权益，取决于这些股份的条款。在按照 IAS 32 优先股被分类为负债的情况下（参见上文第 14.49 段），在得出当期损益时关于此类优先股的任何股利或其他分配（例如：赎回时的应付溢价款）将被作为融资成本处理。[IAS 32 第 35、36 段]。然而，在优先股被分类为权益的情况下，任何股利及其他分配应该会直接借记权益，因此为了计算 EPS 需要作出调整将其从当期利润中扣除，以得出归属于普通股股东的利润。[IAS 33 第 12 段]。无论优先股是作为负债还是权益进行处理，对归属于此类股份的股利及其他分配和调整的金额的计算是相同的，并且在两种情形下，在计算 EPS 时该等金额均应被扣除，以得出归属于普通股股东的利润。

14.53 在优先股享有固定股利的权利的情况下，则这些股利可以是累积的，或者是非累积的。如果优先股股利是累积的，无论股利是否已经宣告，当期股利应当予以考虑。[IAS 33 第 14（b）段]。因此，在公司由于可分配利润

or not it has been declared. [IAS 33 para 14(b)]. Thus, in a year in which the company is unable to pay or declare a cumulative preference dividend, because of insufficient distributable profits (for example, the company has accumulated losses), the undeclared amount of the cumulative preference dividend (net of tax, if applicable) should still be deducted in arriving at earnings for the purposes of the EPS calculation. In the year in which these arrears of preference dividends are paid, they should be ignored in the EPS calculation for that year. [IAS 33 para 14 (b)]. On the other hand, if the preference dividends are non-cumulative, only the amount of dividends declared in respect of the year should be deducted in arriving at the profit attributable to ordinary shareholders. [IAS 33 para 14(a)].

Other appropriations and adjustments in respect of preference shares

14.54 Under IAS 32 (see para 14.49 above) and IAS 39, the charges made in the profit and loss account in respect of preference shares that are treated as financial liabilities will include not only the preference and/or participating dividends, but also other elements such as the amortisation of transaction costs and accrual for any premium payable on redemption. [IAS 39 paras 47, IAS 32 paras 35, 36]. It follows that these other elements should continue to be deducted in arriving at profit for the financial year and the earnings available to ordinary equity holders. In the year in which the preference shares are redeemed, any premium payable on redemption should be ignored in calculating EPS for that year to the extent that it has been accrued (and, therefore, already taken into account) in earlier years.

14.55 In respect of preference shares classified as equity the following adjustments should also be made:

- Any original discount or premium that is amortised to retained earnings using the effective interest method is treated as a preference dividend for the purposes of calculating EPS. [IAS 33 para 15]. An example is non-convertible, non-redeemable preference shares that have been issued at a discount to compensate for non-payment of dividends in earlier years, the discount being amortised to retained earnings. Such shares are often referred to as 'increasing rate preference shares'. (See illustrative example 1 in IAS 33.)

不足（例如：公司有累计亏损）而无力支付或宣告累积优先股股利的年度中，未宣告的累积优先股股利金额（税后金额，如适用）仍应当在得出用于 EPS 计算的收益时予以扣除。在支付这些逾期的优先股股利的年度中，这些股利在该年 EPS 的计算中应当不予以考虑。[IAS 33 第 14（b）段]。另一方面，如果优先股股利是非累积的，只有已宣告的与当年有关的股利金额应当在计算得出归属于普通股股东的利润时予以扣除。[IAS 33 第 14（a）段]。

关于优先股的其他分配和调整

14.54　根据 IAS 32（参见上文第 14.49 段）和 IAS 39，在利润表中被视为金融负债进行处理的优先股所产生的费用将不但包括优先股股利或参加性股利，而且包括诸如交易成本摊销以及预提的任何赎回时的应付溢价款等其他要素。[IAS 39 第 47 段，IAS 32 第 35、36 段]。因此，这些其他要素应当继续在得出财务年度利润以及普通股股东可获得的收益时予以扣除。在优先股被赎回的年度里，计算该年 EPS 时，任何赎回时的应付溢价款只要在以前年度已经预提的范围内（因此，已被列入考虑）应当不予以考虑。

14.55　关于被分类为权益的优先股，还应当作出下列调整：

- 计算 EPS 时，使用实际利率法摊销至留存收益的任何原始折价或溢价作为优先股股利进行处理。[IAS 33 第 15 段]。一个例子是：折价发行以补偿初始数年不支付股利且折价摊销至留存收益的不可转换、不可赎回的优先股。此类优先股经常被称为“增率优先股”。（参见 IAS 33 中的说明性示例 1。）

- On the repurchase of preference shares, any excess of the fair value of consideration given over the carrying amount of the shares is a charge to retained earnings and is deducted in determining the profit, or added in determining the loss, available to ordinary equity holders for the purpose of calculating EPS. [IAS 33 para 16].
- Where preference shares are converted early on favourable terms, the excess of the fair value of ordinary shares or other consideration paid over the fair value of ordinary shares or other consideration payable under the original terms is deducted in determining the profit, or added in determining the loss, available to ordinary equity holders for the purpose of calculating EPS. [IAS 33 para 17].
- Any excess of the carrying amount of preference shares over the fair value of the consideration paid to settle them is added in determining the profit, or deducted in determining the loss, available to ordinary equity holders for the purpose of calculating EPS. [IAS 33 para 18].

14.56 The treatment of preference shares in the EPS calculation is illustrated in the following example:

Example

An entity has the following preference shares in issue at the end of 20X4:

■	5% Redeemable, non-cumulative preference shares, these shares are classified as liabilities under IAS 32. During the year a dividend was paid on the 5% preference shares.	C100,000
■	Increasing rate, cumulative, non-redeemable preference shares issued at a discount in 20X0 with a cumulative dividend rate from 20X5 of 10%. The shares were issued at a discount to compensate the holders, as dividend payments will not commence until 20X5. The accrual for the discount in the current year, calculated using the effective interest method amounted to, say, C18,000. These shares are classified as equity under IAS 32.	C200,000

■ 回购优先股时，所提供对价的公允价值超出该优先股账面价值的部分计入留存收益，并且在确定普通股股东可获得的利润或已遭受的亏损以计算EPS时予以扣除或加回。[IAS 33 第16段]。

■ 在优先股以有利条件提前转换的情况下，所支付的普通股或其他对价的公允价值超出根据原始条款所应支付的普通股或其他对价的公允价值的部分，在确定普通股股东可获得的利润或已遭受的亏损以计算EPS时予以扣除或加回。[IAS 33 第17段]。

■ 优先股账面价值超出为结算该优先股所支付对价的公允价值的部分，在确定普通股股东可获得的利润或已遭受的亏损以计算EPS时予以加回或扣除。[IAS 33 第18段]。

14.56 下列示例说明了在EPS计算中优先股的处理：

示例

某主体在20X4年年末拥有下列已发行优先股：

■ 股利率为5%的可赎回非累积优先股，根据IAS 32这些优先股被分类为负债。在该年度中，对这些股利率为5%的优先股支付了股利。	100,000元
■ 20X0年折价发行的、自20X5年起累积股利率为10%的增率累积不可赎回优先股。因为股利支付自20X5年才开始，对该优先股折价发行以补偿其持有者。使用实际利率法计算的当年预提的折价金额为18,000元。根据IAS 32，这些优先股被分类为权益。	200,000元

■ 8% Non-redeemable, non-cumulative preference shares. At the beginning of the year the entity had C100,000 8% preference shares outstanding, but at 30 June 20X4, it repurchased C50,000 of these at a discount of C1,000.	C50,000
■ 7% Cumulative, convertible preference shares (converted in the year). These shares were classified as equity, until their conversion into ordinary shares at the beginning of the year. No dividend was accrued in respect of the year, although the previous year's dividend was paid immediately prior to conversion. To induce conversion, the terms of conversion of the 7% convertible preference shares were also amended and the revised terms entitled the preference shareholders to an additional 100 ordinary shares on conversion with a fair value of C300.	CNil

The profit attributable to ordinary equity holders for the year 20X4 is C150,000. Adjustments for the purpose of calculating EPS are made as follows:

	C	C
Profit for the year attributable to the ordinary equity holders		150,000
Amortisation of discount on issue of increasing rate preference shares	(18,000)[1]	
Discount on repurchase of 8% preference shares	1,000[2]	
		(17,000)
Profit attributable to ordinary equity holders for basic EPS		133,000

■ 股利率为 8% 的不可赎回非累积优先股。年初时，该主体拥有 100,000 元发行在外的股利率为 8% 的优先股，但是在 20X4 年 6 月 30 日，其折价 1,000 元回购了这些优先股中的 50,000 元。	50,000 元
■ 股利率为 7% 的累积可转换优先股（于当年转换）。这些优先股被分类为权益，直至其在年初时被转换为普通股。就当年而言没有计提股利，尽管在转换前刚支付了前一年度的股利。为促成转换，该股利率为 7% 的可转换优先股的转换条款也被修改，且修改后的条款使得优先股股东有权在转换时获得公允价值为 300 元的额外的 100 股普通股。	0 元

20X4 年归属于普通股股东的利润为 150,000 元。为了计算 EPS 而作出的调整如下：

	元	元
归属于普通股股东的当年利润		150,000
发行增率优先股时的折价摊销	(18,000)[1]	
回购股利率为 8% 的优先股时的折价	1,000[2]	
		(17,000)
用于计算基本 EPS 的归属于普通股股东的利润		133,000

Notes

1. The original discount on issue of the increasing rate preference shares has been amortised to retained earnings, so must be treated as preference dividends for EPS purposes and adjusted against profit attributable to the ordinary equity holders. [IAS 33 para 15]. There is no adjustment in respect of dividends as these do not commence until 20X5. Instead, the finance cost is represented by the amortisation of the discount in the dividend-free period. In future years, the accrual for the dividend of C20,000 will be deducted from profits. [IAS 33 para 14(b)].

2. The discount on repurchase of the 8% preference shares has been credited to equity so must be added to profit. [IAS 33 para 18].

3. The dividend on the 5% preference shares has been charged to the income statement as the preference shares are treated as liabilities, so no adjustment is necessary to profit.

4. No accrual for the dividend on the 8% preference shares is required as they are non-cumulative. Had a dividend been declared for the year it would have been deducted from profit for the purpose of calculating basic EPS as the shares are treated as equity and the dividend would have been charged to equity in the financial statements. [IAS 33 para 14(a)].

5. As the 7% preference shares were converted at the beginning of the year, there is no adjustment in respect of the 7% preference shares as no dividend accrued in respect of the year. The payment of the previous year's cumulative dividend is ignored for EPS purposes as it will have been adjusted for in the prior year. [IAS 33 para 14(b)]. Similarly, the excess of the fair value of additional ordinary shares issued on conversion of the convertible preference shares over fair value of the ordinary shares to which they would have been entitled under the original conversion terms would already have been deducted from profit attributable to the ordinary shareholders and no further adjustment is required.

Participating securities and two-class ordinary shares

14.57 Sometimes, preference shares may be given the right to participate in the

注

1. 发行增率优先股时的原始折价已摊销至留存收益，因此用于计算 EPS 时必须作为优先股股利进行处理，并调减归属于普通股股东的利润。［IAS 33 第 15 段］。就股利而言不作调整，因为自 20X5 年起才开始支付股利。而融资成本体现为无股利期间的折价摊销。在未来年度中，计提的20,000元股利将从利润中予以扣除。［IAS 33 第 14(b)段］。

2. 回购股利率为 8% 的优先股时的折价已经贷记权益，因此必须加回至利润中。［IAS 33 第 18 段］。

3. 股利率为 5% 的优先股的股利已经计入利润表，因为该优先股作为负债处理，因此没有必要对利润进行调整。

4. 无需对股利率为 8% 的优先股计提股利，因为其为非累积优先股。如果当年已宣告股利，为了计算基本 EPS，该股利本应该从利润中扣除，因为这些优先股作为权益处理，其股利在财务报表中应该已经计入权益。［IAS 33 第 14(a)段］。

5. 由于股利率为 7% 的优先股于年初转换，对该股利率为 7% 的优先股没有任何调整，因为当年无应计股利。为了计算 EPS，上年度累积股利的支付不予以考虑，因为其在上年度应该已经作出调整。［IAS 33 第 14（b）段］。类似地，可转换优先股转换时发行的额外普通股的公允价值超出根据原始转换条款这些可转换优先股应该会有权获得的普通股的公允价值的部分，应该是已经从归属于普通股股东的利润中扣除且无需作进一步调整。

参加性证券和两类普通股

14.57　有时，优先股可能被赋予按照预定方案与普通股一起参与利润分配的

profit with ordinary shares according to a predetermined formula, but with an upper limit or cap on the extent of participation by the preference shares. Such participation is usually in addition to a fixed dividend. Participating preference shares would be treated as either financial liabilities or equity instruments under IAS 32, dependent on their terms. Where participating preference shares are classified as liabilities, both the fixed and the participating element would have been charged in arriving at profit or loss attributable to the parent entity and no further adjustments are necessary. Where participating preference shares are classified as equity instruments, IAS 33 contains further guidance that is considered below.

14.58 IAS 33 describes instruments that would include participating preference shares as 'participating equity instruments'. It notes that such instruments include instruments that participate in dividends with ordinary shares according to a predetermined formula (for example, two for one) with, sometimes an upper limit on participation (for example, up to a specified amount per share, but no more). [IAS 33 para A13(a)]. An example might be a participating preference share that receives a fixed dividend of 3% and a variable participation of 20% of the dividend on an ordinary share up to a maximum of C0.5 per participating preference share. Therefore, the total earnings would need to be calculated by reference to the fixed and the participating element in order to calculate the EPS attributable to the participating preference shares.

14.59 In addition to participating equity instruments, an entity could have a class of ordinary shares with a different dividend rate from that of another class of ordinary shares, but without prior or senior rights. [IAS 33 para A13(b)]. IAS 33 describes such instruments as 'two-class ordinary shares'. Where this is the case, the earnings for the period should be apportioned over the different classes of equity shares in issue in accordance with their dividend rights or other rights to participate in undistributed earnings. [IAS 33 para A14]. This means that a company could disclose a number of EPS figures, each attributable to different classes of equity shares and participating equity instruments.

14.60 The steps that should be followed in allocating earnings for the purposes of calculating basic EPS where an entity has different classes of ordinary shares and participating equity instruments that are not convertible into ordinary shares are as follows:

权利，但是优先股的参与程度存在一个上限或限制。此类参与通常是在固定股利之外的。根据 IAS 32，参加性优先股应该是作为金融负债或权益工具进行处理，取决于其条款。在参加性优先股被分类为负债的情况下，在计算得出归属于母公司的损益时，应该是已经同时计入了固定要素和参加性要素，且无需作进一步调整。在参加性优先股被分类为权益工具的情况下，IAS 33 包含了下文所讨论的进一步指引。

14.58　IAS 33 将应该会包含参加性优先股的工具描述为“参加性权益工具”。其指出，此类工具包括按照预定方案（例如：两股对一股）与普通股一起参与股利分配的工具，且有时存在一个参与分配的上限（例如：每股最多可以达到但是不能超出某一规定的金额）。[IAS 33 第 A13(a)段]。收取 3% 的固定股利且参与 20% 变动的普通股股利分配，最多可达每股 0.5 元，这可能是参加性优先股的一个例子。因此，为了计算归属于参加性优先股的 EPS，总收益应该会需要考虑固定要素和参加性要素进行计算。

14.59　除了参加性权益工具之外，主体可能拥有股利率不同于另一类普通股、但是无优先权或更高权利的一类普通股。[IAS 33 第 A13(b)段]。IAS 33 将此类工具描述为“两类普通股”。在这种情况下，当期收益应当在不同类别的已发行普通股之间按照其股利权或其他参与未分配利润分配的权利进行分配。[IAS 33 第 A14 段]。这意味着一家公司可能披露多个 EPS 数值，且每个数值归属于不同类别的普通股和参加性权益工具。

14.60　在主体拥有不同类别的普通股和不可转换为普通股的参加性权益工具的情况下，为了计算基本 EPS 而进行收益分配时应当遵循的步骤如下：

- Profit or loss attributable to ordinary equity holders is adjusted by the amount of dividends declared in the period for each class of shares and by the contractual amount of dividends that must be paid for the period (for example, unpaid cumulative dividends).

- The remaining profit or loss is allocated to ordinary shares and participating equity instruments to the extent that each instrument shares in earnings or losses. The allocation is made as if all the profit or loss has been distributed. The total profit or loss allocated to each class of equity instrument is determined by adding together the amount allocated for dividends and the amount allocated for the participation feature.

- The total amount of profit or loss allocated to each class of equity instrument is divided by the number of outstanding instruments to which the profits or losses are allocated (that is, the instruments in that class) to determine the EPS for that class of instrument.

[IAS 33 para A14].

14.61 Where participating equity instruments (participating preference shares) are convertible into ordinary shares, conversion is assumed if the effect is dilutive. Where this is so, the conversion shares should be included in outstanding ordinary shares for the purposes of calculating diluted EPS (see below under 'Diluted earnings per share'). [IAS 33 para A14].

14.62 The illustrative examples accompanying IAS 33 include a worked example illustrating how the allocation would be done. The following example is based on that example.

Example

An entity has two classes of shares in issue:

5,000 Non-convertible preference shares

10,000 Ordinary shares

The preference shares are entitled to a fixed dividend of C5 per share before any dividends are paid on the ordinary shares. Ordinary dividends are then

■ 归属于普通股股东的损益根据对各类股份当期宣告的股利金额和必须支付的合同约定的当期股利金额（例如：未支付的累积股利）进行调整。

■ 剩余损益将被分配至普通股和参加性权益工具，以各项工具分享的收益或损失为限。该分配进行后就如同所有损益均已分配。分配至各类权益工具的损益总额通过加总用作股利分配的金额和对参加性特征分配的金额予以确定。

■ 通过将分配至每一类权益工具的损益总额除以参与损益分配的发行在外工具（即该类别中的工具）的数量以确定该类工具的 EPS。

[IAS 33 第 A14 段]。

14.61　在参加性权益工具(参加性优先股)可转换为普通股的情况下,如果其影响是具有稀释作用的,则假定已发生转换。在这一情况下,计算稀释 EPS 时,可转换股份应当包括在发行在外的普通股中(参见下文“稀释每股收益”)。[IAS 33 第 A14 段]。

14.62　IAS 33 所附的说明性示例包括了一个处理过的实例来举例说明分配应该是如何进行的。以下示例即以该实例为基础。

示例

某主体拥有两类已发行的股份：

5,000 股不可转换优先股

10,000 股普通股

在向普通股支付任何股利之前，优先股有权享有每股 5 元的固定股利。之后才支付普通股股利，且优先股股东不参与股利分配。随后每股优先

paid in which the preference shareholders do not participate. Each preference share then participates in any additional ordinary dividend above C2 at a rate of 50% of any additional dividend payable on an ordinary share.

The entity's profit for the year is C100,000 and dividends of C2 per share are declared on the ordinary shares.

The calculation of basic EPS using the allocation method described in the previous paragraph is as follows:

	C	C
Profit		100,000
Less dividends payable for the period:		
Preference (5,000 × C5)	25,000	
Ordinary (10,000 × C2)	20,000	(45,000)
Undistributed earnings		55,000
Allocation of undistributed earnings:		
Allocation per ordinary share = A		
Allocation per preference share = B where B = 50% of A		
(A × 10,000) + (50% × A × 5,000) = C55,000		
A = 55,000/(10,000 + 2,500) A = C4.4		
B = 50% of A		
B = C2.2	**Preference shares**	**Ordinary shares**
The basic per share amounts are:		
	C per share	**C per share**
Distributed earnings	5.00	2.00
Undistributed earnings	2.20	4.40
Totals	7.20	6.40
Proof: (5,000 × C7.2) + (10,000 × C6.4) = C100,000		

股以应付每股普通股任何额外股利的 50% 的比例，参与分配任何高于 2 元的额外普通股股利。

该主体当年的利润为 100,000 元，且对普通股宣告每股 2 元的股利。

使用前段所述的分配方法对基本 EPS 进行计算的过程如下：

	元	元
利润		100,000
减当期应付股利：		
优先股(5,000 ×5 元)	25,000	
普通股(10,000 ×2 元)	20,000	(45,000)
未分配利润		55,000

未分配利润的分配：

普通股每股分配 = A

优先股每股分配 = B，B = A 的 50%

(A ×10,000) +(50% ×A ×5,000) = 55,000(元)

A =55,000/(10,000 +2,500) A =4. 4(元)

B = A 的 50%

B =2. 2 (元)

基本每股收益金额为：	**优先股**	**普通股**
	元/每股	元/每股
已分配利润	5. 00	2. 00
未分配利润	2. 20	4. 40
总额	7. 20	6. 40

验证：(5,000 ×7. 2 元) +(10,000 ×6. 4 元) =100,000 元

14.63 IAS 33 implies that the EPS attributable to the participating preference shares (participating equity instrument in IAS 33 terminology) should be disclosed even though only one of its two elements (the participating element) is subordinate to all other classes of equity instrument.

14.64 Table 14.1 illustrates disclosure of EPS for different classes of shares – preferred shares and ordinary shares. The equity note describes the respective dividend rights of the shares.

Table 14.1 – EPS for different classes of shares
Volkswagen AG – annual report and accounts – 31 December 2011
Income statement (extract) of the Volkswagen Group for the period January 1 to December 31, 2011

	Note	2011	2010
Basic earnings per ordinary share in €	11	33.10	15.17
Diluted earnings per ordinary share in €	11	33.10	15.17
Basic earnings per preferred share in €	11	33.16	15.23
Diluted earnings per preferred share in €	11	33.16	15.23

11. Earnings per share

Basic earnings per share are calculated by dividing profit attributable to shareholders of Volkswagen AG by the weighted average number of ordinary and preferred shares outstanding during the reporting period. Earnings per share are diluted by potential shares. These include stock options, although these are only dilutive if they result in the issuance of shares at a value below the average market price of the shares.

A dilutive effect arose in fiscal year 2011 from the eighth tranches of the stock option plan. However, it was so insignificant that it did not affect the reported earnings per share.

	Ordinary		Preferred	
	2011	**2010**	**2011**	**2010**
Weighted average number of shares outstanding-basic	295,068,426	295,024,566	170,142,778	154,905,434
Dilutive potential ordinary shares from the stock option plan	7,508	9,792	—	—
Weighted average number of shares outstanding-diluted	295,075,934	295,034,358	170,142,778	154,905,434

14.63 IAS 33 隐含着归属于参加性优先股（IAS 33 的术语中称之为参加性权益工具）的 EPS 应当予以披露，即使其两项要素中仅有一项（参加性要素）是次于所有其他类别的权益工具的。

14.64 表 14.1 说明了不同类别股份——优先股和普通股—— EPS 的披露。权益附注描述了这些股份各自的股利权。

表 14.1——不同类别股份的 EPS

大众汽车公司——年度报告和报表——2011 年 12 月 31 日

大众集团 2011 年 1 月 1 日至 12 月 31 日期间的利润表（摘录）

	附注	2011 年	2010 年
普通股基本每股收益（欧元）	11	33.10	15.17
普通股稀释每股收益（欧元）	11	33.10	15.17
优先股基本每股收益（欧元）	11	33.16	15.23
优先股稀释每股收益（欧元）	11	33.16	15.23

11. 每股收益

通过将归属于大众汽车公司股东的利润除以报告期间发行在外普通股和优先股的加权平均股数计算基本每股收益。每股收益将被潜在股份所稀释。这些潜在股份包括股票期权，虽然仅当其导致以低于股份平均市价的价格发行股份时，才具有稀释性。

在 2011 财政年度中，稀释作用产生于第 8 批股票期权计划。然而，该稀释作用非常不重大以至于其并不影响报告的每股收益。

	普通股		**优先股**	
	2011 年	**2010 年**	**2011 年**	**2010 年**
发行在外股份的加权平均股数——基本	295,068,426	295,024,566	170,142,778	154,905,434
股票期权计划所产生的稀释性潜在普通股	7,508	9,792	—	—
发行在外股份的加权平均股数——稀释	295,075,934	295,034,358	170,142,778	154,905,434

Con.

	2011	€ million 2010
Profit after tax	15, 799	7, 226
Non-controlling interests	391	392
Profit attributable to shareholders of Volkswagen AG	15, 409	6, 835
Basic earnings attributable to ordinary shares	9, 767	4, 475
Diluted earnings attributable to ordinary shares	9, 767	4, 476
Basic earnings attributable to preferred shares	5, 642	2, 359
Diluted earnings attributable to preferred shares	5, 642	2, 359

	2011	€ 2010
Basic earnings per ordinary share	33. 10	15. 17
Diluted earnings per ordinary share	33. 10	15. 17
Basic earnings per preferred share	33. 16	15. 23
Diluted earnings per preferred share	33. 16	15. 23

23 Equity (extract)

The subscribed capital of Volkswagen AG is composed of no-par value bearer shares with a notional value of € 2. 56. As well as ordinary shares, there are preferred shares that entitle the bearer to a € 0. 06 higher dividend than ordinary shares, but do not carry voting rights.

The subscribed capital increased by a total of € 0. 1 million as a result of the capital increase implemented in the fiscal year due to the exercise of conversion rights from the eighth tranche of the stock option plan. Following the capital increase, the subscribed capital amounted to € 1, 191 million.

The subscribed capital is composed of 295, 089, 817 no-par value ordinary shares and 170, 142, 778 preferred shares.

Authorized capital of up to € 110 million, expiring on May 2, 2016, was approved for the issue of new ordinary bearer shares or preferred shares based on the resolution by the Annual General Meeting on May 3, 2011.

Following the capital increase implemented during the previous year, there is still authorized capital of up to € 179. 4 million, resolved by the Extraordinary General Meeting on December 3, 2009 and expiring on December 2, 2014, to issue up to 70, 095, 502 new no-par value preferred bearer shares.

续表

	2011 年	百万欧元 2010 年
税后利润	15,799	7,226
非控制性权益	391	392
归属于大众汽车公司股东的利润	15,409	6,835
归属于普通股的基本收益	9,767	4,475
归属于普通股的稀释收益	9,767	4,476
归属于优先股的基本收益	5,642	2,359
归属于优先股的稀释收益	5,642	2,359

	2011 年	欧元 2010 年
普通股基本每股收益	33.10	15.17
普通股稀释每股收益	33.10	15.17
优先股基本每股收益	33.16	15.23
优先股稀释每股收益	33.16	15.23

23　权益（摘录）

大众汽车公司的认缴资本由名义金额为 2.56 欧元的无面值不记名股票组成。和普通股一样，还存在使持票人有权获得高于普通股每股 0.06 欧元股利的优先股，但不附有表决权。

由于第 8 批股票期权计划中的转换权的行使，导致在本财政年度中实施增资而使认缴资本共增加 10 万欧元。增资后，认缴资本共计 11.91 亿万欧元。

认缴股本由 295,089,817 股的无面值普通股和 170,142,778 股的优先股组成。

基于 2011 年 5 月 3 日的年度股东大会的决议，最高为 1.1 亿欧元将于 2016 年 5 月 2 日到期的授权资本被批准用于发行新的不记名普通股或优先股。

在上年度实施增资后，仍然存在经 2009 年 12 月 3 日的特别股东大会决定且将于 2014 年 12 月 2 日到期的最高为 1.794 亿欧元的授权资本，可用于发行最多为 70,095,502 股新的无面值不记名优先股。

Con.

The Annual General Meeting on April 22, 2010 resolved to create contingent capital in the amount of up to € 102.4 million expiring on April 21, 2015 that can be used to issue up to € 5 billion in bonds with warrants and/or convertible bonds.

Change in ordinary and preferred shares and subscribed capital

				Shares €
	2011	2010	2011	2010
Balance at January 1	**465,188,345**	**400,243,677**	**1,190,882,163**	**1,024,623,813**
Capital increase	–	64,904,498	–	166,155,515
Stock option plan	44,250	40,170	113,280	102,835
Balance at December 31	**465,232,595**	**465,188,345**	**1,190,995,443**	**1,190,882,163**

Computation of number of ordinary shares

14.65 The denominator of the basic EPS is calculated using the weighted average number of those ordinary shares that are outstanding during the period under review. [IAS 33 para 19].

14.66 Where there have been no changes in capital structure during the year, the relevant denominator is the number of ordinary shares outstanding at the year end. However, if additional ordinary shares have been issued during the year, it would not give a fair presentation to apportion the earnings for the whole of the year over the larger equity base. This is because the capital invested through the issue of the additional shares was available to the entity to increase its earnings only for part of the year. Similar considerations apply where shares have been bought back during the year. In order to take these factors into account, and to permit comparison of EPS with the previous period when there may have been no such change in the issued equity capital, it is necessary to use an average of the number of shares weighted by the number of days outstanding (a 'weighted average ordinary share capital') in the calculation of the denominator. The time-weighting factor should generally be the number of days that the specific shares are outstanding as a

续表

2010年4月22日的年度股东大会决定提供金额最高为1.024亿欧元且将于2015年4月21日到期的或有股本以用于发行最高为50亿欧元的附认股权证的债券或可转换债券。

普通股、优先股及认缴资本的变化

				股份欧元
	2011年	2010年	2011年	2010年
1月1日的余额	**465,188,345**	**400,243,677**	**1,190,882,163**	**1,024,623,813**
增资	–	64,904,498	–	166,155,515
股票期权计划	44,250	40,170	113,280	102,835
12月31日的余额	**465,232,595**	**465,188,345**	**1,190,995,443**	**1,190,882,163**

普通股股数的计算

14.65　使用受审核期间发行在外普通股的加权平均数计算基本EPS的分母。[IAS 33第19段]。

14.66　在当年股本结构未发生改变的情况下，相关的分母为年末时发行在外普通股的股数。然而，如果当年发行了额外的普通股，则将全年的收益在增大了的股本基数上分摊，应该不会提供公允的列报。这是因为通过发行额外股份获得的资本投入仅可供主体用于增加当年部分期间的收益。类似的考虑适用于当年已回购股份的情况。为了将这些因素纳入考虑，并为了允许将EPS与前一期间假定已发行权益资本没有发生变动情况下的EPS进行比较，在分母的计算中有必要使用按发行在外的天数加权的平均股数（“加权平均普通股股本”）。时间权重因数一般应当为特定股份发行在外的天数占总天数的比例，尽管在大多数情况下，一个合理的加权平均数的近似值就足够了。[IAS 33第20段]。

proportion of the total number of days, although a reasonable approximation of the weighted average is adequate in most circumstances. [IAS 33 para 20].

14.67 An example of how the weighted average number of shares should be calculated is given below. The example is derived from the illustrative example in IAS 33.

	Shares issued	Treasury shares	Shares outstanding
1 Jan 20X1 Balance at beginning of year	2,400	–	2,400
31 May 20X1 Issue of new shares for cash	800	–	3,200
1 Dec 20X1 Purchase of shares for cash	–	(200)	3,000
31 Dec 20X1 Balance at end of year	3,200	(200)	3,000

Computation of weighted average:

(2,400 × 5/12) + (3,200 × 6/12) + (3,000 × 1/12) = 2,850 shares

or

(2,400 × 12/12) + (800 × 7/12) – (200 × 1/12) = 2,850 shares

14.68 The general principle under IAS 33 is that shares should be included in the weighted average calculation from the date the consideration is receivable (which is generally the date of their issue). [IAS 33 para 21]. Therefore, shares issued for cash are brought into the calculation from the date the cash is receivable. Where shares are issued as consideration for the acquisition of an asset or a satisfaction of a liability, the shares are included in the averaging calculation from the date the asset is recognised or the liability is settled. In other situations, the date of inclusion should be determined from the terms and conditions attaching to the issue. The substance of any contract associated with the issue should also be considered. The standard provides a number of examples illustrating the timing of inclusion of ordinary shares in the weighted average calculation. These examples are listed below:

- Ordinary shares issued in exchange for cash are included when cash is receivable.
- Ordinary shares issued on the voluntary reinvestment of dividends on ordinary

14.67 下面的示例提供了一个关于应当如何计算股份加权平均数的例子。该示例源自于 IAS 33 中的说明性示例。

	已发行股份	库存股	发行在外股份
20X1 年 1 月 1 日年初股数	2,400	–	2,400
20X1 年 5 月 31 日为获取现金而发行新股	800	–	3,200
20X1 年 12 月 1 日以现金购买股份	–	(200)	3,000
20X1 年 12 月 31 日年末股数	3,200	(200)	3,000

加权平均数的计算：

(2,400 × 5/12) + (3,200 × 6/12) + (3,000 × 1/12) = 2,850(股)

或

(2,400 × 12/12) + (800 × 7/12) – (200 × 1/12) = 2,850(股)

14.68 IAS 33 中的一般原则是股份应当自应收对价之日（通常为股份发行之日）起纳入加权平均数的计算。[IAS 33 第21 段]。因此，为获取现金而发行的股份自应收现金之日起纳入计算。在发行股份作为购买资产或清偿负债的对价的情况下，股份自资产确认或负债结清之日起纳入平均数的计算。在其他情况下，纳入计算的日期应当根据发行所附的条款和条件来确定。与发行相关的任何合同实质也应当予以考虑。该准则提供了一些例子，举例说明将普通股纳入加权平均数计算的时点。这些例子列示如下：

- 为换取现金而发行的普通股当应收现金时被纳入。

- 因普通股或优先股股利的自愿再投资而发行的普通股，当股利再投资时被

or preference shares are included when dividends are reinvested.

- Ordinary shares issued as a result of the conversion of a debt instrument to ordinary shares are included as of the date when interest ceases accruing.
- Ordinary shares issued in place of interest or principal on other financial instruments are included as of the date when interest ceases accruing.
- Ordinary shares issued in exchange for the settlement of a liability of the entity are included as of the settlement date.
- Ordinary shares issued as consideration for the acquisition of an asset other than cash are included as of the date on which the acquisition is recognised.
- Ordinary shares issued for the rendering of services to the entity are included as the services are rendered.
- Ordinary shares issued as part of the cost of a business combination are included from the acquisition date (see para 14.78).

[IAS 33 paras 21, 22].

14.69 The general rule that shares should be included in the basic EPS calculation from the date consideration is receivable does not apply to shares that are issued in partly paid form. Partly paid shares are treated as fractions of shares (payments received to date as a proportion of the total subscription price) and included in the averaging calculation only to the extent that they participate in dividends for the period. [IAS 33 para A15]. Partly paid shares that do not participate in dividends are excluded from the basic EPS calculation, but included in the calculation of diluted EPS (see further para 14.110).

Example

A company issues 100,000 ordinary shares of C1 each for a consideration of C2.50 per share. Calls amounting to C1.75 per share were received by the balance sheet date. The partly paid shares are entitled to participate in dividends for the period in proportion to the amount paid. The number of ordinary share equivalents that would be included in the basic EPS calculation on a weighted basis is as follows:

纳入。

- 因债务工具转换为普通股而发行的普通股，自停止计提利息之日起被纳入。
- 为代替其他金融工具的利息或本金而发行的普通股，自停止计提利息之日起被纳入。
- 为换取主体负债的清偿而发行的普通股，自清偿之日起被纳入。
- 作为购买非现金资产的对价而发行的普通股，自确认购买之日起被纳入。
- 因主体接受服务而发行的普通股，于接受服务之时被纳入。
- 作为业务合并成本的一部分而发行的普通股，自购买日起被纳入（参见第14.78段）。

[IAS 33 第21、22段]。

14.69　股份应当自应收对价之日起被纳入基本EPS计算的一般规则，不适用于以缴纳部分股款形式发行的股份。已缴部分股款的股份作为股份的一小部分（迄今收到的、作为认购总价一部分的付款）处理，并且仅以其参与当期股利分配为限被纳入加权平均数的计算中。[IAS 33 第A15段]。不参与股利分配的已缴部分股款的股份被排除在基本EPS的计算之外，但被包括在稀释EPS的计算中（参见下文第14.110段）。

示例

某公司发行了100,000股普通股，每股面值为1元，对价为每股2.50元。截至资产负债表日止，收到了每股1.75元的股款。已缴部分股款的股份有权按已缴金额的比例参与当期股利的分配。在基于加权平均数的基本EPS的计算中，应该包括的约当普通股的数量如下：

$$100,000 \times \frac{C1.75}{C2.50} = 70,000 \text{ shares}$$

14.70 Whenever changes in ordinary shares occur during the accounting period, an amendment is necessary to the number of shares used in the EPS calculation. In some situations, the EPS in prior periods will also have to be adjusted. Some of the ways in which a company can change its ordinary share capital and the consequential effect on the number of shares used in the EPS calculation are considered below.

Purchase and holding of own shares and ESOPs

14.71 Where a company has purchased its own ordinary shares during the year, there will be a lesser number outstanding after the repurchase. Such repurchases should be reflected in the weighted average number of shares outstanding during the period from the date shares are repurchased as illustrated in paragraph 14.67. Any premium payable on the purchase of a company's own ordinary shares will be charged against reserves and will not affect earnings for the year. No adjustments should be made to the prior year's EPS.

14.72 A company may sometimes hold its own shares in treasury. This situation may arise where it has acquired them in the market, or by forfeiture, or by surrender in lieu of forfeiture, or by way of a gift. Shares held uncancelled in treasury are accounted for as a deduction from shareholders' funds. [IAS 32 para 33; IAS 33 para 20]. Another not uncommon group situation is where a subsidiary continues to hold the shares in the parent that were acquired before it became a group member. Since such shares are no longer available in the market, they are excluded from the weighted average number of ordinary shares for the purpose of calculating EPS. [IAS 33 para 20].

[The next paragraph is 14.75.]

14.75 Another common situation where a company holds its own shares arises where it operates an Employee Share Ownership Plan (ESOP) for the benefit of its employees. For the purpose of calculating EPS these outstanding shares should also be excluded from the calculation to the extent that they have not vested unconditionally in the employees.

$$100,000 \times \frac{1.75\text{元}}{2.50\text{元}} = 70,000\text{股}$$

14.70　在会计期间内无论何时发生普通股的变动，均有必要修改 EPS 计算中所使用的股数。在有些情况下，以前期间的 EPS 也将不得不进行调整。公司能够变更其普通股股本的一些方法及其对在 EPS 计算中所使用的股数的间接影响将在下文中进行讨论。

购买和持有自有股份和职工持股计划

14.71　在公司已于当年购买其自有普通股的情况下，回购后发行在外的股数会减少。如第 14.67 段中所说明的，此类回购应当自回购股份之日起在当期发行在外股份的加权平均数中予以反映。购买公司自有普通股的任何应付溢价款将从权益中的准备中扣除，并且将不会影响当年收益。以前年度的 EPS 不应当予以调整。

14.72　公司有时可能持有其自有股份作为库存股。在公司从市场上购买自有股份，或通过作废，或通过放弃代替作废，或通过赠予的方式取得自有股份的情况下，即可能出现这一情形。所持有的未注销库存股作为股东资金的扣除项进行会计处理。[IAS 32 第 33 段；IAS 33 第 20 段]。另一种并不罕见的涉及集团公司的情形是，子公司继续持有在其成为集团成员之前取得的母公司股份。由于在市场上无法再获得此类股份，因而这些股份不包括在用于计算 EPS 的普通股加权平均数内。[IAS 33 第 20 段]。

[下一段为第 14.75 段。]

14.75　公司持有其自有股份的另一种常见情形出现在公司为了其职工的利益而实行职工持股计划（“ESOP”）的情形。为了计算 EPS，这些发行在外的股份中职工未取得可无条件授予的部分也不应当被包括在计算中。

14.76 An example where a company has excluded treasury shares for the purposes of determining the weighted average number of shares for calculating EPS is given in Table 14.2 below. In this example there were no other issues of shares in the year.

Table 14.2 – Treatment of treasury shares in EPS calculation
Telkom SA Limited – annual report and accounts – 31 March 2011

	Restated 2010	**2011**
12. EARNINGS PER SHARE (extract 1)		
Total operations		
Basic and diluted earnings per share (cents)	7,425.7	**239.9**
The calculation of earnings per share is based on profit attributable to equity holders of Telkom for the year of R1,222 million (2010: R37,458 million) and 509,311,296 (2010: 504,437,832) weighted average number of ordinary shares in issue. **		
12. EARNINGS PER SHARE (extract 2)		
Reconciliation of weighted average number of ordinary shares:		
Ordinary shares in issue (refer to note 24)	520,783,900	**520,783,900**
Weighted average number of treasury shares	(16,346,068)	**(11,472,604)**
Weighted average number of shares outstanding	504,437,832	**509,311,296**
Reconciliation of diluted weighted average number of ordinary shares:		
Weighted average number of shares outstanding	504,437,832	**509,311,296**
Expected future vesting of shares	–	–
Diluted weighted average number of shares outstanding	504,437,832	**509,311,296**

** *The Telkom Conditional Share Plan was concluded with a final vesting in June 2010, therefore there is no adjustment in the weighted average number of shares as a result of the expected future vesting of shares allocated to employees under this plan. Due to the plan being concluded, there is no further dilutive effect on basic earnings per share.*

14.76 下表14.2提供了一个为了确定用于计算EPS的加权平均股数，公司将库存股排除在外的例子。此例中，当年没有其他股份发行。

表14.2——EPS计算中库存股的处理

Telkom SA Limited公司——年度报告和报表——2011年3月31日

	经重述 2010年	**2011年**
12. 每股收益(摘录1)		
经营合计		
基本每股收益和稀释每股收益(分)	7,425.7	**239.9**
每股收益的计算以归属于Telkom权益持有者的年度利润R122,200万(2010年：R3,745,800万)和已发行普通股的加权平均数509,311,296股(2010年：504,437,832股)为基础。**		
12. 每股收益(摘录2)		
普通股加权平均数调节表：		
已发行普通股(参见附注24)	520,783,900	**520,783,900**
库存股的加权平均数	(16,346,068)	**(11,472,604)**
发行在外股份的加权平均数	504,437,832	**509,311,296**
稀释普通股加权平均数调节表：		
发行在外股份的加权平均数	504,437,832	**509,311,296**
预期未来可行权的股份	–	–
稀释发行在外股份的加权平均股数	504,437,832	**509,311,296**

***Telkom附条件的股份计划以2010年6月的最终行权而告终，因此在该计划中分配至职工的预期未来行权的股份，并不导致对加权平均股数的调整。由于该计划已结束，因此对基本每股收益没有进一步的稀释影响。*

Contingently issuable shares

14.77 Contingently issuable shares are ordinary shares that are issuable for little or no cash or other consideration if and when specified conditions in a contingent share agreement have been met. [IAS 33 para 5]. In other words, the consideration for the shares has effectively been received, but the shares remain to be issued – a typical example is contingent consideration on an acquisition payable in shares. Contingently issuable shares are considered to be outstanding and are included in the calculation of basic EPS from the date when all the necessary conditions have been satisfied, that is, the events have occurred. Shares that are issuable solely after the passage of time are not contingently issuable shares, because the passage of time is a certainty and should, therefore, be included in the calculation from inception of the contract. Outstanding ordinary shares that are contingently returnable (that is, subject to recall) are not treated as outstanding, that is they are excluded from the calculation of basic EPS until the date when the shares are no longer subject to recall. [IAS 33 para 24]. Contingently issuable shares are discussed further from paragraph 14.145.

Shares issued as consideration in a business combination

14.78 Where ordinary shares are issued during the financial year as part of the cost of a business combination (for example, in exchange for a majority interest in the equity of another company) – that is, as non-cash consideration, the results of the new subsidiary are included in the consolidation from the acquisition date. Therefore, the shares issued as consideration to obtain those earnings should be included in the EPS calculation on a weighted average basis from the same date. [IAS 33 para 22].

Mandatorily convertible instruments

14.79 An entity may issue a loan note or a preference share that is convertible into ordinary shares of the entity. The instrument may either be mandatorily convertible or convertible at the option of the issuer or holder into a fixed number

或有可发行股份

14.77　或有可发行股份是指如果当满足或有股份协议中的指定条件时，能以极少或不需要现金或其他对价就可发行的普通股。[IAS 33 第 5 段]。换言之，该股份的对价实际上已经收到，但是该股份仍有待发行——一个典型的例子是以股份作为应付收购款中的或有对价。或有可发行股份被认为是发行在外的股份，且自满足所有必要条件（即相关事项已发生）之日起，纳入基本 EPS 的计算。仅仅随着时间的推移即可发行的股份不是或有可发行股份，因为时间的推移是确定事项，因此应当自合同开始起包括在计算中。或有可退回的发行在外普通股（即可被收回）不作为发行在外股份处理，即其不包括在基本 EPS 的计算中，直至这些股份不再可被收回之日。[IAS 33 第 24 段]。自第 14.145 段起将进一步讨论或有可发行股份。

业务合并中作为对价发行的股份

14.78　在财务年度内发行普通股作为业务合并（例如，为换取另一公司的权益中的多数股权）成本的一部分，即作为非现金对价的情况下，新子公司的经营成果自购买日起纳入合并财务报表。因此，作为取得这些收益的对价而发行的股份，应自同一日期起被包括在计算 EPS 的加权平均数中。[IAS 33 第 22 段]。

强制性可转换工具

14.79　主体可能发行可转换为普通股的贷款凭证或优先股。该项工具可能是可强制性转换或者由发行者或持有者选择是否将其转换为固定数量的股份。在某一工具为强制性可转换的情况下，普通股的发行仅仅是取决于时间的推

of shares. Where an instrument is mandatorily convertible, the issue of ordinary shares is solely dependent on the passage of time. Consequently, ordinary shares that are issuable on conversion of a mandatorily convertible instrument should be included in basic EPS from the date that the contract is entered into. [IAS 33 para 23]. On the other hand, debt that is convertible at the option of the holder contains an obligation to issue a fixed number of shares *if* the conversion option is exercised. Such shares are treated as potential ordinary shares as they may never be issued if the conversion option is not exercised. Consequently, such potential shares are not considered outstanding for purposes of calculating basic EPS, but are included in the calculation of diluted EPS (see para 14.114 below).

Example

A company has issued debt that is mandatorily convertible into a fixed number of shares in five years time. Neither the issuer nor the holder has any option to require settlement in cash. Interest is payable (in cash) until conversion. How does it affect EPS?

For the purpose of EPS the potential ordinary shares that would be issued on conversion are included in the weighted average number of ordinary shares used in the calculation of basic EPS (and, therefore, also diluted EPS) from the date of issue of the instrument, since their issue is solely dependent on the passage of time. There is no adjustment to the profit or loss attributable to the ordinary equity holders for consequential interest savings, because the shares are treated as if had already been issued. The interest relates to a separate liability for the interest payments that remain payable.

14.79.1 An entity may have preference shares that are mandatorily convertible when the entity's ordinary share price increases to a specified level. As the conversion is contingent on this uncertain event occuring, the issuable shares are treated in the same ways as an option that is convertible at the option of the issuer or holder. Hence, they are treated as outstanding and are included in the calculation of basic EPS only from the date when all necessary conditions are satisfied (that is, when the ordinary shares have reached the specified share price). [IAS 33 para 24]. Note, that it is still necessary to consider whether these preference shares are themselves participating equity instruments (see para 14.57).

移。因此，一旦强制性可转换工具转换时即可发行的普通股应当自合同订立之日起包括在基本 EPS 计算中。[IAS 33 第 23 段]。另一方面，持有者可选择是否转换的债务中包含了一项如果转换选择权被行使，则需发行固定数量股份的义务。此类股份作为潜在普通股处理，因为*如果*不行使转换选择权，则这些股份可能永远不会发行。因此，在计算基本 EPS 时，此类潜在股份不被认为是发行在外的股份，但包括在稀释 EPS 的计算中（参见下文第 14. 114 段）。

示例

某公司已发行了在五年之内可强制转换为固定数量股份的债务。发行者和持有者均无任何选择权要求以现金结算。直至转换时才应（以现金）支付利息。这将如何影响 EPS？

对于 EPS，转换时应该会发行的潜在普通股自上述工具发行之日起，纳入用于计算基本 EPS（因此，也包括稀释 EPS）的普通股加权平均数中，因为这些潜在普通股的发行仅取决于时间的推移。由于这些股份已经被当作发行的股份进行处理，由此导致的利息节省不需要调整归属于普通股股东的损益。该利息与作为尚待支付利息款的单独负债有关。

14. 79. 1　主体可能拥有当主体的普通股价格上升至指定水平时可强制转换的优先股。由于转换视此不确定事项的发生与否而定，因而该可发行股份以与发行者或持有者拥有转换选择权相同的方式进行处理。因此，这些股份自当且仅当满足所有必要条件（即，当普通股已达到指定股价时）之日起作为发行在外的股份进行处理，被包括在基本 EPS 的计算中。[IAS 33 第 24 段]。应当注意的是，仍有必要考虑这些优先股本身是否为参加性权益工具（参见第 14. 57 段）。

Bonus issue (stock dividends), share split and share consolidation

14.80 The weighted average number of ordinary shares outstanding during the period and for all periods presented should be adjusted for events, other than the conversion of potential ordinary shares, that have changed the number of ordinary shares outstanding, without a corresponding change in resources (see further para 14.169). [IAS 33 para 26]. Where an entity issues new shares by way of a bonus issue or stock dividend during the period, the effect is to increase only the number of shares outstanding after the issue. There is no effect on earnings as there is no flow of funds as a result of the issue. Consequently, the shares should be treated as outstanding as if the issue had occurred at the beginning of the earliest period reported. This means that the earnings for the year should be apportioned over the number of shares after the capitalisation. The EPS figure disclosed for the previous year should be recalculated using the new number of shares in issue. [IAS 33 para 28].

14.81 Similar considerations apply where ordinary shares are split into shares of smaller nominal value (a share of C1 nominal value is divided into four shares of 25c each C1 = 100c) or consolidated into shares of a higher nominal amount (four shares of 25c each are consolidated into one share of C1). In both these situations, the number of shares outstanding before the event is adjusted for the proportionate change in the number of shares outstanding after the event. [IAS 33 para 27].

14.82 The impact on the EPS figure of a bonus issue of shares is illustrated in the following example:

Example

On 31 December 20X7, the issued share capital of a company consisted of C1,000,000 in ordinary shares of 25c each and C500,000 in 10% cumulative preference shares of C1 each. On 1 October 20X8, the company issued 1,000,000 ordinary shares fully paid by way of capitalisation of reserves in the proportion of 1:4 for the year ended 31 December 20X8.

送股（股票股利）、拆股和股份合并

14.80 当期及所有列报期间发行在外普通股的加权平均数，除潜在普通股的转换之外，应当对改变发行在外普通股的股数同时主体资源无相应变化的事项进行调整（参见下文第14.169段）。[IAS 33 第26段]。在主体于当期通过送股或股票股利的方式发行新股的情况下，其影响是仅增加此次发行后发行在外股份的数量。因为此次发行并未导致任何资金流，所以对收益无任何影响。因此，这些股份应当作为已发行在外的股份进行处理，如同该次发行在所列报最早期间的期初已经发生。这意味着当年收益应当按资本变化后的股数进行分配。以前年度披露的 EPS 数值应当使用新的已发行股数进行重新计算。[IAS 33 第28段]。

14.81 类似考虑适用于普通股分割为面值较小的股票（面值1元的1股被分割为每股25分的4股，1元=100分）或合并为面值较高的股票（每股25分的4股被合并为1元的1股）的情况。在这两种情况下，事项发生前发行在外股份的数量均应就事项发生后发行在外股份数量的变化比例进行调整。[IAS 33 第27段]。

14.82 下列示例就送股对 EPS 数值的影响进行了举例说明：

示例

于20X7年12月31日，某公司的已发行股本由每股0.25元的普通股1,000,000元和每股1元股利率为10%的累积优先股500,000元组成。于20X8年10月1日，该公司通过按1∶4的比例将截至20X8年12月31日止年度的权益中的准备转作资本的方式，发行了1,000,000股已全额支付的普通股。

	20X8	20X7
	C'000	**C'000**
Calculation of earnings		
Profit for the year	550	450
Less: preference dividend	(50)	(50)
Earnings	500	400
Number of ordinary shares	No (000)	No (000)
Shares in issue for full year	4,000	4,000
Capitalisation issue at 1 October 20X8	1,000	1,000
Number of shares	5,000	5,000
Earnings per ordinary share of 25c	10.0c	8.0c

The comparative earnings per share for 20X7 can also be calculated by adjusting the previously disclosed EPS in 20X7, in this example 10c, by the following factor:

$$\frac{\text{Number of shares before the bonus issue}}{\text{Number of shares after the bonus issue}}$$

Adjusted EPS for 20X7:

$$10c \times \frac{4,000}{5,000} = 8.0c$$

The above ratio should also be used to restate previous years' EPS and other financial ratios (for example, dividend per share) disclosed in the historical summary.

Issue of shares at full market price

14.83 Where new ordinary shares are issued during the year for cash at full market price, the earnings should be apportioned over the average number of shares outstanding during the period weighted on a time basis.

	20X8 年	20X7 年
	千元	千元
收益计算		
本年利润	550	450
减：优先股股利	(50)	(50)
收益	500	400
普通股股数	千股	千股
全年已发行股份	4,000	4,000
20X8 年 10 月 1 日转作资本发行的股份	1,000	1,000
股数	5,000	5,000
每股 0.25 元的普通股的收益	0.1 元	0.08 元

20X7 年的每股收益比较数也能够通过下列因数调整以前披露的 20X7 年 EPS（此例中为 0.1 元）计算得出：

$$\frac{\text{送股前的股数}}{\text{送股后的股数}}$$

20X7 年调整后的 EPS：

$$0.1\text{ 元}\times\frac{4,000}{5,000}=0.08\text{ 元}$$

上述比率也应当用于重述以前年度的 EPS 和在历史数据汇总中披露的其他财务比率（例如每股股利）。

按完全市场价格发行股份

14.83　在当年按完全市场价格发行以现金购买新普通股的情况下，收益应当按当期发行在外股份的时间的加权平均数进行分配。

Example

On 31 December 20X7, the issued share capital of a company consisted of C1,000,000 in ordinary shares of 25c each and C500,000 in 10% cumulative preference shares of C1 each. On 1 October 20X8, the company issued 1,000,000 ordinary shares at full market price in cash for the year ended 31 December 20X8.

	20X8	20X7
	C'000	C'000
Calculation of earnings		
Profit for the year	550	450
Less: preference dividend	(50)	(50)
Earnings	500	400
Weighted average number of ordinary shares	No (000)	No (000)
Shares in issue for full year	4,000	4,000
Issued on 1 October 20X8(1,000,000 ×3/12)	250	–
Number of shares	4,250	4,000
Earnings per ordinary share of 25c	11.8c	10.0c

The calculation of earnings per share is based on earnings of C500,000 (20X7: C400,000) and on the weighted average of 4,250,000 ordinary shares in issue during the year (20X7: 4,000,000).

[The next paragraph is 14.85.]

Rights issue

14.85 Companies sometimes raise additional capital during the year by issuing shares to existing shareholders on a *pro* rata basis to their existing holdings in the form of a rights issue. The rights shares may either be offered at the current market

示例

20X7 年 12 月 31 日，某公司的已发行股本由每股 0.25 元的普通股 1,000,000 元和每股 1 元的股利率为 10% 的累积优先股 500,000 元组成。于 20X8 年 10 月 1 日，该公司对截至 20X8 年 12 月 31 日止年度按完全市场价格发行了 1,000,000 股付现的普通股。

	20X8 年	20X7 年
	千元	千元
收益计算		
本年利润	550	450
减：优先股股利	(50)	(50)
收益	500	400
普通股加权平均数	数量（000）	数量（000）
全年已发行股份	4,000	4,000
20X8 年 10 月 1 日发行的股份(1,000,000 ×3/12)	250	-
股数	4,250	4,000
每股 0.25 元的普通股的收益	11.8 元	10.0 元

每股收益的计算基于收益 500,000 元（20X7 年：400,000 元）和当年已发行普通股的加权平均数 4,250,000 股(20X7 年:4,000,000 股)。

[下一段为第 14.85 段。]

配股

14.85　公司有时在年度内通过配股的形式向现有股东按其现有持股比例发行股份以筹集额外资本。所配的股份可能按当前市价或低于当前市价的价格发行。如上文第 14.83 段中所讨论的，在股份按完全市场价格发行的情况下，

price or at a price that is below the current market price. Where shares are issued at full market price, the weighting is carried out on a time basis as discussed in paragraph 14.83 above. However, where ordinary shares are issued during the year by way of a rights issue at a discount to the market price, the weighting calculation must reflect the fact that the discount is effectively a bonus (stock dividend) given to the shareholders in the form of shares for no consideration and must, therefore, be taken into account in calculating the weighted average number of shares. [IAS 33 para A2]. In fact, it can be demonstrated (see example below) that a rights issue is equivalent to a capitalisation issue of part of the shares for no consideration and an issue of the remainder of the shares at full market price. The notional capitalisation issue reflects the bonus element inherent in the rights issue and is measured by the following fraction:

$$\frac{\text{Fair value per share immediately before the exercise of rights}}{\text{Theoretical ex-rights fair value per share}}$$

14.86 The fair value per share immediately before the exercise of rights is the *actual* closing price at which the shares are quoted on the last date inclusive of the right to subscribe for the new shares. This is often referred to as the 'cum-rights price', being the price on the last day of quotation cum-rights. The 'ex-rights price', on the other hand, is the *theoretical* price at which, in a perfect market and without any external influences, the shares would trade after the exercise of the rights. Where the rights themselves are publicly traded separately from the shares themselves, as is the case in some countries, the fair value for the purpose of the above calculation is established at the close of the last day on which the shares are traded together with the rights. [IAS 33 para A2].

14.87 The above factor should be used to adjust the number of shares in issue before the rights issue in order to correct for the bonus (stock dividend) element in the rights issue. This correction should be made both for the current period prior to the rights issue and the previous period. The way in which EPS should be calculated following a rights issue and the adjustment that should be made to the comparative EPS figure are considered in the example below.

Example

At 31 December 20X7, the issued capital of a company consisted of 1.8m

以时间为基础进行加权。然而，在年度内通过配股的方式折价发行普通股的情况下，加权计算必须反映以下事实，即该折扣实际上是以零对价股份的形式给予股东的分红（股票股利），因此在计算加权平均股数时必须被考虑在内。[IAS 33 第 A2 段]。事实上，配股能够被证明（参见下面的示例）相当于对一部分股份以零对价进行资本发行并对剩余股份以完全市场价格发行。此名义上的资本发行反映了配股所固有的分红要素，并通过以下系数计量：

$$\frac{\text{行权前的每股公允价值}}{\text{理论上的每股除权公允价值}}$$

14.86　行权前的每股公允价值是在包括认购新股权利的最后日期，对该股份报出的实际收盘价。这通常被称为“含权价”，即最后一天的含权报价。另一方面，“除权价”是指在完全市场中且无任何外部影响的情况下，行权后股份应该会交易的理论价格。在权利本身与股份本身分开进行公开交易的情况下，如在某些国家中的情形，用于上述计算的公允价值在股份与权利一同交易的最后一天的收盘时确定。[IAS 33 第 A2 段]。

14.87　上述因数应当用于调整配股前已发行股份的数量，从而调整配股中的分红（股票股利）要素。应当同时对配股前的当前期间和以前期间作出这一调整。下面的示例讨论了配股后 EPS 的计算方式，以及应当对 EPS 的比较数据作出的调整。

示例

某公司于 20X7 年 12 月 31 日的已发行股本包括 1,800,000 股每股 0.1 元

ordinary shares of 10c each, fully paid. The profit for the year ended 31 December 20X7 and 20X8 amounted to C630,000 and C875,000 respectively. On 31 March 20X8, the company made a rights issue on a 1 for 4 basis at 30c. The market price of the shares immediately before the rights issue was 60c.

Calculation of theoretical ex rights price

	No		c
Initial holding	4	Market value	240
Rights taken up	1	Cost	30
New holding	5	Theoretical price	270

Theoretical ex rights price $\frac{270}{5} = 54c$

The market price is the fair value of the shares immediately prior to the exercise of rights, that is, the actual cum-rights price of 60c.

Cost is the amount payable for each new share under the rights issue.

Calculation of bonus element

The bonus element of the rights issue is given by the fraction:

$$\frac{\text{Market price before rights issue}}{\text{Theoretical ex-rights price}} \quad \frac{60}{54} = \frac{10}{9}$$

This corresponds to a bonus issue of 1 for 9. The bonus ratio will usually be greater than 1, that is the market price of the shares immediately prior to the exercise of rights is greater than the theoretical ex-rights price. If the ratio is less than 1 it may indicate that the market price has fallen significantly during the rights period, which was not anticipated when the rights issue was announced. In this situation, the rights issue should be treated as an issue of shares for cash at full market price (see para 14.83 above).

As stated in paragraph 14.85 above, it can be demonstrated, using the figures in the example, that a rights issue of 1 for 4 at 30c is equivalent to a bonus issue of 1 for 9 combined with an issue of shares at full market price of 54c

的已全额支付的普通股。截至20X7年12月31日和截至20X8年12月31日止年度的利润分别为630,000元和875,000元。于20X8年3月31日，该公司以0.3元的价格进行配股，每4股配1股。配股前的股份市价为0.6元。

理论除权价的计算

	数量		元
初始持股	4	市场价格	2.4
配股	1	成本	0.3
最新持股	5	理论价格	2.7

理论除权价　$\frac{2.7}{5}=0.54$ 元

市场价格是股份行权前的公允价值，即实际含权价0.6元。

成本是为配发的每股新股支付的金额。

分红要素的计算

配股的分红要素由以下分式得出：

$$\frac{\text{配股前市价}}{\text{理论除权价}} \quad \frac{0.6}{0.54}=\frac{10}{9}$$

这相当于每9股配1股的分红配股。分红比率通常会大于1，即行权前的股份市场价格大于理论除权价。如果该比率小于1，可能表明在此配股期间市价已大幅下跌，这在宣布配股时未被预料到。在这种情况下，配股应当作为按完全市场价格发行要求付现的股份处理（参见上文第14.83段）。

如上文第14.85段所述，使用本例中的数值可以证明以0.3元的价格每4股配1股相当于每9股配1股的分红配股，同时按每股0.54元的完全市价发行新股。考虑某一个人股东持有180股股份。

per share. Consider an individual shareholder holding 180 shares.

	No	Value	C
Original holding	180	Value at 60c per share	108.00
Rights shares (1:4)	45	Value at 30c per share	13.50
Holding after rights issue	225	Value at 54c per share	121.50

The additional 45 rights shares at 30C can be shown to be equivalent to a bonus issue of 1 for 9 on the original holding followed by an issue of 1 : 8 at full market price of 54c following the bonus issue as follows:

	No	Value	C
Original holding	180	Value at 60c per share	108.00
Bonus issue of 1 for 9	20	Value nil	nil
	200	Value at 54c per share	108.00
Issue of 1 for 8 at full price	25	Value at 54c per share	13.50
Total holding	225	Value at 54c per share	121.50

The shareholder is, therefore, indifferent as to whether the company makes a rights issue of 1 for 4 at 30c per share or a combination of a bonus issue of 1 for 9 followed by a rights issue of 1 for 8 at full market price of 54c per share.

Having calculated the bonus ratio, the ratio should be applied to adjust the number of shares in issue before the rights issue both for the current year and for the previous year. Therefore, the weighted average number of shares in issue for the current and the previous period, adjusted for the bonus element would be:

Weighted average number of shares

	20X8	20X7
Number of actual shares in issue before rights	1,800,000	1,800,000
Correction for bonus issue (1:9)	200,000	200,000
Deemed number of shares in issue before rights issue(1.8m × 10/9)	2,000,000	2,000,000

	数量	价值	元
初始持股	180	价值为每股 0.6 元	108.00
配股（1:4）	45	价值为每股 0.3 元	13.50
配股后持股	225	价值为每股 0.54 元	121.50

以 0.3 元的价格额外配送的 45 股可以被显示为相当于在初始持股的基础上每 9 股分红 1 股，并在此次分红配股之后按 1:8 以完全市价 0.54 元发行股份，如下：

	数量	价值	元
初始持股	180	价值为每股 0.6 元	108.00
每 9 股分红 1 股	20	价值为零	零
	200	价值为每股 0.54 元	108.00
以 1:8 按完全市价发行	25	价值为每股 0.54 元	13.50
持股总数	225	价值为每股 0.54 元	121.50

因此，股东并不关心公司是以每股 0.3 元的价格每 4 股配 1 股，还是每 9 股分红 1 股之后再按每股 0.54 元的完全市价每 8 股配 1 股。

计算出分红比率之后，应当将该比率用于调整配股前本年度和以前年度已发行的股份数量。因此，根据分红要素调整的当期和以前期间的已发行股份的加权平均数应该是：

加权平均股数

	20X8 年	**20X7** 年
配股前实际已发行股份的数量	1,800,000	1,800,000
校正分红配股（1:9）	200,000	200,000
配股前已发行股份的认定数量(1,800,000 × 10/9)	2,000,000	2,000,000

The number of shares after the rights issue would be:
1.8m × 5/4 = 2,250,000

Therefore, the weighted average number of shares would be:

2.0m for the whole year		2,000,000
2.0m × 3/12 (before rights issue)	500,000	–
2.25m × 9/12 (after rights issue)	1,687,500	–
Weighted average number	2,187,500	2,000,000

Calculation of EPS following a rights issue

	20X8	20X7 (as previously stated)
Basic EPS	C875,000	C630,000
	2,187,500	1,800,000
	40.0c	35.0c
Basic EPS for 20X7 (as restated)		C630,000
		2,000,000
		31.5c

The restated EPS for 20X7 can also be calculated by adjusting the earnings per share figure of the previous year by the *reciprocal* of the bonus element factor as shown below.

$$35c \times 9/10 = 31.5c$$

In practice, the EPS for the corresponding period can be adjusted directly using the reciprocal of the bonus element factor above.

14.88 A question arises as to whether the averaging calculation in a rights issue made during the year should be performed from the announcement date, or from the last date of acceptance of the subscription price, or from the share issue date following despatch of the share certificates. Depending on the circumstances of

配股后的股数应该是：
1,800,000 × 5/4 = 2,250,000

因此，加权平均股数应该是：

全年 200 万股		2,000,000
200 万 ×3/12（配股前）	500,000	–
225 万 ×9/12（配股后）	1,687,500	–
加权平均数	2,187,500	2,000,000

配股后 EPS 的计算

	20X8 年	20X7 年 （如前所述）
基本 EPS	875,000 元	630,000 元
	2,187,500	1,800,000
	0.4 元	0.35 元
20X7 年的基本 EPS（经重述）		630,000 元
		2,000,000
		0.315 元

2007 年经重述的 EPS 如下所示，也可以通过分红要素因子的*倒数*调整以前年度的每股收益数值进行计算。

0.35 元 ×9/10 = 0.315 元

在实务中，相应期间的 EPS 可以直接使用上述分红要素因子的倒数进行调整。

14.88 问题在于年度中发生配股的平均数的计算应自宣告日、接受认购价的最后日期，还是派发股份证书后的股份发行日起开始计算。根据具体情况，配股宣告日与股份发行日之间通常存在 60 至 80 天的延迟。根据 IAS 33 第 21 段中股份一般应当自应收对价之日起纳入计算的原则，可以得出平均数计算

each case, there is often a delay of between 60 to 80 days between the date of announcement of the rights issue and the share issue date. Following the principle in paragraph 21 of IAS 33 that shares should generally be included from the date consideration is receivable, it follows that the averaging calculation should be performed from the day following the last date of acceptance of the subscription price, which is also the date when the rights are legally exercised. This is because the company begins to generate income from all the proceeds received from that date, which is often midway between the announcement date and the share issue date. Therefore, the new shares should be included in the EPS calculation from the day following the last date on which proceeds are received and not from the announcement date or from the date when the new shares are actually issued. An example of a rights issue (and a share consolidation – see para 14. 81 above) is Table 14. 2. A.

Table 14. 2. A – Effect of rights issue on earnings per share

SEGRO plc – Annual report – 31 December 2009

14. EARNINGS AND NET ASSETS PER SHARE

The earnings per share calculations use the weighted average number of shares and the net assets per share calculations use the number of shares in issue at year end. Both earnings per share and net assets per share calculations exclude 1. 3 million shares held on trust for employee share schemes (2008 1. 5 million).

On 7 April 2009, the Company issued 5, 240. 7 million new ordinary shares (pre-share consolidation) through a rights issue. The rights issue was offered at 10 pence per share and represented a discount to the fair value of the existing shares. The number of shares used for prior year calculations of earnings per share and net assets per share shown below have been adjusted for the discounted rights issue in order to provide a comparable basis for the current year. An adjustment factor of 6. 92 has been applied based on the Company's share price of 136. 5 pence per share on 20 March 2009, the day before the new shares commenced trading on the London Stock Exchange and the theoretical ex-rights price at that date of 19. 73 pence per share. In addition, the impact of the 10 for 1 share consolidation has also resulted in an adjustment to the prior period comparables. Note 25 provides further detail on the rights issue and the share consolidation. As discussed in note 1, these adjustments to comparative earnings per share and net assets per share calculations have not impacted the income statement or balance sheet and therefore, since it has not changed from the previously presented figures, a balance sheet at 31 December 2007 has not been shown.

应自接受认购价的最后一天的次日起开始，这一天也是法律意义上的行权日。这是因为公司自该日起开始从收到的所有价款中产生收益，且该日通常处于宣告日与股份发行日的中间。因此，新股应自获得价款的最后一天的次日起，而非自宣告日或新股的实际发行日起纳入 EPS 的计算。表 14. 2. A 是配股的一个例子（股份合并参见上文第 14. 81 段）。

表 14. 2. A——配股对每股收益的影响

SEGRO plc 公司——年度报告——2009 年 12 月 31 日

14. 每股收益和每股净资产

每股收益的计算使用加权平均股数,每股净资产的计算使用年末已发行股份的数量。每股收益和每股净资产的计算均不包括由信托持有的职工持股计划的 1,300,000 股股份(2008 年 1,500,000 股)。

本公司于 2009 年 4 月 7 日通过配股发行 5,240,700,000 股新普通股(股份合并前)。配股以每股 10 便士发行,相当于现有股份公允价值的一定折扣。以下所示用于以前年度每股收益和每股净资产计算的股数已对该折价配股进行调整,从而为当年提供一个可比的基础。基于本公司 2009 年 3 月 20 日(新股开始在伦敦证券交易所交易的前一天)每股 136. 5 便士的股价和当天每股 19. 73 便士的理论除权价,使用了调整因子 6. 92。此外,10 股并 1 股的股份合并的影响也导致了调整以前期间的比较数。附注 25 提供了关于配股和股份合并的进一步详细情况。如附注 1 所讨论,这些对每股收益和每股净资产比较数计算的调整并未影响利润表或资产负债表,因此由于与以前列报的数值未发生变化,2007 年 12 月 31 日的资产负债表未被列示。

Con.

14(i) – Earnings per ordinary share(extract)

	2009			2008		
	Earnings £m	Shares million	Pence per share	Earnings £m	Shares million	Pence per share
Basic EPS	(233.1)	563.8	(41.3)	(938.1)	300.5	(312.2)
Dilution adjustments:						
Share options and save as you earn schemes	–	0.2	–	–	–	–
Diluted EPS	(233.1)	564.0	(41.3)	(938.1)	300.5	(312.2)

25. SHARE CAPITAL AND SHARE – BASED PAYMENTS (extract 1)

On 7 April 2009, the Company issued 5,240.7 million new ordinary shares (pre share consolidation) at 10 pence per share on the basis of 12 new ordinary shares for every 1 existing ordinary share to raise £500 million (net of expenses).

25. SHARE CAPITAL AND SHARE – BASED PAYMENTS (extract 2)

At the General Meeting held on 28 July 2009:

(a) an ordinary resolution was passed to conduct a share consolidation, consolidating and re-classifying 10 of each existing authorised and existing issued shares of the Company of 1 pence each into 1 share of 10 pence each. The purpose of the share consolidation was to reduce the number of the Company's shares in issue so that the likely share price is appropriate for a Company of SEGRO's size. The share consolidation took effect on 31 July 2009.

Issue of shares at less than market price

14.88.1 Sometimes shares may be issued at a discount to the market price, such as for the acquisition of an asset or the cancellation of a liability. Although the standard does not specifically deal with this situation, it would be appropriate to calculate the inherent bonus element in the issue for the purposes of adjusting the number of shares before the issue. This treatment is implicit in the wording in paragraph 27(b) of IAS 33, which makes reference to a bonus element in *any other issue*.

续表

14(i)——普通股每股收益(摘录)

	2009 年			2008 年		
	收益	股份	便士	收益	股份	便士
	百万英镑	百万	每股	百万英镑	百万	每股
基本 EPS	(233.1)	563.8	(41.3)	(938.1)	300.5	(312.2)
稀释调整:						
股份期权和即赚即储计划	–	0.2	–	–	–	–
稀释 EPS	(233.1)	564.0	(41.3)	(938.1)	300.5	(312.2)

25. 股本和以股份为基础的支付(摘录 1)

本公司于 2009 年 4 月 7 日以每股 10 便士、按每 1 股现有普通股发行 12 股新普通股,发行 5,240,700,000 股新普通股(股份合并前)以筹集 5 亿英镑(已扣除费用)。

25. 股本和以股份为基础的支付(摘录 2)

在 2009 年 7 月 28 日召开的股东大会上:

(a)通过了一项普通决议,决定进行股份合并,将每 10 股每股 1 便士的本公司现有经授权和现有已发行股份合并和重新分类为每股 10 便士的股份 1 股。股份合并的目的在于减少本公司已发行股份的数量,从而使股价容易适合于 SEGRO 此等规模的公司。股份合并于 2009 年 7 月 31 日生效。

以低于市场价格发行股份

14.88.1 股份有时可能以市场价格的折价发行，例如为购买一项资产或取消一项负债。虽然准则未明确涉及这一情况，但是为了调整发行前股数，计算发行的内在分红要素应该是适当的。这一处理隐含在 IAS 33 第 27（b）段的措辞中，提及了分红要素存在于*任何其他发行*中。

Dividends payable in shares or cash

14.89 Where a company pays its dividends in the form of shares or gives the shareholder the option to receive a dividend in either cash or shares (sometimes referred to as scrip dividends or enhanced scrip dividends), the shares issued increase the weighted average number of shares used in the EPS calculation.

14.90 Under IAS 33, paragraphs 5 and 7 and paragraphs 58 to 61 'Contracts that may be settled in ordinary shares or cash', scrip dividends may be regarded as potential ordinary shares (see para 14.98 below) that entitle the recipient to ordinary shares. These potential ordinary shares are converted into ordinary shares when the scrip shares are issued, which is after the balance sheet date. Since shares are included in the weighted average from the date consideration is receivable, ordinary shares issued on the voluntary reinvestment of dividends on ordinary or preference shares should be included on a weighted average basis at the date when the dividends are reinvested. [IAS 33 para 21 (b)]. In practice, for scrip dividends, this is the dividend payment date.

14.91 Furthermore, the cash dividend foregone by the shareholders electing to take a scrip dividend of shares is taken to be the consideration paid for those shares, which is normally equivalent to the current market value of the shares. The rationale for this is that the cash dividend foregone by the shareholders electing to take shares instead of cash is effectively reinvested in the company as fully paid up shares at market value. As a result, the earnings figure in the numerator already reflects the income generated by the additional cash retained from the dividend payment date. Consequently, for the purposes of the EPS calculation the issue of scrip shares should be treated as an issue at full market price and the relevant number of shares should be included in the denominator on a weighted basis from the dividend reinvestment date.

[The next paragraph is 14.93.]

Special dividend followed by share consolidation

14.93 Companies sometimes return surplus cash to shareholders. This is normally

以股份或现金支付的股利

14.89 在公司以股份的形式支付其股利或者给予股东收取现金或股份股利（有时被称为股票股利或超值股票股利）的选择权的情况下，所发行的股份增加了 EPS 计算中所使用的加权平均股数。

14.90 根据 IAS 33 第 5 和 7 段以及第 58 至 61 段“可以普通股或现金结算的合同”，股票股利可能可以被视为潜在普通股使接受者有权获得普通股（参见下文第 14.98 段）。当作为股利的股份发行时，即资产负债表日后，这些潜在普通股被转换为普通股。由于股份自应收对价之日起被包括在加权平均数中，因此为普通股或优先股股利的自愿再投资而发行的普通股应于股利再投资之日以加权平均数被包括在内。[IAS 33 第 21（b）段]。在实务中，对于股票股利，此即股利支付日。

14.91 此外，选择接受股票股利的股东所放弃的现金股利被视作为这些股份支付的对价，其通常相当于该股份的当前市场价值。这一论述的理由是，选择接受股份而非现金的股东所放弃的现金股利，实际是按市场价格全额支付的股份再次投资至公司。因此，分子中的收益数值已经反映出自股利支付日起，留存的额外现金所产生的收益。所以对于 EPS 的计算，股票股利的发行应当按完全市价的发行进行处理，相关的股份数量应当自股利再投资日起以加权平均数包括在分母中。

[下一段为第 14.93 段。]

支付特别股利后进行股份合并

14.93 公司有时会向股东返还现金盈余。这通常通过股份回购或者综合股份

effected by means of a share repurchase or by a synthetic share repurchase that is achieved by the payment of a special dividend to shareholders followed by a consolidation of share capital, for example, changing five 20c shares into four 25c shares.

14.94 IAS 33 deals specifically with the effect on EPS of a special dividend accompanied by a share consolidation. Where a share consolidation is combined with a special dividend and the overall effect of the combined transaction is a share repurchase at fair value the reduction in the number of ordinary shares outstanding is the result of a corresponding reduction in resources. The weighted average number of ordinary shares outstanding for the period in which the combined transaction takes place is adjusted for the reduction in the number of ordinary shares from the date the special dividend is recognised. [IAS 33 para 29].

Example

A company has in issue 10,000 shares with a nominal value of 10c each. At the beginning of 20X8, it decides either to launch a share repurchase of 1,000 shares at the current market price of C1 per share or pay a special dividend of 10c per share (net) followed by a share consolidation of 9 new shares for 10 old shares. The profit after tax for 20X7 and 20X8 (before the effect of the share transactions) is C2,000. Interest rates are 8% per annum and the company pays corporation tax at 31%.

	Balance sheet before transactions	**Repurchase of 1,000 shares at C1 per share**	**Special dividend of 10c per share followed by share consolidation of 10:9**
	C	**C**	**C**
Net assets	5,000	4,000	4,000
Share capital 10,000 shares at 10c each	1,000		

回购来实现，且后者通过在向股东支付特别股利后进行股本合并（例如，将5股0.2元的股份变为4股0.25元的股份）来完成。

14.94　IAS 33特别阐述了伴有股份合并的特别股利对EPS的影响。在股份合并与特别股利这一组合交易的总体影响是主体资产相应减少，结果相等于以公允价值进行股份回购发行在外普通股股数。上述组合交易发生期间发行在外普通股的加权平均数，需根据特别股利确认之日起普通股股数的减少而进行调整。[IAS 33第29段]。

示例

某公司已发行股票10,000股，每股面值0.1元。于20X8年年初，其决定以当时的市价每股1元回购1,000股股份，或者在支付每股0.1元（净额）的特别股利后进行10股旧股并为9股新股的股份合并。20X7年和20X8年的税后利润（在股份交易产生影响前）为2,000元。每年的利率为8%，且公司按31%的税率缴纳公司税。

	交易前的资产负债表	**以每股1元回购1,000股股份**	**支付每股0.1元的特别股利后按10:9进行股份合并**
	元	**元**	**元**
净资产	5,000	4,000	4,000
10,000股股本，每股0.1元	1,000		

Con.

9,000 shares at 10c each		900	
9,000 shares at 11. 1c each			1,000
Capital redemption reserve		100	
Profit and loss account	4,000	3,000	3,000
	5,000	4,000	4,000
Net assets per share	C0. 50	C0. 44	C0. 44

Effect on earnings per share-share repurchase

	20X8 C	20X7 C
Profit for the year	2,000. 00	2,000. 00
Loss of interest on cash paid out (C 1,000 ×0. 08 ×0. 69)	55. 20	–
Earnings	1,944. 80	2,000. 00
Number of shares in issue	9,000	10,000
EPS	21. 61c	20. 00c

Effect on earnings per share-special dividend followed by share consolidation

The total nominal value of the shares remain unchanged, but whereas before there were 10,000 shares of 10C each there are now 9,000 shares of 11. 1c each.

	20X8 C	20X7 C
Profit for the year	2,000. 00	2,000. 00
Loss of interest on cash paid out (C1,000 ×0. 08 ×0. 69)	55. 20	–
Earnings	1,944. 48	2,000. 00
Number of shares in issue (unadjusted)	9,000	10,000

续表

9,000 股股份，每股 0.1 元		900	
9,000 股股份，每股 0.111 元			1,000
资本赎回准备		100	
损益账户	4,000	3,000	3,000
	5,000	4,000	4,000
每股净资产	0.50 元	0.44 元	0.44 元

股份回购对每股收益的影响

	20X8 年 元	**20X7 年 元**
本年利润	2,000.00	2,000.00
因支付现金而损失的利息（1,000 元 ×0.08 ×0.69）	55.20	-
收益	1,944.80	2,000.00
已发行股份的数量	9,000	10,000
EPS	0.261 元	0.2 元

支付特别股利后进行股份合并对每股收益的影响

股份的总面值不变，但是之前有 10,000 股每股 0.1 元的股份，而现在有 9,000 股每股 0.111 元的股份。

	20X8 年 元	**20X7 年 元**
本年利润	2,000.00	2,000.00
因支付现金而损失的利息（1,000 元 ×0.08 ×0.69）	55.20	-
收益	1,944.48	2,000.00
已发行股份的数量（未调整）	9,000	10,000

Con.

EPS unadjusted (correct treatment)	21.61c	20.00c
Number of shares in issue (adjusted for consolidation)	9,000	9,000
EPS adjusted (incorrect treatment)	21.61c	22.22c

14.95 As can be seen from the above example, the economic effect, in terms of net asset per share, of an actual share repurchase is identical to a synthetic share repurchase that is achieved by the combination of a special dividend with a share consolidation. It follows that the earnings per share figures for the two transactions should also be identical. If an adjustment were made to the previous year's EPS for the share consolidation as shown above, there would be an apparent dilution of 2.75% ((22.22 - 21.61)/22.22) that would make the share repurchase look significantly more attractive than the special dividend route. But this would be misleading as the economic effect of the two transactions is identical. Therefore, no adjustment to prior year's EPS should be made for the share consolidation. [IAS 33 para 29].

14.96 In the above example, it was assumed for simplicity that the combined transaction took place at the beginning of the year and so the new shares were treated as outstanding for a full year. If the combined transaction takes place part way through the year, the weighted average number of ordinary shares outstanding for the period in which the combined transaction takes place should be adjusted for the reduction in the number of shares from the date the special dividend is paid, that is, when resources leave the entity. [IAS 33 para 29]. An example of a company that has treated the payment of an exceptional dividend and a share consolidation carried out at the same time as equivalent to a share buy-back is given in the Table 14.3 below. The company is an investment company and also shows net assets per share (based on shares in issue at the period end).

续表

未经调整的 EPS（正确处理）	0.2161 元	0.2 元
已发行股份的数量（因合并而调整）	9,000	9,000
调整后的 EPS（错误处理）	0.2161 元	0.2222 元

14.95 从上述示例可以看出，就每股净资产而言，实际股份回购的经济影响等同于通过特别股利与股份合并的结合而实现的综合股份回购的经济影响。因此，两种交易的每股收益数值也应相等。如果如上所示就股份合并对前一年度的 EPS 作出调整，则会产生 2.75% 的明显稀释(0.2222 - 0.2161)/0.2222，使得股份回购较支付特别股利的方式显得明显更具吸引力。但是这应该是具有误导性的，因为两种交易的经济影响是相同的。因此，不应就股份合并调整以前年度的 EPS。[IAS 33 第 29 段]。

14.96 在上述示例中，为简单起见，假设组合交易发生于年初，因此新股作为全年发行在外的股份处理。如果该组合交易发生在年度中间，则组合交易发生期间发行在外普通股的加权平均数，应当对支付特别股利之日（即当资源离开主体时）起股数的减少进行调整。[IAS 33 第 29 段]。下面的表 14.3 是关于公司将支付特别股利并同时执行股份合并视同于股份回购进行处理的一个例子。该公司是一家投资公司，同时基于期末的已发行股份列示了每股净资产。

Table 14. 3—Effect on EPS of special dividend and share consolidation

Mitchells & Butlers plc—Annual report—29 September 2007

12. Dividends

	2007 52 weeks £m	2006 52 weeks £m
Amounts paid and recognised in equity		
In respect of the 53 weeks ended 1 October 2005:		
– Final dividend of 7. 55p per share	–	38
In respect of the 52 weeks ended 30 September 2006:		
– Interim dividend of 3. 65p per share	–	18
– Final dividend of 8. 60p per share	35	–
In respect of the 52 weeks ended 29 September 2007:		
– Special interim dividend of 100. 0p per share	486	–
– Interim dividend of 4. 25p per share	17	–
	538	56
Proposed final dividend of 10. 0p (2006 8. 60p) per share	40	35

The payment of the special interim dividend amounting to £486m was made on 25 October 2006. The shareholders approved, at an Extraordinary General Meeting on 17 October 2006, the consolidation of the share capital of the Company by the issue of 34 new ordinary shares of 8 13/24p each for every 41 existing shares of 7 1/12p each.

The Board recommended on 28 November 2007 the proposed final dividend for the 52 weeks ended 29 September 2007. This did not qualify for recognition in the financial statements at 29 September 2007 as it had not been approved by the shareholders at that date.

13. Earnings per ordinary share

Basic earnings per share (EPS) has been calculated by dividing the profit or loss for the financial period by the weighted average number of ordinary shares in issue during the period, excluding own shares held in treasury and by employee share trusts.

For diluted earnings per share, the weighted average number of ordinary shares is adjusted to assume conversion of all dilutive potential ordinary shares.

表 14.3——特别股利和股份合并对 EPS 的影响

Mitchells & Butlers plc 公司——年度报告——2007 年 9 月 29 日

12. 股利

	2007 年 52 周 百万英镑	2006 年 52 周 百万英镑
支付并在权益中确认的金额		
对于截至 2005 年 10 月 1 日的 53 周：		
——期末股利每股 7.55 便士	–	38
对于截至 2006 年 9 月 30 日的 52 周：		
——中期股利每股 3.65 便士	–	18
——期末股利每股 8.60 便士	35	–
对于截至 2007 年 9 月 29 日的 52 周：		
——特别中期股利每股 100.0 便士	486	–
——中期股利每股 4.25 便士	17	–
	538	56
拟派期末股利每股 10.0 便士（2006 年为 8.60 便士）	40	35

金额为 4.86 亿英镑的特别中期股利于 2006 年 10 月 25 日支付。股东在 2006 年 10 月 17 日的特别股东大会上批准，通过对每 41 股每股 7 1/12 便士的现有股份发行 34 股每股 8 13/24 便士的新普通股，将本公司的股本进行合并。

董事会于 2007 年 11 月 28 日建议，拟对截至 2007 年 9 月 29 日的 52 周派发期末股利。这并不符合在 2007 年 9 月 29 日的财务报表中进行确认的条件，因为在该日其尚未经股东批准。

13. 普通股每股收益

基本每股收益已通过将财务期间的损益除以该期间已发行普通股（不包括库存股和由职工股份信托持有的自身股份）的加权平均数计算得出。

对于稀释每股收益，普通股的加权平均数以假设所有稀释性潜在普通股均已转换进行调整。

Con.

Earnings per ordinary share amounts are presented before exceptional items (see note 9) in order to allow a better understanding of the underlying trading performance of the Group.

	Profit/(loss) £m	Basic EPS pence per ordinary share	Diluted EPS pence per ordinary share
52 weeks ended 29 September 2007			
Loss for the period	(10)	(2.5) p	(2.5) p*
Exceptional items, net of tax	155	38.0p	36.9p
Profit before exceptional items	145	35.5p	34.4p
52 weeks ended 30 September 2006			
Profit for the period	195	39.7p	38.8p
Exceptional items, net of tax	(51)	(10.4) p	(10.2) p
Profit before exceptional items	144	29.3p	28.6p

* The 2007 diluted EPS per ordinary share is unchanged from the basic EPS, as the inclusion of the dilutive potential ordinary shares would reduce the loss per share and is therefore not dilutive.

The weighted average number of ordinary shares used in the calculations above are as follows:

	2007 52 weeks millions	2006 52 weeks millions
For basic EPS calculations	408	491
Effect of dilutive potential ordinary shares:		
Contingently issuable shares	8	7
Other share options	5	5
For diluted EPS calculations	421	503

On 17 October 2006, shareholders approved a share capital consolidation together with a Special Dividend of 100.0p per ordinary share. The overall effect of the transaction was that of a share repurchase at fair value, therefore no adjustment has been made to comparative data.

续表

普通股每股收益以扣除特殊项目前的金额(见附注9)列报,从而使得使用者更好地了解本集团的相关贸易业绩。

	利润/(亏损) 百万英镑	基本 EPS 普通股 每股便士	稀释 EPS 普通股 每股便士
截至2007年9月29日的52周			
本期亏损	(10)	(2.5) 便士	(2.5) 便士*
特殊项目，税后金额	155	38.0 便士	36.9 便士
扣除特殊项目前的利润	145	35.5 便士	34.4 便士
截至2006年9月30日的52周			
本期利润	195	39.7 便士	38.8 便士
特殊项目，税后金额	(51)	(10.4) 便士	(10.2) 便士
扣除特殊项目前的利润	144	29.3 便士	28.6 便士

*2007年的普通股每股稀释 EPS 跟基本 EPS 一样，因为将稀释性潜在普通股纳入计算将减少每股亏损，因而其并非稀释性的。

上述计算中所使用的普通股加权平均数如下:

	2007年 52周 百万	2006年 52周 百万
用于基本 EPS 的计算	408	491
稀释性潜在普通股的影响:		
或有的可发行股份	8	7
其他股份期权	5	5
用于稀释 EPS 的计算	421	503

2006年10月17日，股东批准了股本合并以及普通股每股100.0便士的特别股利。该交易的总体影响与以公允价值进行股份回购相同，因此比较数据未作调整。

Con.

At 29 September 2007, nil (2006 nil) contingently issuable shares and 1,034,538 (2006 965,822) other share options were outstanding that could potentially dilute basic EPS in the future but were not included in the calculation of diluted EPS as they are antidilutive for the periods presented.

24. Called up share capital

	2007		2006	
	Number of shares	£m	Number of shares	£m
Authorised				
Ordinary shares of 8 13/24p each	1,181,130,148	101	–	–
Ordinary shares of 7 1/12p each	–	–	1,424,304,003	101
	1,181,130,148	101	1,424,304,003	101
Called up, allotted and fully paid				
Ordinary shares of 8 13/24p each:				
At start of the financial period	486,910,806	34	500,438,040	35
Share capital consolidation	(83,131,113)	–	–	–
Repurchase and cancellation	–	–	(13,527,234)	(1)
At end of the financial period	403,779,693	34	486,910,806	34

All of the ordinary shares rank equally with respect to voting rights and rights to receive ordinary and special dividends. There are no restrictions on the rights to transfer shares.

On 17 October 2006, shareholders approved a share capital consolidation on the basis of 34 new ordinary shares for every 41 existing ordinary shares. This provided for all of the authorised ordinary shares of 7 1/12p each (whether issued or unissued) to be consolidated into new ordinary shares of 8 13/24p each, which became effective on 18 October 2006.

Details of options granted under the Group's share schemes are contained in note 7.

续表

于2007年9月29日，没有或有的可发行股份（2006年0股）以及其他股份期权1,034,538份（2006年965,822份）发行在外且其在未来可能对基本EPS作出潜在稀释，但因其在所列报期间具有反稀释性而不被纳入稀释EPS的计算。

24. 已催缴股本

	2007年		2006年	
	股数	百万英镑	股数	百万英镑
已授权				
普通股每股8 13/24便士	1,181,130,148	101	–	–
普通股每股7 1/12便士	–	–	1,424,304,003	101
	1,181,130,148	101	1,424,304,003	101
已催缴、分配和全额支付				
普通股每股8 13/24便士：				
在财务期间的期初	486,910,806	34	500,438,040	35
股本合并	(83,131,113)	–	–	–
回购及取消	–	–	(13,527,234)	(1)
在财务期间的期末	403,779,693	34	486,910,806	34

所有普通股在表决权及获得普通股利和特别股利的权利上等级相同。股份转让的权利不存在任何限制。

2006年10月17日，股东批准按对每41股现有普通股发行34股新普通股进行股本合并。这就使得所有经授权的每股7 1/12便士的普通股（无论已发行还是未发行）被合并为每股8 13/24便士的新普通股，并于2006年10月18日生效。

在集团股份计划中授予的期权的详情包含于附注7中。

Diluted earnings per share

Measurement

14.97 As discussed from paragraph 14.65 above, the basic EPS is calculated on the number of ordinary shares outstanding in respect of the period. Sometimes companies may have 'potential ordinary shares' in issue. The standard defines a 'potential ordinary share' as a financial instrument or other contract that may entitle its holder to ordinary shares. [IAS 33 para 5]. Examples given in the standard are:

Financial liabilities or equity instruments, including preference shares, that are convertible into ordinary shares.

Options (including employee share options) and warrants.

Shares that would be issued on satisfaction of certain conditions that result from contractual arrangements, such as the purchase of a business or other assets.

[IAS 33 para 7].

14.98 In addition IAS 33, clarifies that contracts that may result in the issue of ordinary shares of the entity to the holder of the contract at the option of the issuer or the holder are potential ordinary shares. [IAS 33 paras 58 to 61]. Such contracts are dealt with from paragraph 14.159 below.

14.99 In each of these situations, the effect of the conversion into ordinary shares may be to dilute future EPS. It should be noted that not all potential ordinary shares in issue will have a diluting effect (see further para 14.126). Any potential dilution, however, is of considerable interest to existing ordinary shareholders. This is because it indicates the possible reduction in current earnings that may be distributed to them by way of dividends in the future and the possible increase in the number of shares over which the total market value of the company may be divided.

14.100 The standard, therefore, requires the calculation of diluted EPS, in

稀释每股收益

计量

14.97　如上文第 14.65 段起所讨论，基本 EPS 按当期发行在外普通股的股数计算得出。有时公司可能有已发行的“潜在普通股”。准则将“潜在普通股”定义为可使其持有者有权获得普通股的金融工具或其他合同。［IAS 33 第 5 段］。准则中给出的示例为：

金融负债或权益工具，包括可转换为普通股的优先股。

期权（包括职工股份期权）和认股权证。

因合同安排在满足某些条件诸如购买业务或其他资产时将发行的股份。

［IAS 33 第 7 段］。

14.98　此外，IAS 33 明确根据发行者或持有者的选择可能导致向合同持有者发行主体的普通股的合同为潜在普通股。［IAS 33 第 58 至 61 段］。下文第 14.159 段起对此类合同进行讨论。

14.99　在上述各种情况下，转换为普通股的影响可能是稀释未来的 EPS。应当注意的是，并非所有已发行潜在普通股均将产生稀释作用（参见下文第 14.126 段的进一步讨论）。然而，对于现有普通股股东，任何潜在稀释都是与其利益相关的。这是因为其表明了未来可能通过股利的方式分配至这些股东的现行收益因而可能导致减少，以及公司总市场价值所除以的股数可能会增加。

14.100　因此，准则要求除基本 EPS 外，还应对归属于母公司普通股股东的

addition to the basic EPS (see para 14.46), for profit or loss attributable to the parent entity's ordinary equity holders and separately for each of continuing and discontinued operations where these are presented in accordance with IFRS 5. For the purpose of calculating diluted EPS, the profit or loss for the period attributable to ordinary equity holders adjusted for the effects of all dilutive potential ordinary shares should be divided by the sum of the weighted average number of ordinary shares used in the basic EPS calculation and the weighted average number of shares that would be issued on the conversion of all the dilutive potential ordinary shares into ordinary shares. [IAS 33 paras 30 to 32, 36].

14.101 It should be noted that although existing ordinary shareholders are interested in future dilution, the diluted EPS figure calculated in accordance with the standard is not intended to be a predictor of dilution, or a forward - looking number. It is seen as an additional historical measure. The IASB and the FASB concluded that as the objective of basic EPS is to measure performance over the reporting period, the objective of diluted EPS should be consistent with that objective while giving effect to all dilutive potential ordinary shares that were outstanding during the period. A past performance method of computing diluted EPS will aid comparison between diluted EPS of different periods. In addition, presenting diluted EPS with undiluted EPS that are calculated on a consistent basis will enable users to view the spread between the two figures as representing a reasonable estimate of the potential dilution that exists in the entity's capital structure.

Computation of earnings

14.102 For the purpose of calculating diluted EPS, the profit or loss attributable to the parent entity's ordinary equity holders should be adjusted for the after-tax effect of:

- Dividends or other items related to dilutive potential ordinary shares that have been deducted in arriving at profit attributable to ordinary equity holders for the purpose of calculating basic EPS, such as dividends on dilutive convertible preference shares.

损益计算稀释 EPS（参见第 14.46 段），且在持续经营和终止经营按照《国际财务报告准则第 5 号》列报的情况下，分开计算持续经营和终止经营的稀释 EPS。为计算稀释 EPS，已对所有稀释性潜在普通股的影响作出调整的当期损益，应当除以基本 EPS 的计算中所使用的普通股加权平均数与所有稀释性潜在普通股转换为普通股时应该会发行的普通股的加权平均数之和。[IAS 33 第 30 至 32 段、第 36 段]。

14.101　应注意的是，尽管现有普通股股东对未来的股份稀释感兴趣，但是按照准则计算稀释 EPS 数值的目的并不在于作为稀释的预报或是前瞻性的数字。其被视为一项额外的历史计量。IASB 和 FASB 得出结论认为，由于基本 EPS 的目的在于计量报告期间的业绩，因而对该期间发行在外的所有稀释性潜在普通股所产生的影响，稀释 EPS 的目的应与该目的一致。采用以往业绩计算稀释 EPS 的方法将有助于不同期间稀释 EPS 的比较。此外，将采用一致基础计算的稀释 EPS 和未稀释 EPS 一同列示，将使得使用者能够将这两个数值之间的差额视为对主体资本结构中所存在的潜在稀释的合理估计。

收益的计算

14.102　为计算稀释 EPS，归属于母公司普通股股东的损益应对下列事项的税后影响进行调整：

- 在得出用于计算基本 EPS 的归属于普通股股东的利润时已扣除的与稀释性潜在普通股有关的股利或其他项目，例如稀释性可转换优先股的股利。

- Interest recognised in the period on dilutive potential ordinary shares, such as interest on dilutive convertible debt.
- Any other changes in income or expense that would result from the conversion of the dilutive potential ordinary shares.

[IAS 33 paras 32(a), 33].

14.103 Once potential ordinary shares are converted into ordinary shares during the period, the dividends, interest and other expense associated with those potential ordinary shares will no longer be incurred. The effect of the conversion, therefore, is to increase profit (or reduce losses) attributable to ordinary equity holders as well as the number of shares in issue. This is illustrated in paragraph 14.114 dealing with convertible securities. Adjustments to profit or loss attributable to ordinary equity holders also include any transaction costs, discounts or premiums on potential ordinary shares that are allocated to periods in accordance with the effective interest method in paragraph 9 of IAS 39, that is, the adjustment to earnings should add back the issue costs (or similar) amortised in the period, in addition to the interest/dividend cost.

14.104 The adjustments to earnings include not only the direct savings in debt servicing cost or dividends and other appropriations and adjustments in respect of convertible preference shares and the related tax effects, but also any other consequential changes in other income or expense arising as a result of the conversion. A situation that often arises in practice is where the equity conversion option in a foreign currency convertible bond, which is treated as a liability, is marked to market through profit or loss. The marked-to-market adjustment needs to be removed from profit or loss for the purposes of calculating diluted EPS. IAS 33 also mentions, as an example, an increase in an employee non-discretionary profit sharing plan as a result of the savings in after-tax interest cost following conversion of convertible debt. [IAS 33 paras 34, 35]. The example given below illustrates such an adjustment. When calculating tax for the purposes of diluted EPS the standard tax rate rather than the entity's effective tax rate should be used. This is because the effective tax rate may be influenced by factors (such as group relief) that affect the entity's results other than the expenses associated with the potential ordinary shares.

■ 当期对稀释性潜在普通股确认的利息，例如稀释性可转换债务的利息。

■ 稀释性潜在普通股的转换所将导致收益或费用的任何其他变化。

[IAS 33 第 32（a）段、第 33 段]。

14.103　一旦潜在普通股在当期被转换为普通股，则与这些潜在普通股相关的股利、利息及其他费用将不再发生。因此，转换的影响是增加（或减少）归属于普通股股东的利润（或亏损）以及已发行股份的数量。这在讨论可转换证券的第 14.114 段中予以说明。对归属于普通股股东的损益的调整也包括按 IAS 39 第 9 段中的实际利率法分配至相关期间的潜在普通股的任何交易费用、折价或溢价，即除利息/股利成本之外，对收益的调整还应当加回当期摊销的发行成本（或类似成本）。

14.104　对收益的调整不仅包括债务服务成本或股利的直接节省和对可转换优先股的其他分配与调整及相关税收影响，还包括转换所导致的任何对其他收益或费用的相应变化。在实务中经常出现的一种情况是，作为负债处理的外币可转换债券中的权益转换期权，通过损益按市值计价。为计算稀释 EPS，按市值计价所作的调整需从损益中扣除。IAS 33 还举例提及了可转换债务转换后税后利息费用的节省所导致的非酌情选择的职工利润分享计划增加的情况。[IAS 33 第 34、35 段]。下文给出的示例说明了此类调整。当计算用于稀释 EPS 计算的税款时，应当使用标准税率而非主体的实际税率。这是因为除与潜在普通股相关的费用外，实际税率也可能受到影响主体经营成果的其他因素所影响（例如集团税收减免）。

Example

Entity A has in issue 25,000 4% debentures with a nominal value of C1. The debentures are convertible to ordinary shares at a rate of 1:1 at any time until 20X9. The entity's management receives a bonus based on 1% of profit before tax.

Entity A's results for 20X2 showed a profit before tax of C80,000 and a profit after tax of C64,000 (for simplicity a tax rate of 20% is assumed in this example).

For the purpose of calculating diluted EPS, the earnings should be adjusted for the reduction in the interest charge that would occur if the debentures were converted and for the increase in the bonus payment that would arise from the increased profit.

This is illustrated below:

	C
Profit after tax	64,000
Add: Reduction in interest cost[1]	
25,000 × 4%	1,000
Less tax expense 1,000 × 20%	(200)
Less: Increase in management bonus	
1,000 × 1%	(10)
Add tax benefit 10 × 20%	2
Earnings for the purposes of diluted EPS	64,792

[1] Note that for simplification, this example does not illustrate the classification of the components of the convertible debenture as liabilities and equity as required by IAS 32.

14.105 It should be noted that the requirement in paragraph 14.102 above refers to adjusting the profit attributable to ordinary equity holders. This figure is after deducting dividends on convertible preference shares and is the figure used for the purpose of calculating basic EPS. In some cases those dividends will be charged as

示例

主体 A 已发行 25,000 份面值为 1 元利率为 4% 的债券。20X9 年前，债券可随时以 1:1 的比例转换为普通股。该主体的管理层按税前利润的 1% 获得奖金。

主体 A 在 20X2 年的经营成果显示税前利润为 80,000 元，税后利润为 64,000 元（为简单起见，本例中假设税率为 20%）。

为计算稀释 EPS，收益应当就债券转换应该会发生的利息费用减少和利润增加应该会导致的奖金支出增加进行调整。

对此说明如下：

	元
税后利润	64,000
加：利息费用的减少[1]	
25,000 ×4%	1,000
减：税费 1,000 ×20%	(200)
减：管理层奖金的增加	
1,000 ×1%	(10)
加：税务利益 10 ×20%	2
用于计算稀释 EPS 的收益	64,792

[1] 需注意的是，为简单起见，此例并未说明按 IAS 32 的要求将可转换债券的组成部分分类为负债和权益的情况。

14.105 应当注意的是，上文第 14.102 段中的要求提及调整归属于普通股股东的利润。这一数值是扣除可转换优先股股利后并被用于计算基本 EPS 的数值。在有些情况下，在得出年度利润时这些股利将计入财务费用（在 IAS 32 中作为金融负债处理的优先股）且得出归属于普通股股东的利润时无需作出

finance costs in arriving at profit for the year (preference shares treated as a financial liability under IAS 32) and no adjustment will be necessary to arrive at profit attributable to ordinary shareholders. In other cases they will be classified in equity (preference shares treated as equity instruments under IAS 32) and an adjustment will be made to profit for the year to arrive at profit attributable to ordinary equity holders. In either case, however, if the convertible preference shares are dilutive, the profit attributable to ordinary shareholders for the purpose of calculating diluted EPS is before deducting the preference dividend.

Computation of number of ordinary shares

14.106 As noted in paragraph 14.100, the denominator of diluted EPS should be calculated as the sum of the weighted average number of ordinary shares used in the basic EPS calculation and the weighted average number of ordinary shares that would be issued on the conversion of all the dilutive potential ordinary shares into ordinary shares. [IAS 33 para 36].

14.107 Entities may have more than one type of potential ordinary share in issue at the reporting date. Whether all these potential ordinary shares actually will be converted into ordinary shares in the future is usually not determinable at the reporting date. The standard requires the assumption that all potential ordinary shares have been converted into ordinary shares at the beginning of the period or, if not in existence at the beginning of the period, the date of the issue of the financial instrument or the granting of the rights by which they are generated. [IAS 33 para 36]. This is sometimes referred to as the 'if converted' method.

14.108 The conversion into ordinary shares should be determined from the terms of the financial instrument or the rights granted and this determination should assume the most advantageous conversion rate or exercise price from the standpoint of the holder of the potential ordinary shares. [IAS 33 para 39]. The effect is to ensure that the diluted EPS is based on the maximum number of new shares that would be issuable under the instrument's terms. In practice, it may be that not all conversion rights or warrants are exercised, in which case the dilutive effect in reality would be less than the diluted figure suggests. Where an instrument has variable conversion terms such that it is convertible at reducing rates over its life

调整。在其他情况下，其将被分类为权益（在 IAS 32 中作为权益工具处理的优先股），且得出归属于普通股股东的利润时将作出调整。但在以上两种情况下，如果可转换优先股具有稀释性，则用于计算稀释 EPS 的归属于普通股股东的利润是在扣除优先股股利之前的利润。

普通股股数的计算

14.106　如第 14.100 段中所述，稀释 EPS 的分母应当为基本 EPS 的计算中所使用的普通股加权平均数与所有稀释性潜在普通股转换为普通股时应该会发行的普通股的加权平均数之和。[IAS 33 第 36 段]。

14.107　在报告日，主体可能拥有一种以上类型的已发行潜在普通股。所有这些潜在普通股在未来是否确实会转换为普通股在报告日通常无法确定。准则要求假设所有潜在普通股在期初均已转换为普通股，或者如果其在期初并不存在，则假设其在该金融工具发行之日或导致其生成的权利授予之日已转换。[IAS 33 第 36 段]。这有时被称为“假设转换法”。

14.108　转换为普通股应当根据该金融工具的条款或所授予的权利确定，且应当假设采用从潜在普通股持有者的角度看最有利的转换率或行权价格。[IAS 33 第 39 段]。其影响是为了确保稀释 EPS 基于按金融工具的条款应该会发行新股的最大数量。在实务中，可能并非所有转换权或认股权证均被行使，在这一情况下，实际的稀释作用应该会比稀释数值所表明的小。在某一工具具有可变转换条款从而在其存续期间以逐渐降低的转换率进行转换的情况下（参见下文第 14.115 段中的示例），其影响为用期末转换率确定转换时应该会发行的股份数量。这是因为确定可发行新股的最大数量时不会考虑前期较高的转换率，因为该工具不能再以这些较高的转换率进行转换。

(see the example in para 14. 115 below), the effect is that the conversion rate at the end of the period is used to determine the number of shares that would be issued on conversion. This is because the maximum number of new shares would not take into consideration the higher conversion rates in previous periods, because the instrument could no longer be converted at those higher rates.

14. 109 Potential ordinary shares are included in the diluted EPS calculation on a weighted basis only for the period they were outstanding. Therefore, potential ordinary shares that are issued during the year are included on a weighted basis from the date of issue to the balance sheet date. Where potential ordinary shares that are outstanding at the beginning of the period are converted during the year, they are included on a weighted average basis from the beginning of the year to the date of conversion. This is illustrated in the examples in paragraph 14. 115. The new ordinary shares that are issued on conversion are included from the date of conversion in both basic and diluted EPS on a weighted basis. The same principles apply where potential ordinary shares, instead of being converted, are cancelled or allowed to lapse during the reporting period. [IAS 33 para 38].

14. 110 In computing diluted EPS, only potential ordinary shares that are dilutive are considered in the calculation. Potential ordinary shares should be treated as dilutive when, and only when, their conversion to ordinary shares would decrease profit per share or increase loss per share from *continuing operations* attributable to ordinary equity holders. [IAS 33 para 41]. The effects of anti – dilutive potential ordinary shares are ignored in calculating diluted EPS. [IAS 33 para 43]. Where a company has a number of different types of potential ordinary shares in issue, each one would need to be considered separately rather than in aggregate. The way in which this should be done is considered further from paragraph 14. 126 below.

[The next paragraph is 14. 112.]

14. 112 As noted in paragraph 14. 110, potential ordinary shares are either dilutive or anti-dilutive based on profit or loss from continuing operations attributable to ordinary equity holders. If the potential ordinary shares are dilutive at this level they must be treated as dilutive for all other EPS calculations (that is, total EPS, discontinued operations EPS and any additional EPS given) whether or not they are actually dilutive at the relevant level of profit (see further para

14.109　潜在普通股仅在其发行在外的期间按加权平均数纳入稀释 EPS 的计算。因此，年度中发行的潜在普通股自发行日起至资产负债表日止按加权平均数纳入计算。在期初发行在外的潜在普通股在年内被转换的情况下，其自年初起至转换日止按加权平均数纳入计算。第 14.115 段的示例对此进行了说明。转换时发行的新普通股自转换日起按加权平均数纳入基本 EPS 和稀释 EPS。相同的原则适用于潜在普通股在报告期内被取消或被允许失效、而非被转换的情况。[IAS 33 第 38 段]。

14.110　计算稀释 EPS 时，在计算过程中仅考虑稀释性的潜在普通股。当且仅当潜在普通股转换为普通股将减少归属于普通股股东的持续经营所产生的每股利润或增加每股亏损时，才应当被视为具有稀释性的。[IAS 33 第 41 段]。反稀释性潜在普通股的影响在计算稀释 EPS 时忽略不计。[IAS 33 第 43 段]。在一家公司拥有若干不同类型的已发行潜在普通股的情况下，各种股票将需要单独考虑，而非合并考虑。这应当如何进行处理，在下文第 14.126 段中进一步讨论。

[下一段为第 14.112 段。]

14.112　如第 14.110 段所述，基于归属于普通股股东的持续经营损益，潜在普通股具有稀释性或反稀释性。如果潜在普通股在这一层面具有稀释性，则无论其对于相关层面的利润实际是否具有稀释性，对于所有其他 EPS 的计算（即 EPS 总额，终止经营的 EPS 及任何给定的额外 EPS），均应作为具有稀释性处理（参见下文第 14.126 段）。[IAS 33 第 A3 段]。

14. 126). [IAS 33 para A3].

Partly paid shares

14. 113 As stated in paragraph 14. 69, partly paid shares are included in the computation of basic EPS to the extent that they rank for dividends during the period. Partly paid shares that do not rank for dividends during the period - for example, they do not rank until they are fully paid - are regarded as the equivalent of share options and warrants. That is, the unpaid balance should be assumed to be the proceeds used to purchase shares under the treasury stock method (see further para 14. 117). The number of shares included in diluted EPS is the difference between the number of partly paid shares already in issue and the number of shares assumed to be purchased at average market price during the period. [IAS 33 para A16].

Convertible securities

14. 114 Where a company has issued instruments in the form of debentures, loan stocks or preference shares that are convertible into ordinary shares of the entity, the instrument's terms will specify the dates, the number of shares and, in effect, the conversion price or prices at which the new shares will be issued. Convertible preference shares are dilutive when the amount of dividend on such shares declared or accrued in the period per ordinary share obtainable on conversion is below basic EPS for continuing operations (where it exceeds basic EPS, the convertible preference shares are anti-dilutive). Convertible debt is dilutive when the interest, net of tax and other changes in income or expense, per ordinary share obtainable on conversion is lower than basic EPS for continuing operations (where it exceeds basic EPS, the convertible debt is anti-dilutive). [IAS 33 para 50]. However, see paragraph 14. 130 for situations where there is more than one class of potential ordinary share.

14. 115 A convertible security is a particularly good example to illustrate the application of the principles discussed from paragraphs 14. 102 to 14. 110 above for calculating diluted EPS.

Example 1

已缴部分股款的股份

14.113　如第 14.69 段所述，已支付部分股款的股份以其在当期参与股利分配的部分为限被纳入基本 EPS 的计算。当期不参与股利分配的已支付部分股款的股份——例如，全额支付股款前不参与股利分配——被视为股份期权和认股权证的等价物。即，未支付余额应当被假定为根据库存股法用于购买股份的价款（参见第 14.117 段的进一步讨论）。纳入稀释 EPS 计算的股数为已发行的已支付部分股款的股份数量与当期假设以平均市价购买的股份数量之间的差额。［IAS 33 第 A16 段］。

可转换证券

14.114　在某一公司以债券、贷款股或优先股的形式发行了可转换为主体普通股的工具的情况下，该工具的条款将明确说明日期、股数和实际上的转换价格或所将发行新股的价格。当可转换优先股在当期宣告或计提的股利除以转换可获得的普通股股数低于持续经营所产生的基本 EPS 时，此类可转换优先股具有稀释性（在其超出基本 EPS 的情况下，可转换优先股具有反稀释性）。当可转换债务的利息扣除税款及收益或费用的其他变化后的金额除以转换可获得的普通股股数低于持续经营所产生的基本 EPS 时，该可转换债务具有稀释性（在其超出基本 EPS 的情况下，可转换债务具有反稀释性）。［IAS 33 第 50 段］。但对于存在一种以上潜在普通股的情况，参见第 14.130 段。

14.115　对于说明上文第 14.102 段至第 14.110 段所讨论的用于计算稀释 EPS 的原则的应用，可转换证券是一个特别好的例子。

示例 1

No conversion during the year

At 30 June 20X1, the issued share capital of a company consisted of 1,500,000 ordinary shares of C1 each. On 1 October 20X1 the company issued C1,250,000 of 8% convertible loan stock for cash at par. Each C100 nominal of the loan stock may be converted at any time during the years ended 20X6/X9 into the number of ordinary shares set out below:

30 June 20X6 135 ordinary shares
30 June 20X7 130 ordinary shares
30 June 20X8 125 ordinary shares
30 June 20X9 120 ordinary shares

If the loan stocks are not converted by 20X9, they would be redeemed at par. There are two different ways of assessing these instruments under IAS 32. The conversion option to convert to a number of shares which varies only with time may be viewed as either an option to convert to a variable or fixed number of shares and recognised as either a liability or equity respectively. See chapter 7 of IFRS Manual of Accounting – Financial Instruments for more details. This example assumes the written equity conversion option is accounted for as a derivative liability and marked to market through profit or loss. The change in the options' fair value reported in 20X2 and 20X3 amounted to a loss of C2,500 and C2,650 respectively. It is assumed that there are no tax consequences arising from these losses.

The profit before interest and taxation for the year ended 30 June 20X2 and 20X3 amounted to C825,000 and C895,000 respectively and relate wholly to continuing operations. The rate of tax for both periods is 33%.

	20X3	**20X2**
Trading results	**C**	**C**
Profit before interest and tax	895,000	825,000
Interest on 8% convertible loan stock		
(20X2: 9/12 × C100,000)	(100,000)	(75,000)
Change in fair value of embedded option	(2,650)	(2,500)
Profit before tax	792,350	747,500
Taxation @ 33%	(262,350)	(247,500)
Profit after tax	530,000	500,000

年度中无转股

20X1 年 6 月 30 日，某公司的已发行股本包括 1,500,000 股每股 1 元的普通股。20X1 年 10 月 1 日，该公司按票面价格发行 1,250,000 元利率为 8% 的可转换贷款股以获取现金。每 100 元面值的贷款股可于 20X6 至 X9 年期间任意转换为下列数量的普通股：

20X6 年 6 月 30 日 135 股普通股
20X7 年 6 月 30 日 130 股普通股
20X8 年 6 月 30 日 125 股普通股
20X9 年 6 月 30 日 120 股普通股

如果截至 20X9 年贷款股未被转换，则将按票面价格被赎回。按照 IAS 32，评估这些工具有两种不同的方法。可转换为若干股份（数量仅随时间改变）的可转换期权，可被视为可转换为变动或固定数量股份的选择权，并分别被确认为负债或权益。更多详情，参见《国际财务报告准则实务指引——金融工具系列》第七章。此例假设签出的权益转换期权作为衍生负债进行会计处理，并通过损益按市价计价。20X2 年和 20X3 年报告的期权公允价值的变化分别为损失 2,500 元和 2,650 元。假设这些损失不产生任何税务后果。

截至 20X2 年 6 月 30 日止年度和截至 20X3 年 6 月 30 日止年度的息税前利润的分别为 825,000 元和 895,000 元，且全部与持续经营相关。两个期间的税率均为 33%。

	20X3 年	**20X2 年**
交易成果	**元**	**元**
息税前利润	895,000	825,000
利率 8% 的可转换贷款股的利息		
(20X2 年：9/12 × 100,000 元)	(100,000)	(75,000)
嵌入期权的公允价值变动	(2,650)	(2,500)
税前利润	792,350	747,500
按 33% 税率计算的税金	(262,350)	(247,500)
税后利润	530,000	500,000

Calculation of basic EPS

Number of equity shares outstanding	1,500,000	1,500,000
Basic EPS	C530,000	C500,000
	1,500,000	1,500,000
	35.3c	33.3c

Calculation of diluted EPS

Test whether convertibles are dilutive:

The saving in after-tax earnings resulting from the conversion of C100 nominal of loan stock amounts to C100 × 8% × 67% + C2,650/12,500 = C5.36 + C0.21 = C5.57. There will then be 135 extra shares in issue. Therefore, the incremental earnings per share = 4.12c (that is, C5.57/135). As this incremental earnings per share is less than the basic EPS at the continuing level, it this will have the effect of reducing the basic EPS of 35.3c. Hence the convertibles are dilutive (see further para 14.131).

	20X3	**20X2**
Adjusted earnings	**C**	**C**
Profit for basic EPS	530,000	500,000
Add: interest and other charges on earnings saved as a result of the conversion	102,650	77,500
Less: tax relief thereon	(33,000)	(24,750)
Adjusted earnings for equity	599,650	552,750

Adjusted number of shares

From the conversion terms, it is clear that the maximum number of shares issuable on conversion of C1,250,000 loan stock after the end of the financial year would be at the rate of 135 shares per C100 nominal, that is, 1,687,500 shares.

Number of equity shares for basic EPS	1,500,000	1,500,000
Maximum conversion at date of issue 1,687,500 × 9/12	–	1,265,625
Maximum conversion after balance sheet date	1,687,500	–
Adjusted capital	3,187,500	2,765,625
Diluted EPS	C599,650	C552,750
	3,187,500	2,765,625
	18.8c	20.0c

基本 EPS 的计算

发行在外的普通股股数	1,500,000	1,500,000
基本 EPS	530,000 元	500,000 元
	1,500,000	1,500,000
	0.353 元	0.333 元

稀释 EPS 的计算

测试可转换贷款股是否具有稀释性：

转换面值 100 元的贷款股所导致税后收益的节省为 100 元 ×8% ×67% +2,650 元/12,500 = 5.36 元 + 0.21 元 = 5.57 元。之后将发行额外股份 135 股。因此，增量每股收益 = 0.412 元（即，5.57 元/135）。由于该增量每股收益小于持续经营层面的基本 EPS，因而将产生使基本 EPS0.353 元减少的影响。所以，该可转换贷款股具有稀释性（参见第 14.131 段的进一步讨论）。

	20X3 年	**20X2 年**
调整后的收益	元	元
用于计算基本 EPS 的利润	530,000	500,000
加：因转换而节省的计入收益的利息		
及其他费用	102,650	77,500
减：相应抵减的税额	(33,000)	(24,750)
调整后的权益收益	599,650	552,750

调整后的股数

从转换条款来看，明确了财务年度结束后 1,250,000 元贷款股转换时可发行股份的最大数量应该是按每 100 元面值的贷款股转换为 135 股股份的比例转换，即 1,687,500 股股份。

用于计算基本 EPS 的普通股股数	1,500,000	1,500,000
发行日的最大转换量 1,687,500 ×9/12	–	1,265,625
资产负债表日后的最大转换量	1,687,500	–
调整后的资本	3,187,500	2,765,625
稀释 EPS	599,650 元	552,750 元
	3,187,500	2,765,625
	0.188 元	0.200 元

Example 2

Partial conversion during the year

The facts are the same as set out in the previous example, but at 1 January 20X6, the holders of half the loan stock exercised their right of conversion.

	20X6	20X5
Trading results	**C**	**C**
Profit before interest and tax	1,220,000	1,000,000
Interest on 8% convertible loan stock	(75,000)*	(100,000)
Change in fair value of embedded option	(2,750)	(5,000)
Profit before tax	1,142,250	895,000
Taxation @ 33%	(377,850)	(297,000)
Profit after tax	764,400	598,000

* Interest = (C1,250,000 × 8% × ½) + (C625,000 × 8% × ½) = C75,000

	20X6	20X5
Calculation of basic EPS		
Adjusted number of shares:		
Number outstanding before conversion	1,500,000	1,500,000
Weighted average shares issued on conversion at 1 January 20X6 = 843,750/2	421,875	–
Adjusted number of shares	1,921,875	1,500,000
Basic EPS	C764,400	C598,000
	1,921,875	1,500,000
	39.8c	39.9c
Calculation of diluted EPS		
Adjusted earnings	**C**	**C**
Profit for basic EPS	764,400	598,000
Add: interest and other charges on earnings saved as a result of conversion	77,750	105,000
Less: tax relief thereon	(24,750)	(33,000)
Adjusted earnings	817,400	670,000

示例 2

年度中部分转换

情况与前面示例情况相同,但是半数贷款股的持有者于 20X6 年 1 月 1 日行使了其转换权。

	20X6 年	20X5 年
交易成果	元	元
息税前利润	1,220,000	1,000,000
利率 8% 的可转换贷款股的利息	(75,000)*	(100,000)
嵌入期权的公允价值变动	(2,750)	(5,000)
税前利润	1,142,250	895,000
按 33% 税率计算的税金	(377,850)	(297,000)
税后利润	764,400	598,000

* 利息 =(1,250,000 元 ×8% ×½)+(625,000 元 ×8% ×½)=75,000 元

基本 EPS 的计算		
调整后的股数:		
转换前发行在外股份的数量	1,500,000	1,500,000
20X6 年 1 月 1 日转换时所发行股份的加权平均数 =843,750/2	421,875	–
调整后的股数	1,921,875	1,500,000
基本 EPS	764,400 元 / 1,921,875	598,000 元 / 1,500,000
	0.398 元	0.399 元
稀释 EPS 的计算		
调整后的收益	元	元
用于计算基本 EPS 的利润	764,400	598,000
加:因转换而节省的计入收益的利息及其他费用	77,750	105,000
减:相应抵减的税额	(24,750)	(33,000)
调整后的收益	817,400	670,000

Adjusted number of shares		
Number of equity shares for basic EPS	1,921,875	1,500,000
Assumed conversion of C1,250,000 loan stock outstanding at the beginning of the year at the maximum rate of 135 shares per C100 of stock up to 1 January 20X6 (6 months)	843,750	–
Assumed conversion of C625,000 of remaining stock outstanding at 30 June 20X6 at the maximum rate of 135 shares per C100 of stock (6 months)	421,875	–
Maximum conversion after balance sheet date at the rate of 135 shares per C100 of stock	–	1,687,500
Adjusted number of shares	3,187,500	3,187,500
Diluted EPS	C817,400	C670,000
	3,187,500	3,187,500
	25.6c	21.0c

Example 3

Final conversion during the year

The facts are the same as set out in the previous example, but the holders of half of the loan stock had exercised their right of conversion on 1 January 20X6 at 135 shares per C100 stock and the remaining stock was converted on 30 June 20X7 at 130 shares per C100 stock.

	20X7	**20X6**
Trading results	**C**	**C**
Profit before interest and tax	1,450,000	1,220,000
Interest on 8% convertible loan stock	(50,000) *	(75,000)
Change in fair value of embedded option	(3,500)	(2,750)
Profit before tax	1,396,500	1,142,250
Taxation @ 33%	(462,000)	(377,850)
Profit after tax	934,500	764,400
* Interest = C625,000 × 8% = C50,000		

调整后的股数		
用于计算基本 EPS 的普通股股数	1,921,875	1,500,000
假设以每 100 元股票转换为 135 股股份的最大比例转换截至 20X6 年 1 月 1 日的年初发行在外的贷款股 1,250,000 元（6 个月）	843,750	–
假设以每 100 元股票转换为 135 股股份的最大比例转换在 20X6 年 6 月 30 日发行在外的剩余股票 625,000 元（6 个月）	421,875	–
以每 100 元股票转换为 135 股股份的比例得出资产负债表日后的最大转换量	–	1,687,500
调整后的股数	3,187,500	3,187,500
稀释 EPS	817,400 元	670,000 元
	3,187,500	3,187,500
	0.256 元	0.210 元

示例 3

年度中最终转换

情况与前面示例所述相同，但是半数贷款股的持有者于 20X6 年 1 月 1 日按每 100 元股票转换为 135 股股份行使其转换权，且剩余贷款股于 20X7 年 6 月 30 日按每 100 元股票转换为 130 股股份进行转换。

	20X7 年	**20X6 年**
交易成果	**元**	**元**
息税前利润	1,450,000	1,220,000
利率 8% 的可转换贷款股的利息	(50,000)*	(75,000)
嵌入期权的公允价值变动	(3,500)	(2,750)
税前利润	1,396,500	1,142,250
按 33% 税率计算的税金	(462,000)	(377,850)
税后利润	934,500	764,400

* 利息 = 625,000 元 × 8% = 50,000 元

Calculation of basic EPS		
Adjusted number of shares:		
Number outstanding before conversion	1,500,000	1,500,000
Weighted average shares issued on conversion at 1 January 20X6	843,750	421,875
Weighted average shares issued on conversion at 30 June 20X7	–	–
Adjusted number of equity shares	2,343,750	1,921,875
	C934,500	C764,400
Basic EPS	2,343,750	1,921,875
	39.9c	39.8c
Calculation of diluted EPS		
Adjusted earnings	**C**	**C**
Profit for basic EPS	934,500	764,400
Add: interest and other charges on earnings saved as a result of conversion	53,500	77,750
Less: tax relief thereon	(16,500)	(24,750)
Adjusted earnings	971,500	817,400
Adjusted number of shares		
Number of equity shares for basic EPS	2,343,750	1,921,875
Assumed conversion of C1, 250, 000 loan stock outstanding at the beginning of the year at the maximum rate of 135 shares per C100 of stock up to 1 January 20X6 (6 months)	–	843,750
Assumed conversion of C625, 000 of remaining stock outstanding at 30 June 20X6 at the maximum rate of 135 shares per C100 of stock (6 months)	–	421,875
Assumed conversion of C625, 000 of stock outstanding at the maximum rate of 130 shares per C100 of stock†	812,500	–
Adjusted number of shares	3, 156, 250	3, 187,500

† Deemed to be outstanding for the whole year because the remaining loan stock of C625,000 was redeemed on the last day of the financial year, that is, on 30 June 20X7.

	C971,500	C817,400
Diluted EPS	3, 156, 250	3, 187,500
	30.8c	22.6c

基本EPS 的计算		
调整后的股数		
转换前发行在外股份的数量	1,500,000	1,500,000
20X6 年 1 月 1 日转换时所发行股份的加权平均数	843,750	421,875
20X7 年 6 月 30 日转换时所发行股份的加权平均数	–	–
调整后的普通股股数	2,343,750	1,921,875
	934,500 元	764,400 元
基本EPS	2,343,750	1,921,875
	0.399 元	0.398 元
稀释 EPS 的计算		
调整后的收益	元	元
用于计算基本 EPS 的利润	934,500	764,400
加：因转换而节省的计入收益的利息及其他费用	53,500	77,750
减:相应抵减的税额	(16,500)	(24,750)
调整后的收益	971,500	817,400
调整后的股数		
用于计算基本 EPS 的普通股股数	2,343,750	1,921,875
假设以每 100 元股票转换为 135 股股份的最大比例转换截至 20X6 年 1 月 1 日的年初发行在外的贷款股 1,250,000 元(6 个月)	–	843,750
假设以每 100 元股票转换为 135 股股份的最大比例转换在 20X6 年 6 月 30 日发行在外的剩余股票 625,000 元(6 个月)	–	421,875
假设以每 100 元股票转换为 130 股股份的最大比例转换发行在外的股票 625,000 元†	812,500	–
调整后的股数	3,156,250	3,187,500

† 被视为在整个年度发行在外的,因为剩余的 625,000 元贷款股于该财务年度的最后一天即 20X7 年 6 月 30 日被赎回。

	971,500 元	817,400 元
稀释EPS	3,156,250	3,187,500
	0.308 元	0.226 元

14.116 Table 14.4 shows the presentation of adjustments made for the purpose of diluted EPS that result from dilutive convertible debt. The extract also illustrates disclosure of continuing, total and discontinued EPS, the treatment of own shares held and the effect on diluted EPS of share options issued by a subsidiary, Genentech (see para 14.134).

Table 14.4 – Effect of potential ordinary shares on diluted EPS

Roche Holding Ltd – Annual Report and Accounts – 31 December 2007

29. Earnings per share and non-voting equity security

Basic earnings per share and non-voting equity security

For the calculation of basic earnings per share and non-voting equity security, the number of shares and nonvoting equity securities is reduced by the weighted average number of its own non-voting equity securities held by the Group during the period.

Basic earnings per share and non-voting equity security

	Continuing businesses		Group	
	2007	2006	2007	2006
Net income attributable to Roche shareholders (millions of CHF)	9,761	7,860	9,761	7,880
Number of shares (millions)	160	160	160	160
Number of non-voting equity securities (millions)	703	703	703	703
Weighted average number of own non-voting equity securities held (millions)	(4)	(11)	(4)	(11)
Weighted average number of shares and non-voting equity securities in issue (millions)	859	852	859	852
Basic earnings per share and non-voting equity security (CHF)	11.36	9.22	11.36	9.24

Diluted earnings per share and non-voting equity security

For the calculation of diluted earnings per share and non-voting equity security, the net income and weighted average number of shares and non-voting equity securities outstanding are adjusted for the effects of all dilutive potential shares and non-voting equity securities.

14.116　表 14.4 显示了由稀释性可转换债务导致为计算稀释 EPS 而作出的调整的列报。该摘录同时说明了持续经营所产生 EPS、EPS 总额和终止经营 EPS 的披露，持有自身股份的处理以及子公司基因泰克所发行股份期权对稀释 EPS 的影响（参见第 14.134 段）。

表 14.4——潜在普通股对稀释 EPS 的影响

罗氏控股有限公司——年度报告和报表——2007 年 12 月 31 日

29. 股份和无表决权权益性证券的每股收益

股份和无表决权权益性证券的基本每股收益

对于股份和无表决权权益性证券的基本每股收益的计算，股份和无表决权权益性证券的数量减去了本集团在当期持有的自身无表决权权益性证券的加权平均数。

股份和无表决权权益性证券的基本每股收益

	持续经营		本集团	
	2007 年	2006 年	2007 年	2006 年
归属于罗氏股东的净收益（百万瑞士法郎）	9,761	7,860	9,761	7,880
股数（百万）	160	160	160	160
无表决权权益性证券的数量（百万）	703	703	703	703
持有自身无表决权权益性证券的加权平均数（百万）	(4)	(11)	(4)	(11)
已发行股份和无表决权权益性证券的加权平均数（百万）	859	852	859	852
股份和无表决权权益性证券的基本每股收益（瑞士法郎）	11.36	9.22	11.36	9.24

股份和无表决权权益性证券的稀释每股收益

对于股份和无表决权权益性证券的稀释每股收益的计算，净收益和发行在外股份和无表决权权益性证券的加权平均数对所有稀释性潜在股份和无表决权权益性证券的影响进行了调整。

Con.

Potential dilutive effects arise from the convertible debt instruments and the employee stock option plans. If the outstanding convertible debt instruments were to be converted then this would lead to a reduction in interest expense and an increase in the number of shares which may have a net dilutive effect on the earnings per share. The exercise of outstanding vested employee stock options would have a dilutive effect. The exercise of the outstanding vested Genentech employee stock options would have a dilutive effect if the net income of Genentech is positive. The diluted earnings per share and non-voting equity security reflects the potential impacts of these dilutive effects on the earnings per share figures.

Diluted earnings per share and non-voting equity security

	Continuing businesses		Group	
	2007	2006	2007	2006
Net income attributable to Roche shareholders (millions of CHF)	9,761	7,860	9,761	7,880
Elimination of interest expense, net of tax, of convertible debt instruments, where dilutive (millions of CHF)	4	25	4	25
Increase in minority share of Group net income, net of tax, assuming all outstanding Genentech stock options exercised (millions of CHF)	(141)	(100)	(141)	(100)
Net income used to calculate diluted earnings per share (millions of CHF)	9,624	7,785	9,624	7,805
Weighted average number of shares and non-voting equity securities in issue (millions)	859	852	859	852
Adjustment for assumed conversion of convertible debt instruments, where dilutive (millions)	1	7	1	7
Adjustment for assumed exercise of equity compensation plans, where dilutive (millions)	2	3	2	3
Weighted average number of shares and non-voting equity securities in issue used to calculate diluted earnings per share (millions)	862	862	862	862
Diluted earnings per share and non-voting equity security (CHF)	11.16	9.03	11.16	9.05

续表

可转换债务工具和职工股票期权计划产生潜在稀释作用。如果发行在外的可转换债务工具被转换，将导致利息费用的减少和股数的增加，这可能对每股收益产生稀释的净影响。发行在外的已授予的职工股票期权的行使应该会产生稀释作用。如果基因泰克的净收益为正数，则发行在外的已授予的基因泰克职工股票期权的行使应该会产生稀释作用。股份和无表决权权益性证券的稀释每股收益反映了这些稀释作用对每股收益数值的潜在影响。

股份和无表决权权益性证券的稀释每股收益

	持续经营		本集团	
	2007 年	2006 年	2007 年	2006 年
归属于罗氏股东的净收益（百万瑞士法郎）	9,761	7,860	9,761	7,880
抵销可转换债务工具（在具有稀释性的情况下）税后利息费用（百万瑞士法郎）	4	25	4	25
假设所有发行在外的基因泰克股票期权均被行使，少数股东所享有集团税后净收益份额的增加（百万瑞士法郎）	(141)	(100)	(141)	(100)
用于计算稀释每股收益的净收益（百万瑞士法郎）	9,624	7,785	9,624	7,805
已发行股份和无表决权权益性证券的加权平均数（百万）	859	852	859	852
对可转换债务工具（在具有稀释性的情况下）的假设转换所作的调整（百万）	1	7	1	7
对权益报酬计划（在具有稀释性的情况下）的假设行使所作的调整（百万）	2	3	2	3
用于计算稀释每股收益的已发行股份和无表决权权益性证券的加权平均数（百万）	862	862	862	862
股份和无表决权权益性证券的稀释每股收益（瑞士法郎）	11.16	9.03	11.16	9.05

Con.

28. Equity attributable to Roche shareholders (extract)

Share capital

As of 31 December 2007, the authorized and issued share capital of Roche Holding Ltd, which is the Group's parent company, consisted of 160,000,000 shares with a nominal value of 1.00 Swiss franc each, as in the preceding year. The shares are bearer shares and the Group does not maintain a register of shareholders. Based on information supplied to the Group, a shareholder group with pooled voting rights owns 50.0125% (2006: 50.0125%) of the issued shares. This is further described in Note 33. Based on information supplied to the Group, Novartis International Ltd, Basel, and its affiliates 33.3330% (participation below 3 31/3%) of the issued shares (2006: 33.3330%).

Non-voting equity securities (*Genussscheine*)

As of 31 December 2007, 702,562,700 non-voting equity securities have been authorised and were in issue as in the preceding year. Under Swiss company law these non-voting equity securities have no nominal value, are not part of the share capital and cannot be issued against a contribution which would be shown as an asset in the balance sheet of Roche Holding Ltd. Each non-voting equity security confers the same rights as any of the shares to participate in the net profit and any remaining proceeds from liquidation following repayment of the nominal value of the shares and, if any, participation certificates. In accordance with the law and the Articles of Incorporation of Roche Holding Ltd, the Company is entitled at all times to exchange all or some of the non-voting equity securities into shares or participation certificates.

Own equity instruments (extract)

Holdings of own equity instruments *in equivalent number of non-voting equity securities*

	31 December 2007 (millions)	31 December 2006 (millions)
Non-voting equity securities	0.4	0.2
Low Exercise Price Options	1.9	6.8
Derivative instruments	9.3	8.2
Total own equity instruments	11.6	15.2

Own equity instruments are recorded within equity at original cost of acquisition.

续表

28. 归属于罗氏股东的权益(摘录)

股本

截至2007年12月31日，本集团的母公司罗氏控股有限公司的已授权和已发行股本由160,000,000股面值为每股1.00瑞士法郎的股份组成，与前一年度相同。这些股份为不记名股份且本集团并未保留股东名册。基于向本集团提供的信息，某一股东集团拥有已发行股份的50.0125%（2006年：50.0125%）的集体表决权。附注33中对此予以进一步描述。基于向本集团提供的信息，巴塞尔的诺华国际有限公司及其附属公司拥有已发行股份的33.3330%（参与权低于33 1/3%）(2006年：33.3330%)。

无表决权权益性证券(德语为"*Genussscheine*")

截至2007年12月31日，702,562,700股无表决权权益性证券已经授权并发行，与前一年度相同。根据瑞士的公司法，这些无表决权权益性证券没有面值，并非股本的一部分，也不能针对在罗氏控股有限公司的资产负债表中显示为资产的出资发行。每份无表决权权益性证券授予与任何股份相同的参与分配净利润的权利以及参与分配偿还股份（如有参与权证书）面值后的任何剩余清算价款的权利。按照法律和罗氏控股有限公司的章程，公司始终有权将所有或部分无表决权权益性证券转换为股份或参与权证书。

自身权益工具（摘录）

持有与无表决权权益性证券*相同数量的自身权益工具的情况*

	2007年12月31日（百万）	2006年12月31日（百万）
无表决权权益性证券	0.4	0.2
低行权价格期权	1.9	6.8
衍生工具	9.3	8.2
自身权益工具总额	11.6	15.2

自身权益工具以原始取得成本计入权益。

Con.

8. Discontinued businesses (extract)

The 2006 results include 20 million Swiss francs of profit from discontinued businesses. This consisted of income of 28 million Swiss francs relating to the release of certain accruals and provisions that were no longer required less 5 million Swiss francs of expenses for the unwinding of the discounted provisions and 3 million Swiss francs of income tax expenses. This had an impact of 0.02 CHF on earnings per share and non-voting equity security (basic and diluted).

Share warrants, options and other potential ordinary shares

14.117 Where a company has issued warrants to subscribe for shares at fixed prices on specified dates in the future or granted share options to directors and employees, these and other potential ordinary shares should be taken into account in the calculation of diluted EPS if they are dilutive. [IAS 33 para 45]. Warrants or options are defined as financial instruments that give the holder the right to purchase ordinary shares. [IAS 33 para 5]. They are dilutive when they would result in the issue of ordinary shares for less than the average market price of ordinary shares during the period. Under IAS 33, the expected proceeds from the exercise of the dilutive share warrants and options are deemed to be used by the company in purchasing as many of its ordinary shares as possible in the open market, using an average market price for the period. Since these shares are fairly priced and are neither dilutive or anti-dilutive, they are ignored in the diluted EPS calculation. They are, therefore, deducted from the number of shares to be issued under the options or warrants to give the number of shares deemed to be issued at no consideration. As these shares are dilutive, they are added to the number of ordinary shares outstanding in the computation of diluted EPS. [IAS 33 paras 45 to 47].

14.118 The method reflects more dilution as the value of options and warrants increases relative to the value of the underlying share. That is, as the average market price for the underlying share increases, the assumed proceeds from exercise will buy fewer shares, thus increasing the number of shares issued for nil consideration and, hence, the denominator. This method of accounting for share

续表

8. 已终止的业务(摘录)
2006 年的经营成果包括已终止的业务所产生的 2 千万瑞士法郎的利润。这由某些不再需要的预提费用和预计负债转回的 2 千 8 百万瑞士法郎收益，减去这些预计负债折现释放的 5 百万瑞士法郎的费用和 3 百万瑞士法郎的所得税构成。这对股份和无表决权权益性证券的每股收益（基本每股收益和稀释每股收益）产生 0. 02 瑞士法郎的影响。

认股权证、期权及其他潜在普通股

14. 117　在公司已发行用于在未来指定日期以固定价格认购股份的认股权证或授予董事和职工股份期权的情况下，如果这些认股权证、期权及其他潜在普通股具有稀释性，则在稀释 EPS 的计算中应被考虑在内。[IAS 33 第 45 段]。认股权证或期权被定义为给予持有者购买普通股权利的金融工具。[IAS 33 第 5 段]。当其将导致以低于当期普通股平均市价的价格发行普通股时，其具有稀释性。根据 IAS 33，行使稀释性认股权证和期权所产生的预期价款被视为公司用于在公开市场中以当期平均市价购买尽可能多的普通股。由于上述股份定价公允且既不具有稀释性也不具有反稀释性，因而在计算稀释 EPS 时忽略不计。从根据认股权证或期权所将发行股份的数量中扣除该股份数量，从而得出被视为将以零对价发行的股份数量。由于这些将以零对价发行的股份具有稀释性，因而在计算稀释 EPS 时，将其加至发行在外的普通股股数中。[IAS 33 第 45 至 47 段]。

14. 118　当期权和认股权证的价值相对于相关普通股股份的价值有所增加时，该方法体现了更高的稀释性。即由于相关股份的平均市价增加，假设行使期权和认股权证的价款仅能购买较少的股份，从而将增加以零对价发行的股份数量，也就是分母。这一对认股权证和期权及其他股份购买协议进行会计处理的方法通常被称为“库存股法”。然而，尽管一段时期内股价的增加可能增

warrants and options and other share purchase agreements is often referred to as 'the treasury stock method'. However, although increases in the share price over a number of periods may increase the dilutive effect, the standard makes it clear that previously reported EPS figures are not retrospectively adjusted to reflect changes in share prices. [IAS 33 para 47].

14.119 It should be noted that the fair value of share options and warrants under the treasury stock method should always be calculated on the basis of the average price of an ordinary share for the period rather than the period end market price. The use of the average stock price is consistent with the objective of diluted EPS to measure earnings per share for the period based on period information and that use of end-of-period data or estimates of the future is inconsistent with the objectives as discussed in paragraph 14.101 above. The standard indicates that a pragmatic basis of calculation, such as a simple average of weekly or monthly prices should be adequate for calculating the average price for the period. Also, closing market prices are adequate for calculating the average market price, but where prices fluctuate wildly an average of the high and low prices generally produces a more representative price. The method should be used consistently, unless it becomes unrepresentative due to changed market conditions. For example, an entity that had used closing market prices to calculate the average market price during several years of relatively stable prices might change to using an average of high and low prices, if prices began to fluctuate wildly and closing prices no longer produced a representative average price. [IAS 33 paras A4, A5].

14.120 Paragraph 41 of IAS 33 says that potential shares are treated as dilutive when they decrease profit or increase loss per share from continuing operations attributable to ordinary equity holders. Where an entity is making profits from continuing operations, share options will always be additionally dilutive if the exercise price is below the average of the share price during the period (that is, the options are 'in the money'). However, where an entity has incurred a loss from continuing operations, options that are in the money would only be dilutive if they increased the loss per share from continuing operations, that is, made the loss per share more negative. But as the effect of bringing in more shares will be to increase the denominator and therefore reduce the loss per share, in the money options will be anti-dilutive and so are not included in the diluted EPS.

加稀释作用，但准则明确指出不能追溯调整以前报告的 EPS 数值来反映股价的变化。[IAS 33 第 47 段]。

14.119　值得注意的是，库存股法中股份期权和认股权证的公允价值应始终以当期普通股的平均价格而非期末市场价格为基础进行计算。使用平均股价的做法与稀释 EPS 的目标一致，即基于期间信息计量当期每股收益，而使用期末数据或采用对未来估计的做法则与上文第 14.101 段中所述目标不一致。准则指出一种务实的计算方法，例如每周或每月价格的简单平均数应足以计算当期的平均价格。此外，收盘价足以用于计算平均市价，但如果价格波动极大，则最高价和最低价的平均数一般能得出一个更具代表性的价格。这一方法应被一贯地运用，除非由于市场条件的变化使其变得不具代表性。例如，某主体在价格相对稳定的以往数年中历来使用收盘价来计算平均市价，如果价格开始大起大落且收盘价不再能够计算得出具有代表性的平均价格，则其可能改为使用最高价和最低价的平均数。[IAS 33 第 A4、A5 段]。

14.120　IAS 33 第 41 段指出，当潜在股份减少归属于普通股股东的持续经营所产生的每股利润或增加每股亏损时，其被视为具有稀释性。在主体通过持续经营盈利的情况下，如果股份期权的行权价格低于当期股价的平均数（即期权为“价内期权”），则这些股份期权始终将具有额外的稀释性。然而，在主体持续经营产生了亏损的情况下，仅当价内期权增大持续经营所产生的每股亏损（即，导致每股亏损的负数金额更大）时，其才具有稀释性。但由于将更多股份纳入计算的影响将是增加分母并由此减少每股亏损，因而价内期权将具有反稀释性，从而不被包括在稀释 EPS 的计算中。

14.121 An example that illustrates the mechanics of calculating diluted EPS where a company has granted options is given below.

Example

At 31 December 20X7 and 20X8, the issued share capital of a company consisted of 4,000,000 ordinary shares of 25c each. The company has granted options that give holders the right to subscribe for ordinary shares between 20Y6 and 20Y9 at 70c per share. Options outstanding at 31 December 20X7 and 20X8 were 630,000. There were no grants, exercises or lapses of options during the year. The profit after tax attributable to ordinary equity holders for the years ended 31 December 20X7 and 20X8 amounted to C500,000 and C600,000 respectively (wholly relating to continuing operations).

Average market price of share:
Year ended 31 December 20X7 = C1.20
Year ended 31 December 20X8 = C1.60

Calculation of basic EPS		
	20X8	**20X7**
Basic EPS	C600,000 / 4,000,000	C500,000 / 4,000,000
	15.0c	12.5c
Calculation of diluted EPS		
Adjusted number of shares		
Number of shares under option:		
Issued at full market price:		
(630,000 × 0.70) ÷ 1.20		367,500
(630,000 × 0.70) ÷ 1.60	275,625	
Issued at nil consideration – dilutive	354,375	262,500
Total number of shares under option	630,000	630,000
Number of equity shares for basic EPS	4,000,000	4,000,000
Number of dilutive shares under option	354,375	262,500
Adjusted number of shares	4,354,375	4,262,500
Diluted EPS	C600,000 / 4,354,375	C500,000 / 4,262,500
	13.8c	11.7c
Percentage dilution	8.00%	6.40%

Note – If options had been granted or exercised during the period, then the number of 'nil consideration' shares in respect of these options would be included in the diluted EPS calculation on a weighted average basis for the period prior to exercise.

14.121　下列示例说明了在某公司已授予期权的情况下稀释 EPS 的计算方式。

示例

20X7 年 12 月 31 日和 20X8 年 12 月 31 日，某公司的已发行股本中包括 4,000,000 股每股 0.25 元的普通股。该公司已授予将给予持有者在 20X6 年至 20X9 年间按每股 0.70 元认购普通股的权利的期权。20X7 年 12 月 31 日和 20X8 年 12 月 31 日，发行在外的期权为 630,000 份。当年并无新授予、行使或失效的期权。截至 20X7 年 12 月 31 日止年度和截至 20X8 年 12 月 31 日止年度归属于普通股股东的税后利润分别为 500,000 元和 600,000 元（全部与持续经营相关）。

股份的平均市价：
截至 20X7 年 12 月 31 日止年度 =1.20 元
截至 20X8 年 12 月 31 日止年度 =1.60 元

基本 EPS 的计算

	20X8 年	**20X7 年**
基本 EPS	600,000 元	500,000 元
	4,000,000	4,000,000
	0.15 元	0.125 元
稀释 EPS 的计算		
调整后的股数		
期权项下的股数：		
以完全市场价格发行：		
(630,000×0.70)÷1.20		367,500
(630,000×0.70)÷1.60	275,625	
以零对价发行—稀释性	354,375	262,500
期权项下的总股数	630,000	630,000
用于计算基本 EPS 的普通股股数	4,000,000	4,000,000
期权项下的稀释性股份数量	354,375	262,500
调整后的股数	4,354,375	4,262,500
稀释 EPS	600,000 元	500,000 元
	4,354,375	4,262,500
	0.138 元	0.117 元
稀释百分比	8.00%	6.40%

注—如果期权在当期被授予或行使，则这些期权所对应的“零对价”股份数量将在行权前按当期的加权平均数纳入稀释 EPS 的计算中。

14.122 Table 14.5 illustrates the disclosure of the effect of options on diluted EPS.

Table 14.5 – Effect of share options on diluted EPS

Syngenta AG – Annual Report and Accounts – 31 December 2011

Consolidated Income Statement (extract)

(for the years ended December 31, 2011, 2010 and 2009)

(US $ million, except share and per share amounts)	**Notes**	**2011**	**2010**	**2009**[a]
Earnings per share (US $):				
Basic earnings per share	8	**17.40**	**15.07**	15.11
Diluted earnings per share	8	**17.31**	**14.99**	15.01
Weighted average number of shares:				
Basic		**91,892,275**	**92,687,903**	93,154,537
Diluted		**92,383,611**	**93,225,303**	93,760,196

8. Earnings per share

Basic earnings per share amounts are calculated by dividing net income for the year attributable to ordinary shareholders of Syngenta AG by the weighted average number of ordinary shares outstanding during the year.

Diluted earnings per share amounts are calculated by dividing the net income attributable to ordinary shareholders of Syngenta AG by the sum of the weighted average number of ordinary shares outstanding during the year plus the weighted average number of ordinary shares that would be issued on the conversion of all the dilutive potential ordinary shares into ordinary shares.

Treasury shares are deducted from total shares in issue for the purposes of calculating earnings per share.

The calculation of diluted earnings per share for the year ended December 31, 2011 excluded 558,727 (2010: 373,365; 2009: 226,897) of Syngenta AG shares and options granted to employees, as their inclusion would have been antidilutive.

14.122　表 14.5 说明了期权对稀释 EPS 影响的披露。

表 14.5——股份期权对稀释 EPS 的影响

先正达股份公司——年度报告及报表——2011 年 12 月 31 日

合并利润表（摘录）

（截至 2009、2010 和 2011 年 12 月 31 日止年度）

(百万美元,股数和每股金额除外)	附注	2011 年	2010 年	2009 年[a]
每股收益(美元):				
基本每股收益	8	**17.40**	**15.07**	15.11
稀释每股收益	8	**17.31**	**14.99**	15.01
加权平均股数:				
基本		**91,892,275**	**92,687,903**	93,154,537
稀释		**92,383,611**	**93,225,303**	93,760,196

8. 每股收益

基本每股收益的金额通过将归属于先正达股份公司普通股股东的当年净利润除以当年发行在外的普通股加权平均数计算得出。

稀释每股收益的金额通过将归属于先正达股份公司普通股股东的净利润除以当年发行在外的普通股加权平均数加上所有稀释性潜在普通股转换为普通股时所将发行的普通股加权平均数之和计算得出。

为计算每股收益,应将库存股从已发行股份的总数中予以扣除。

截至 2011 年 12 月 31 日止年度的稀释每股收益的计算不包括授予职工的 558,727（2010 年：373,365；2009 年：226,897）份先正达股份公司的股份和期权，因为将其包括在内将具有反稀释性。

Con.

(US $ million, except number of shares)	2011	2010	2009[a]
Net income attributable to Syngenta AG shareholders	**1,599**	**1,397**	1,408
Weighted average number of shares			
Weighted average number of shares – basic	**91,892,275**	92,687,903	93,154,537
Adjustments for dilutive potential ordinary shares:			
Grants of options over Syngenta AG shares under employee share participation plans	**261,100**	328,437	396,027
Grants of Syngenta AG shares under employee share participation plans	**230,236**	208,963	209,632
Weighted average number of shares – diluted	**92,383,611**	**93,225,303**	93,760,196

14.123 Although the standard does not specifically say so, it should be assumed that the average price for the period means the average price during the period covered by the financial statements. However, where options are issued during the period the average price should be taken to be the average price during the period for which the options were in issue. This may affect whether the options are dilutive or anti-dilutive.

Example

An entity issued share options on 1 January 20X3. The share options are exercisable upon issue. The exercise price of the share options is 20c. The average share price during the year was as follows:

Average share price 1 January 20X3 to 30 June 20X3	8c
Average share price 1 July 20X3 to 31 December 20X3	22c
Average share price for the year to 31 December 20X3	15c

Management is preparing the financial statements for the year ended 31 December 20X3 and is considering the effect on diluted EPS of the following

续表

（百万美元，股数除外）	**2011 年**	**2010 年**	**2009 年**[a]
归属于先正达股份公司股东的净利润	**1, 599**	**1, 397**	1, 408
加权平均股数			
加权平均股数——基本	**91, 892, 275**	92, 687, 903	93, 154, 537
就稀释性潜在普通股所作的调整：			
根据职工参股计划授予先正达股份公司的股份期权	**261, 100**	328, 437	396, 027
根据职工参股计划授予先正达股份公司的股份	**230, 236**	208, 963	209, 632
加权平均股数——稀释	**92, 383, 611**	**93, 225, 303**	93, 760, 196

14. 123　尽管准则并未特别说明，但应假设当期的平均价格是指财务报表所涵盖期间的平均价格。然而，如果期权在当期发行，则平均价格应被视为期权发行期间的平均价格。这可能会影响到期权具有稀释性还是反稀释性。

示例

某主体于 20X3 年 1 月 1 日发行股份期权。该股份期权发行时即可行使。该股份期权的行权价格为 0. 2 元。年度平均股价如下：

20X3 年 1 月 1 日至 20X3 年 6 月 30 日的平均股价	0. 08 元
20X3 年 7 月 1 日至 20X3 年 12 月 31 日的平均股价	0. 22 元
截至 20X3 年 12 月 31 日止年度的平均股价	0. 15 元

管理层正在编制截至 20X3 年 12 月 31 日止年度的财务报表并正考虑以下两种情况的年末股价对稀释 EPS 的影响。

two scenarios for year-end share prices:

(a) the share price is 18c at 31 December 20X3; or
(b) the share price is 23c at 31 December 20X3.

(a) The fact that the year end share price is less than the exercise price is not relevant because the standard requires the comparison to be made between the exercise price and the average market price of the shares for the period, not with the price at the year end. [IAS 33 para 45]. The share options should not be included in the diluted EPS calculation as they are out-of-the money, that is, the exercise price (20c) is higher than the average price of the ordinary shares for the period (15c).

(b) Similarly the fact that the year end share price is more than the exercise price is not relevant. There is no change in the answer from that given in (a) above, because the extent of dilution is calculated by reference to the exercise price and the average share price during the period. The exercise price is 20c and the average fair value of the shares is 15c and, therefore, the options are still out of the money for the purpose of the diluted EPS calculation.

14.124 The basic method of including options or warrants in the EPS computation is the treasury stock method described in paragraph 14.117 above. However, the treasury stock method may not always be applicable for calculating the dilutive effects of options or warrants. Sometimes options or warrants may require or permit the tendering of debt or other securities of the entity in payment of all or part of the exercise price. In computing diluted EPS:

■ Those options or warrants are assumed to be exercised and the debt or other securities are assumed to be tendered.

■ Interest (net of tax) on any debt assumed to be tendered is added back as an adjustment to the numerator.

■ If tendering cash would be more advantageous to the option holder or warrant holder and the contract permits tendering cash, the tendering of cash should be assumed.

（a）股价于20X3 年 12 月 31 日为0. 18 元；或
（b）股价于20X3 年 12 月 31 日为0. 23 元。

（a）年末股价低于行权价格的事实与稀释每股收益的计算并不相关，因为准则要求将行权价格与股份的当期平均市价而非年末价格进行比较。［IAS 33 第 45 段］。该股份期权不应被纳入稀释 EPS 的计算，因为其为价外期权，即行权价格（0. 2 元）高于普通股的当期平均价格（0. 15 元）。

（b）类似地，年末股价高于行权价格的事实也不相关。答案与上文（a）中给出的相同，因为稀释程度是通过参考行权价格和当期平均股价计算得出的。行权价格为 0. 2 元且股份的平均公允价值为 0. 15 元，因此在计算稀释 EPS 时该期权仍为价外期权。

14. 124　将期权或认股权证纳入 EPS 计算的基本方法为上文第 14. 117 段中所述的库存股法。然而，库存股法可能并非总是适用于计算期权或认股权证的稀释作用。有时期权或认股权证可能要求或允许所有或部分采用主体的债务或其他证券作为对价予以偿付。在计算稀释 EPS 时：

■ 假设这些期权或认股权证将行使且债务或其他证券将作为对价进行偿付。

■ 假设将作为偿付对价的任何债务的利息（税后金额）作为分子的调整项被加回。

■ 如果提供现金对于期权持有者或认股权证持有者将更为有利且合同允许提供现金，则应假设提供现金作为偿付对价。

[IAS 33 Para A7].

Example

An entity issued 50,000 warrants at the beginning of the year. Each warrant may be exercised to purchase 10 ordinary shares by tendering either C100 cash or C100 nominal of outstanding 6% debentures of the entity. The market value of the debentures at the balance sheet date is C92 and the average market price of the entity's share for the period and at the balance sheet date is C9.50 and C9.60 respectively.

In the calculation of diluted EPS, it is first necessary to consider whether the warrants are dilutive. The warrants would be dilutive if either:

(a) The warrants are exercised for cash and the average market price of the related ordinary shares for the period exceeds the exercise price. This is not the case here as the average share price of C95 (10 shares @ C9.50) is less than the exercise price of C100.

(b) The warrants are exercised by tendering the entity's debentures and the selling price of the debenture to be tendered is below that at which the debenture may be tendered under the warrant agreement and the resulting discount establishes an effective exercise price below the market price of the ordinary shares obtained upon exercise. This is the case here as the market value of the debentures of C92 (nominal value C100) is less than the market price of the shares obtained of C96 at the balance sheet.

Therefore, the warrants are dilutive, and it is assumed that debentures will be tendered because it will be more advantageous to the warrant holder to surrender the entity's debentures that have a market value of C92 rather than pay cash of C100 to obtain 10 ordinary shares with a market value of C96.

For the purposes of calculating diluted EPS, the company will increase the numerator by the after-tax interest saved of C210,000 (C5m @ 6% less tax @ 30%) on effectively repurchasing C5m (C100 nominal for each 50,000 warrants) of the entity's outstanding debentures. In addition, the full amount of 500,000 shares to be issued following the exercise of warrants, (rather

［IAS 33 第 A7 段］。

示例

某主体于年初发行 50, 000 份认股权证。可以 100 元现金或主体发行在外的面值 100 元利率 6% 的债券行使一份认股权证以购买 10 股普通股。资产负债表日债券的市场价值为 92 元，且主体股份在当期平均市价和资产负债表日的市价分别为 9. 50 元和 9. 60 元。

在计算稀释 EPS 时，首先需要考虑该认股权证是否具有稀释性。若满足下列条件之一，则认股权证将具有稀释性：

（a）认股权证以现金行使，且相关普通股的当期平均市价高于行权价格。此处的情况并非如此，因为平均股价 95 元（10 股，每股 9. 50 元）低于行权价格 100 元。

（b）认股权证通过偿付主体的债券行使，且所偿付债券的售价低于认股权证协议中规定可偿付债券的价格，其所产生的折扣使得实际行权价格低于行权时所获普通股的市价。此处的情况满足此要求，因为债券的市场价值 92 元（面值 100 元）低于所获股份在资产负债表中的市价 96 元。

因此，该认股权证具有稀释性，并且假设认股权证持有者将通过偿付债券来行使期权，因为对其而言，放弃市场价值为 92 元的债券较支付 100 元的现金以获得 10 股市场价值为 96 元的普通股更为有利。

在计算稀释 EPS 时，公司将通过因实际回购该主体发行在外的债券 5 百万元（50, 000 份每份面值 100 元的认股权证）而节省的税后利息 210, 000 元（5 百万元乘以 6% 减 30% 的税）来增加分子。此外，行使认股权证后所将发行 500, 000 股股份的全部金额（而非根据库存股法以等同于债券市场价值 92 元的实际行权价格和平均股价 9. 50 元计算得出的

than the number computed under the treasury stock method using an effective exercise price equal to the market value of C92 for the debenture and an average share price of C9.50), is included in the denominator. This treatment reflects the fact that a repurchase of debt with the warrant/option proceeds followed by an issue of shares under the warrant/option agreement is in substance equivalent to a traditional or conventional debt instrument that is convertible into a fixed number of shares.

On the other hand, if the tendering of cash is considered to be more advantageous to the warrant holder, for instance, if cash tendered in the above example was C90 for each warrant, tendering of cash would be considered to be dilutive as the exercise price is less than the average share price. In that situation, the number of dilutive shares included in the denominator would be calculated under the treasury stock method in the normal way for options and warrants.

Furthermore, where both cash and debt instruments are tendered, the number of dilutive shares included in the denominator would be the sum of (a) the amount calculated using the treasury stock method to the cash proceeds and (b) the amount calculated by treating the debt tendered as a conventional convertible debt.

14.125 In some circumstances, the proceeds from the exercise of options or warrants may be required to be applied to redeem the entity's existing debt instruments. Upon the assumed exercise of such options or warrants, the proceeds are applied to purchase the debt at its market price rather than to purchase ordinary shares under the treasury stock method. The treasury stock method is applied, however, for the excess proceeds received from the assumed exercise of the options or warrants over the amount used for the assumed purchase of debt. Interest, net of income tax, on any debt assumed to be purchased is added back as an adjustment to the numerator. [IAS 33 Para A9].

Example

An entity granted 500,000 new options at the beginning of the year to its debenture holders that also own all of the entity's 6% redeemable 20,000

数字）被计入分母。这一处理反映了以下事实，即根据认股权证/期权协议，以认股权证/期权发行价款回购债务之后发行股份的做法，实质上等同于可转换为固定数量股份的传统或常规债务工具。

另一方面，如果以现金作为对价进行偿付被视为对认股权证持有者更为有利，例如，如果上述示例中每份认股权证的现金偿付价格为 90 元，则以现金偿付的方式将被视为具有稀释性，因为其行权价格低于平均股价。在这一情况下，分母中所包含的稀释性股份数量将根据通常库存股法对期权和认股权证采用的方式来计算。

此外，如果同时存在以现金和债务工具作为偿付方式的情况，则分母中所包含的稀释性股份数量将为：（a）对现金价款采用库存股法计算得出的金额与（b）将债务偿付作为常规可转换债务处理计算得出的金额之和。

14.125　在某些情况下，行使期权或认股权证所产生的价款可能需被用于赎回主体的现有债务工具。在假设行使此类期权或认股权证时，相关价款假设被用于以市价购买债务而非根据库存股法购买普通股。然而，对于假设行使期权或认股权证所取得的价款超出假设购买债务所使用的金额的部分，则采用库存股法。假设购买的任何债务的所得税后利息均应作为分子的调整项被加回。［IAS 33 第 A9 段］。

示例

某主体于年初授予其债券持有者 500,000 份新期权，这些债券持有者同时持有主体全部 20,000 份利率为 6%、面值为 100 元的可赎回债券。该

nominal C100 debentures. The exercise price of the option is C6. 50. The terms of the options require the company to use the proceeds received from the exercise of options to repurchase the company's outstanding debentures. The average market price of nominal C100 debenture and an ordinary share for the period are C105 and C8 respectively.

For the purposes of calculating diluted EPS, the above options are assumed to be exercised and the proceeds of C3, 250, 000 (500, 000 @ 6. 50) are applied to purchase all the outstanding 20, 000 nominal debentures at the average price of C105 for C2, 100, 000. The excess proceeds of C1, 150, 000 are deemed to be applied to purchase shares in the market at C8 per share, that is, 143,750 shares. Therefore, the number of dilutive shares that are included in the denominator under the treasury stock method is 500, 000 - 143, 750 = 356, 250.

In addition, the entity would increase the numerator by the after-tax interest saved on the assumed repurchase of the debentures, that is, C84, 000 (C2m @ 6% less tax @ 30%).

The incremental earnings per share = C84, 000 ÷ 356, 250 = C0. 24.

The options would be included in the diluted EPS calculation if the incremental earnings per share of C0. 24 is less than the basic EPS at the continuing operations level.

Calculating diluted EPS

14. 126 As stated in paragraph 14. 110 above, only potential ordinary shares that are dilutive are considered in the calculation of diluted EPS. Potential ordinary shares should be treated as dilutive when, and only when, their conversion to ordinary shares would decrease profit or increase loss per share from continuing operations attributable to ordinary equity holders. [IAS 33 paras 41, 43]. The profit from continuing operations is the profit for the period after deducting preference dividends (and other appropriations and adjustments in respect of preference shares) and excluding items relating to discontinued operations. This means that the entity would need to calculate a basic earnings per share from

期权的行权价格为 6. 50 元。期权条款要求公司使用行使期权所取得的价款回购公司发行在外的债券。面值为 100 元的债券和普通股的当期平均市价分别为 105 元和 8 元。

为计算稀释 EPS，假设行使上述期权的价款 3, 250, 000 元（500, 000 乘以 6. 50）被用于购买所有发行在外的 20, 000 份平均价格为 105 元、共计 2, 100, 000 元的债券。超额价款 1, 150, 000 元被视为用于购买市场中每股 8 元的股份，即 143, 750 股股份。因此，根据库存股法分母中所包含的稀释性股份的数量为 500, 000 - 143 ,750 = 356, 250。

此外，主体将通过假设回购债券时节省的税后利息即 84, 000 元（2, 000, 000 元乘以 6% 减 30% 的税）来调增分子。

增量每股收益 = 84, 000 元 ÷ 356, 250 = 0. 24 元。

如果增量每股收益 0. 24 元小于持续经营层面的基本 EPS，则期权将被包括在稀释 EPS 的计算中。

稀释 EPS 的计算

14. 126　正如上文第 14. 110 段中所述，仅将具有稀释性的潜在普通股考虑在稀释 EPS 的计算中。当且仅当潜在普通股向普通股的转换将减少归属于普通股股东的持续经营所产生的每股利润或增加每股亏损时，其才应被视为具有稀释性。[IAS 33 第 41、43 段]。持续经营所产生的利润为扣除优先股股利（及其他与优先股有关的分配和调整）并排除了与终止经营相关的项目后的当期利润。这意味着主体将需计算持续经营所产生的基本每股收益。如果假设潜在普通股转换为普通股将导致上述持续经营所产生的每股收益降低至基本水平之下，则其应具有稀释性。另一方面，如果其影响是将每股收益增至基本水平之上，则这一证券并不具有稀释性，因而应排除在稀释 EPS 的计算之

continuing operations. A potential ordinary share would be dilutive if its assumed conversion results in reducing this earnings per share from continuing operations below the basic level. On the other hand, if the effect is to increase this earnings per share above the basic level, the security is not dilutive and should be excluded from the diluted EPS calculation. [IAS 33 para 42].

14.127 It follows from the above that on no account should the dilution be tested by reference to whether the conversion of a potential ordinary share reduces the standard basic EPS calculated on the total profit or loss for the period. The reason for choosing, as a control number, the 'profit from continuing operations' is because this level of profit, unaffected by discontinued operations, is likely to remain stable over time and reflect the earnings that will exist in the future when the dilution occurs. This is a sensible approach for the following reason. If there is a loss from discontinued operations and this turns the overall earnings per share attributable to ordinary equity holders into a loss per share, the exercise of, say, an option will increase the denominator and result in a lower overall loss per share. This is because the loss is 'shared' among a higher number of shares. In that situation, the option is anti-dilutive at this level, but may well be dilutive at the continuing operations level.

Example

A company has a profit from continuing activities, but a loss for the year overall because of losses on discontinued operations. Options are dilutive when considered at continuing operations profit level as the diluted EPS at that level decreases profit per share. However, at the overall loss for the year level, applying the dilution caused by the options decreases loss per share. Is it still correct to show the effect of the options in the diluted EPS?

Yes. If the options are dilutive at the profit from continuing operations level then they should be included in the diluted EPS calculation at the loss for the year level. If that reduces loss per share then so be it, but the company should explain the circumstances. A form of explanation might be '*Options are dilutive at the profit from continuing operations level and so, in accordance with IAS 33, have been treated as dilutive for the purpose of diluted earnings per share. The diluted loss per share is lower than basic loss per share*

外。[IAS 33 第 42 段]。

14.127　承上所述，稀释性与否绝不应通过参照潜在普通股的转换是否降低以当期损益总额计算的标准基本 EPS 来测试。选择“持续经营所产生的利润”作为控制数是因为其不受终止经营的影响，并可能在一段时间内保持稳定并反映未来稀释实际发生时所存在的收益。基于下列原因，这是一种敏感的方法。如果存在终止经营所导致的亏损，并且其使归属于普通股股东的总体每股收益变为每股亏损，则期权的行使将会增加分母并导致更低的总体每股亏损。这是因为亏损由更大数量的股份分担。在这种情况下，期权在这一层面具有反稀释性，但很有可能在持续经营层面具有稀释性。

示例

某公司持续经营活动盈利，但由于终止经营的亏损导致年度的总体亏损。在持续经营利润层面考虑时，期权具有稀释性，因为该层面的稀释 EPS 降低了每股利润。然而，在全年总体亏损的层面，应用期权的稀释性减少了每股亏损。在稀释 EPS 中体现期权的影响是否仍然正确？

是。如果期权在持续经营利润层面具有稀释性，则其应被包括在全年总体亏损层面的稀释 EPS 的计算中。如果由此降低了每股亏损，也只能如此处理，但公司应对该情况进行解释。一种解释方式可能是“*期权在持续经营利润层面具有稀释性，因此根据 IAS 33，在计算稀释每股收益时已作为稀释性期权处理。由于终止经营亏损的影响，稀释每股亏损低于基本每股亏损*”。

because of the effect of losses on discontinued operations'.

In addition to disclosing basic and diluted EPS for the overall loss for the year, the entity would also be required to disclose basic and diluted EPS at the continuing operations level on the face of the income statement and the basic and diluted EPS for discontinued operations either on the face of the income statement or in the notes (see further para 14.173 onwards). [IAS 33 paras 66, 68].

[The next paragraph is 14.130.]

14.130 In order to determine whether a particular convertible instrument, option or warrant will have a dilutive effect, it is necessary to consider each of them separately rather than in aggregate. This consideration is complicated and involves the following steps:

- The entity first calculates the profit or loss from continuing operations attributable to ordinary equity holders.
- The entity next calculates the earnings per incremental share for each type of potential ordinary share. The earnings per incremental share is the increase in profit or loss (or less commonly the decrease) that would result from the exercise or conversion of the security divided by the weighted average increase in the number of ordinary shares that would result from the conversion.
- The entity next ranks all potential ordinary shares from the most dilutive (lowest earnings per incremental share) to the least dilutive (highest earnings per incremental share). Options and warrants are generally included first because they do not affect the numerator of the calculation and, hence, are most dilutive.
- The entity then calculates a basic EPS using profit or loss from continuing operations attributable to ordinary equity holders as the numerator.
- The most dilutive potential ordinary share with the lowest earnings per incremental share is then included and a new EPS as indicated above is calculated. If this new figure is lower than the previous one, the entity recalculates EPS including the potential shares with the next lowest earnings per

除披露全年总体亏损的基本 EPS 和稀释 EPS 外，主体还须在利润表主表中披露持续经营层面的基本 EPS 和稀释 EPS，并在利润表主表或附注中披露终止经营的基本 EPS 和稀释 EPS（参见下文自 14.173 段起的段落）。[IAS 33 第 66、68 段]。

[下一段为第 14.130 段。]

14.130　为确定某项特定可转换工具、期权或认股权证是否具有稀释性，有必要分别进行单独考虑而非作为一个整体合并考虑。这一考虑颇为复杂并涵盖下列步骤：

- 主体首先计算归属于普通股股东的持续经营所产生的损益。
- 其次，主体计算各种类型潜在普通股的增量每股收益。增量每股收益是该证券的行使或转换所将导致损益的增加（或在较少见的情况下，损益的减少）除以转换所将导致普通股加权平均股数的增加的结果。
- 主体随后将所有潜在普通股按最具稀释性（最低的增量每股收益）至具最少稀释性（最高的增量每股收益）进行排序。期权和认股权证一般最先被包括在内，因为其并不影响计算式中的分子，因而最具稀释性。
- 然后主体使用归属于普通股股东的持续经营所产生的损益作为分子计算基本 EPS。
- 具有最低增量股每股收益的最具稀释性的潜在普通股随后被纳入并计算得出上文所述的新 EPS。如果这一新数值低于原数值，则主体应通过将具有次低增量股每股收益的潜在普通股包括在内来重新计算 EPS。

incremental share.

- The above process of including increasingly less dilutive shares continues until the resulting EPS figure increases or there are no more potential ordinary shares to consider.
- Any potential ordinary share that has the effect of increasing the cumulative EPS from continuing operations is considered to be anti-dilutive and is excluded from the diluted per share calculation.
- All other potential ordinary shares with higher rankings are considered to be dilutive potential ordinary shares and are included in the diluted EPS calculation in the normal way.

[IAS 33 Para 44].

In most instances, where there is a loss from continuing operations, there would be no difference between the basic and diluted EPS as potential ordinary shares would be anti-dilutive.

14.131 The sequence of including each issue or series of potential ordinary shares from the most dilutive to the least dilutive guarantees that the final diluted EPS figure expresses maximum dilution of the basic EPS. A numerical example depicting the above steps is shown below.

Example

The issued share capital of C plc at 31 December 20X7 and 20X8 comprises 2,000,000 ordinary shares of 10c each. The company granted options over 100,000 ordinary shares in 20X6. The options can be exercised between 20X9 and 20Y1 at 60c per share. The average market price of C plc's shares during 20X8 was 75c.

In addition, C plc has 800,000 8% C1 convertible cumulative preference shares (treated as an equity instrument under IAS 32) and C1,000,000 5% convertible bonds in issue throughout 20X8. Each preference share and bond is convertible into 2 ordinary shares.

The company's results for the year ended 31 December 20X8 comprised

■ 上述将稀释性越来越小的股份包括在内的过程持续至所计算的 EPS 数值较原数值有所增加或再无潜在普通股可纳入考虑。

■ 任何具有增加持续经营 EPS 影响的潜在普通股均被视为具有反稀释性，因而被剔除出稀释每股收益的计算中。

■ 所有其他排序较前的潜在普通股均被视为稀释性潜在普通股，并以通常方式纳入稀释 EPS 的计算。

[IAS 33 第 44 段]。

在大多数情况下，如果持续经营产生亏损，则基本 EPS 与稀释 EPS 之间将不存在差异，因为潜在普通股将具有反稀释性。

14.131 按最具稀释性至最不具稀释性的顺序纳入各次发行或各个系列的潜在普通股的做法，确保最终稀释 EPS 数值体现基本 EPS 最大程度的稀释效果。描述上述步骤的数值示例如下。

示例

C 公众有限公司于 20X7 年 12 月 31 日和 20X8 年 12 月 31 日已发行在外 2,000,000 股普通股，每股面值 0.1 元。该公司于 20X6 年授予可用于购买 100,000 股普通股的期权。该期权可在 20X9 年与 20Y1 年间以每股 0.60 元行权。C 公众有限公司在 20X8 年的平均市价为 0.75 元。

此外，C 公众有限公司在 20X8 年已发行在外的潜在普通股包括 800,000 股面值为 1 元，利率为 8% 的可转换累积优先股（根据 IAS 32 作为权益工具处理）和票面金额为 1,000,000 元，利率为 5% 的可转换债券。1 股优先股和 1 份债券可转换为 2 股普通股。

该公司截至 20X8 年 12 月 31 日止年度的经营成果包括持续经营所产生的

operating profit from continuing operations of C300, 000 and operating profit from discontinued operations of C100, 000. Interest and tax at 30% amounted to C100, 000 and C90, 000 respectively. The profit for the year was C210, 000.

The necessary steps to calculate C plc's diluted earnings per share for 20X8 are set out below. Comparative figures for 20X7 have not been included in this example.

1 Calculation of profit from continuing operations

	Total	Continuing operations	Discontinued operations
	C	C	C
Operating profit from continuing operations	300,000	300,000	
Operating profit from discontinued operations *	100,000		100,000
Profit before interest	400,000	300,000	100,000
Interest **	100,000	76,000	24,000
Profit after interest	300,000	224,000	76,000
Tax @ 30% **	90,000	67,200	22,800
Profit	210,000	156,800	53,200
Less: Preference dividend	64,000	64,000	–
Profit attributable to ordinary equity holders	146,000	92,800	53,200

* The above workings are for illustrative purposes and do not show the discontinued operations as they are required to be presented in the income statement by IAS 1 – and IFRS 5. The presentation of discontinued operations is dealt with in chapter 26.

** Interest has been allocated to the discontinued operation on the basis of the debt that has been attributed to the discontinued operation. Taxation has been attributed on the basis of the taxation actually payable by the discontinued operation.

营业利润300,000元和终止经营所产生的营业利润100,000元。利息和采用30%税率计算的税款分别为100,000元和90,000元。年度利润为210,000元。

计算C公众有限公司20X8年稀释每股收益所需的步骤如下。20X7年的比较值并未包括在此例中。

1. 计算持续经营所产生的利润

	总计	持续经营	终止经营
	元	元	元
持续经营所产生的营业利润	300,000	300,000	
终止经营所产生的营业利润*	100,000		100,000
息前利润	400,000	300,000	100,000
利息**	100,000	76,000	24,000
息后利润	300,000	224,000	76,000
以30%的税率计算的税款**	90,000	67,200	22,800
利润	210,000	156,800	53,200
减：优先股股利	64,000	64,000	–
归属于普通股股东的利润	146,000	92,800	53,200

* 上述计算仅供说明而未显示终止经营，因为IAS 1和IFRS 5要求将其列报在利润表中。终止经营的列报在第二十六章中阐述。

** 利息已按归属于终止经营的债务分配至终止经营。税款已按实际应由终止经营支付的税款进行分配。

2 Determine earnings per incremental share for each class of potential ordinary share and rank them from the most dilutive to least dilutive

	Increase in earnings C	Increase in number of ordinary shares	Earnings per incremental share c	Rank (note)
Options				
Increase in earnings	nil			
Incremental shares issued for nil consideration				
100,000 × (75 − 60)/75		20,000	nil	1
8% Convertible preference shares				
Increase in earnings 8% × C800,000	64,000			
Incremental shares 2 × 800,000		1,600,000	4.00	3
5% Convertible bonds				
Increase in earnings after taxes 1,000,000 × 5% × 70%	35,000			
Incremental shares 1,000,000 × 2		2,000,000	1.75	2

Note: Ranking is in ascending order of earnings per incremental share.

Since the options, convertible preference shares and convertible bonds have been in issue throughout 20X8, the increase in number of ordinary shares is also their weighted average for the year. If options are granted during the year, they are brought into the averaging calculation from the date of grant.

If there were more than one series, say, of options these would have to be ranked by series.

2. 确定各类潜在普通股的增量股每股收益并按最具稀释性至具最少稀释性对其进行排序

	收益的增加 元	普通股 股数的 增加	增量股 每股收益 元	排序 (注)
期权				
收益的增加	0			
零对价发行的				
增量股				
100,000×(75－60)/75		20,000	0	1
股利率为 8%的可转换优				
先股				
收益的增加 8%　×				
800,000 元	64,000			
增量股 2×800,000		1,600,000	0.04	3
利率为 5% 的可转换债券				
税后收益的增加				
1,000,000×5%×70%	35,000			
增量股				
1,000,000×2		2,000,000	0.0175	2

注:按增量股每股收益升序排列。

由于期权、可转换优先股和可转换债券在整个 20X8 年度均发行在外,因而普通股股数的增加也是其当年的加权平均数。如果期权于当年方被授予,则将其自授予日起纳入平均数的计算。

如果存在一个以上系列的期权,则应按系列进行排序。

3 Calculate the cumulative dilution effect on profit per share from continuing operations

	Profit from continuing operations C	Weighted average number of shares	Profit from continuing operations per share(c)	
Profit	92,800	2,000,000	4.64	
Options	–	20,000		
	92,800	2,020,000	4.59	Dilutive
5% Convertible bonds	35,000	2,000,000		
	127,800	4,020,000	3.18	Dilutive
8% Convertible preference shares	64,000	1,600,000		
	191,800	5,620,000	3.41	Anti-dilutive

Since diluted earnings per share from continuing operations is increased when taking the convertible preference shares into account (from 3.18 to 3.41), the convertible preference shares are anti-dilutive and are ignored in the calculation of diluted earnings per share.

4 Calculate diluted earnings per share including only dilutive potential ordinary shares

	Earnings C	Weighted average number of shares	Earnings per share (c)
Profit attributable to ordinary equity holders	146,000	2,000,000	7.30
Options		20,000	–
	146,000	2,020,000	–
5% Convertible bonds	35,000	2,000,000	–
Diluted earnings	181,000	4,020,000	4.50

3. 计算对持续经营所产生每股利润的累计稀释影响

	持续经营所产生的利润 元	加权平均股数	持续经营所产生的每股利润 元	
利润	92,800	2,000,000	0.0464	
期权	–	20,000		
	92,800	2,020,000	0.0459	稀释性
5% 可转换债券	35,000	2,000,000		
	127,800	4,020,000	0.0318	稀释性
8%可转换优先股	64,000	1,600,000		
	191,800	5,620,000	0.0341	反稀释性

由于纳入可转换优先股时持续经营所产生的稀释每股收益增加(从0.0318增至0.0341)，因而该可转换优先股具有反稀释性，因此在稀释每股收益的计算中忽略不计。

4. 计算稀释每股收益时仅纳入稀释性潜在普通股

	收益 元	加权平均股数	每股收益 元
归属于普通股股东的利润	146,000	2,000,000	0.073
期权		20,000	—
	146,000	2,020,000	—
5%可转换债券	35,000	2,000,000	—
稀释收益	181,000	4,020,000	0.045

The final diluted EPS is calculated by reference to profit attributable to ordinary equity holders, but the dilution test is carried out by using the profit from continuing operations as the 'control number' (see para 14.132 below) as set out in step three above.

The above example deals only with the calculation of the diluted EPS for the total profit attributable to ordinary equity holders. However, IAS 33 also requires disclosure of the basic and diluted EPS attributable to continuing and to discontinued operations. The figures to be disclosed would be as follows.

	Basic EPS (c)	Diluted EPS (c)
Profit attributable to ordinary equity holders	7.30	4.50
Profit from continuing operations	4.64[1]	3.18[1]
Profit from discontinued operations	2.66[2]	1.32[2]

Notes:

[1] As per step 3 above, Basic = 92,800/2,000,000 = 4.64; Diluted = 127,800/4,020,000 = 3.18

[2] Basic = 53,200/2,000,000 = 2.66; Diluted = 53,200/4,020,000 = 1.32

Note that the income statement effect of the convertible bonds is not adjusted against the discontinued operations results, because it relates to continuing operations. The additional shares are taken into account because the discontinued operation EPS is measured as one element of the EPS for the total entity result. Also, the sum of the continuing operations EPS and discontinued operations EPS (for both basic and diluted) equals the EPS calculated on the profit attributable to ordinary equity holders.

14.132 Paragraph A3 of the standard illustrates the application of the 'control number' with a useful example. The following example is derived from that example.

Example

An entity has a profit from continuing operations of C4m, a loss from discontinued operations of C7m, a loss for the year attributable to equity

通过参考归属于普通股股东的利润计算得出最终的稀释 EPS，但如上文步骤 3 中所示，通过使用持续经营所产生的利润作为“控制数”（参见下文第 14.132 段）进行稀释测试。

以上示例仅涉及归属于普通股股东的总利润的稀释 EPS 的计算。然而，IAS 33 还要求披露归属于持续经营的基本 EPS、稀释 EPS 和归属于终止经营的基本 EPS、稀释 EPS。需要披露的数值如下。

	基本 EPS（元）	稀释 EPS（元）
归属于普通股股东的利润	0.073	0.045
持续经营所产生的利润	0.0464[1]	0.0318[1]
终止经营所产生的利润	0.0266[2]	0.0132[2]

注：

[1] 按照上文步骤 3，基本 EPS = 92,800/2,000,000 = 0.0464；稀释 EPS = 127,800/4,020,000 = 0.0318

[2] 基本 EPS = 53,200/2,000,000 = 0.0266；稀释 EPS = 53,200/4,020,000 = 0.0132

值得注意的是，可转换债券对利润表的影响并未针对终止经营的结果进行调整，因为其与持续经营相关。然而视同额外发行的股份会被纳入考虑，因为终止经营的 EPS 是计量主体总经营成果的 EPS 的一项要素。此外，持续经营的 EPS 与终止经营的 EPS（包括基本 EPS 和稀释 EPS）之和等于就归属于普通股股东的利润计算的 EPS。

14.132　准则第 A3 段通过一个有用的示例说明了“控制数”的应用。下列示例即源自于该示例。

示例

某主体持续经营所产生的利润为 4 百万元，终止经营所产生的亏损为 7 百万元，归属于普通股股东的年度亏损为 3 百万元，发行在外普通股股

holders of C3m and C4m ordinary shares and C1m potential ordinary shares outstanding.

The entity's basic EPS for continuing operations is C1 for continuing operations, a (C1.75) loss for discontinued operations and (C0.75) for the loss for the year.

The C1m potential ordinary shares are included in the diluted EPS calculation because (assuming no income statement effect for the potential ordinary shares) their effect on the EPS calculation for continuing operations is dilutive. On that assumption, the resulting diluted EPS for continuing operations is C0.8. Because the profit from continuing operations is the control number, the potential ordinary shares are also included in the calculation of the diluted EPS for loss from discontinued operations and for the total loss for the year attributable to equity holders. The resultant diluted EPS figures are respectively (C1.4) for discontinued operations and (C0.6) for the loss attributable to equity holders. This is despite the fact that these figures are anti-dilutive to their comparable basic EPS figures of (C1.75) and (C0.75).

EPS for interim periods

14.133 IAS 33 states that dilutive potential ordinary shares should be determined independently for each period presented. The number of dilutive potential ordinary shares included in the year to date period should not be a weighted average of the dilutive potential ordinary shares included in each interim computation. [IAS 33 para 37]. In other words, the number of dilutive potential ordinary shares should be determined for each interim period based on the year to date position at the end of the interim period.

Example

An example of this principle might be where an entity made an acquisition in the previous year and entered into an agreement to issue 1,000 additional ordinary shares for each C50,000 of consolidated profit in excess of C1,000,000 in the following year, based on the entity's consolidated financial

为 4 百万元和潜在普通股为 1 百万元。

该主体持续经营的基本 EPS 为 1 元，终止经营的基本 EPS 对应终止经营的亏损 -1.75 元，归属于普通股股东的 EPS 对应年度亏损 -0.75 元。

1 百万元的潜在普通股被纳入稀释 EPS 的计算，因为（假设潜在普通股对利润表无影响）其对持续经营 EPS 的计算具有稀释性的影响。根据这一假设，持续经营的稀释 EPS 为 0.8 元。由于持续经营所产生的利润是控制数，因而潜在普通股也被纳入终止经营所产生亏损的稀释 EPS 以及归属于权益持有者的年度总亏损的稀释 EPS 的计算。上述稀释 EPS 数值分别为终止经营所对应的 -1.4 元和归属于权益持有者的亏损所对应的 -0.6 元，尽管这些数值对其比较基本 EPS 数值 -1.75 元和 -0.75 元而言具有反稀释性。

中期 EPS

14.133 IAS 33 指出稀释性潜在普通股应当针对各列报期间单独确定。计入当期的稀释性潜在普通股股数不应为纳入各个中期计算的稀释性潜在普通股的加权平均数。[IAS 33 第 37 段]。换言之，应基于年初至中期期末的情况确定各个中期的稀释性潜在普通股股数。

示例

这一原则的示例可能是某主体在上一年度进行收购并签订协议，约定主体下一年度合并财务报表的合并利润超出 1,000,000 元时，每超过 50,000 元则额外发行 1,000 股普通股。该主体公布季度报告。各个季度的结果如下：

statements. The entity reports quarterly. The results for each quarter are as follows:

		Cumulative
	C	C
First quarter	600,000	600,000
Second quarter	700,000	1,300,000
Third quarter	(200,000) *	1,100,000
Fourth quarter	400,000	1,500,000

* includes a loss from discontinued operations of C300,000.

The company has 100,000 ordinary shares outstanding during the year.

The EPS and diluted EPS for each quarter are as follows:

	Quarter 1	Quarter 2	Quarter 3	Quarter 4	Year
Numerator C	600,000	700,000	(200,000)	400,000	1,500,000
Denominator:					
Ordinary shares	100,000	100,000	100,000	100,000	100,000
Basic EPS *	C6	C7	(C2)	C4	C15
Potential ordinary shares	–	6,000	2,000 **	10,000	10,000
Total denominator for diluted EPS	100,000	106,000	102,000	110,000	110,000
Diluted EPS	C6	C6.6	(C1.96)	C3.64	C13.64

* The potential ordinary shares are not included in the calculation of the basic EPS, because there is no certainty that the condition will be satisfied until the end of the period.

** In quarter 3 there is a profit from continuing operations of C100,000 and a loss from discontinued operations of C300,000 and as the potential ordinary shares are dilutive at the continuing operations level they are taken into account in the diluted EPS, even though they are anti-dilutive at the total loss level.

The above example demonstrates that the diluted EPS for the year differs from any average or weighted average of the diluted EPS figures reported in the individual quarterly accounts. This is simply because the denominator used in each of the first three quarters differs from the denominator at the year end. Under the rules in the standard the diluted EPS figure for the year should be based on the year to date figures, that is, at the year end the figure should be disclosed as C13.64.

	元	累计 元
第一季度	600,000	600,000
第二季度	700,000	1,300,000
第三季度	(200,000)*	1,100,000
第四季度	400,000	1,500,000

* 包括终止经营所产生的亏损300,000元。

该公司当年发行在外的普通股股数为100,000股。

各季度的EPS和稀释EPS如下：

	第1季度	第2季度	第3季度	第4季度	年度
分子元	600,000	700,000	(200,000)	400,000	1,500,000
分母：					
普通股	100,000	100,000	100,000	100,000	100,000
基本EPS*	6元	7元	(2元)	4元	15元
潜在普通股	–	6,000	2,000**	10,000	10,000
稀释EPS的分母					
总额	100,000	106,000	102,000	110,000	110,000
稀释EPS	6元	6.6元	(1.96元)	3.64元	13.64元

* 由于在期末前无法确定是否能满足相关条件，潜在普通股未纳入基本EPS的计算。

** 在第三季度，持续经营产生利润100,000元，终止经营导致亏损300,000元，由于潜在普通股在持续经营层面具有稀释性，因而将纳入稀释EPS，尽管其在总亏损层面具有反稀释性。

以上示例说明了年度稀释EPS不同于各份季度报表中所报告的稀释EPS数值的平均数或加权平均数。这仅仅是因为前三季度的各个季度中所使用的分母不同于年末时的分母。根据准则的规定，当年的稀释EPS数值应基于年初至今的数值，即年末时该数值应披露为13.64元。

Securities of subsidiaries, joint ventures and associates

14.134 A subsidiary, joint venture or associate may issue potential ordinary shares to parties other than the parent, venturer or investor. These potential ordinary shares may be convertible into either ordinary shares of the subsidiary, joint venture or associate or they may be convertible into shares of the parent, venturer or investor (the reporting entity). If the potential ordinary shares have a dilutive effect on the reporting entity's basic EPS, they should be included in the calculation of the reporting entity's diluted EPS. [IAS 33 para 40].

14.135 If the potential ordinary shares issued by a subsidiary enable their holders to obtain ordinary shares in the subsidiary, then those potential ordinary shares should be included in computing the subsidiary's EPS figures (if indeed the subsidiary is calculating an EPS figure). In any event, those earnings per share amounts would be included in the consolidated EPS based on the group's holdings of the subsidiary's securities. On the other hand, if the potential shares issued by the subsidiary enable their holders to obtain ordinary shares in the parent, then these potential ordinary shares should be considered along with the other potential ordinary shares issued by the parent in the computation of consolidated diluted EPS. The same considerations apply where potential ordinary shares issued by an associate or a joint venture are exchangeable into ordinary shares of the associate or joint venture, or into ordinary shares of the reporting entity. They should be included in the EPS computation of the reporting entity if they are considered to be dilutive. [IAS 33 para A11].

Example

A parent entity has profit attributable to ordinary shareholders of C100,000 (excluding any earnings of the subsidiary). There are 10,000 ordinary shares outstanding. The parent owns 800 ordinary shares in the subsidiary representing 80% of the subsidiary's ordinary share capital. It also owns 200 convertible preference shares in the subsidiary representing 50% of the subsidiary's preference share capital (which is treated as an equity instrument under IAS 32). The parent also has 20 warrants exercisable to purchase ordinary shares in the subsidiary.

子公司、合营企业和联营企业的证券

14.134　子公司、合营企业或联营企业可能向母公司、合营者或投资者之外的第三方发行潜在普通股。这些潜在普通股可能转换为子公司、合营企业或联营企业的普通股，也可能转换为母公司、合营者或投资者（报告主体）的股份。如果潜在普通股对报告主体的基本 EPS 具有稀释作用，则应将其纳入报告主体的稀释 EPS 的计算。[IAS 33 第 40 段]。

14.135　如果子公司所发行的潜在普通股使其持有者能获得该子公司的普通股，则计算子公司的 EPS 数值时（如果子公司的确也计算 EPS 数值）应包含这些潜在普通股。在任何情况下，这些每股收益的金额均将基于集团所持有的子公司证券纳入合并 EPS 的计算。另一方面，如果子公司所发行的潜在普通股使其持有者能获得母公司的普通股，则在计算合并稀释 EPS 时这些潜在普通股应连同母公司所发行的其他潜在普通股一起加以考虑。同样的考虑也适用于联营企业或合营企业所发行的可转换为该联营企业或合营企业普通股，或可转换为报告主体普通股的潜在普通股的情形。如果这些潜在普通股被视为具有稀释性，则应将其纳入报告主体 EPS 的计算。[IAS 33 第 A11 段]。

示例

某母公司归属于普通股股东的利润为 100,000 元（不包括子公司的任何收益）。该母公司发行在外的普通股股数为 10,000。该母公司持有 800 股子公司的普通股，占子公司普通股股本的 80%。其同时持有 200 股子公司的可转换优先股，占子公司优先股股本的 50%（在 IAS 32 中作为权益工具处理）。该母公司还拥有 20 份认股权证，行权后可以购买子公司普通股。

The subsidiary has profit attributable to ordinary shareholders of C6, 000. Its ordinary share capital consists of 1, 000 ordinary shares and it has 400 convertible (one for one) preference shares in issue. It has also issued 150 warrants exercisable to subscribe for ordinary shares of the subsidiary, with an exercise price of C5 per warrant. The average market price of one ordinary share of the subsidiary was C10. Dividends on the preference shares are C1 per share. There were no inter-company transactions or eliminations other than dividends. Tax has been ignored for the purposes of this example.

Subsidiary's earnings per share

Basic EPS $\frac{6,000 - 400}{1,000} = \text{C}5.6$

This is calculated as the subsidiary's profit from which is deducted the preference dividend that had been charged to retained earnings. The result is divided by the number of the subsidiary's ordinary shares.

Diluted EPS $\frac{6,000}{1,000 + 75 + 400} = \text{C}4.07$

This is the subsidiary's profit (preference dividends are not deducted as they would be saved on conversion of the preference shares) divided by the number of ordinary shares plus the ordinary shares that would be issued on conversion of the preference shares on the basis of one for one and the number of ordinary shares that would be issued for nil consideration on exercise of the warrants calculated as follows:

Proceeds of warrants 150 × C5 = C750.

Number of ordinary shares that could be issued at fair value C750 ÷ C10 = 75

Number of ordinary shares that would be issued at nil consideration 150 − 75 = 75

Consolidated earnings per share

Basic EPS $\frac{100,000 + 4,680}{10,000} = \text{C}10.47$

The earnings are calculated as the profit attributable to ordinary shareholders,

子公司归属于普通股股东的利润为6,000元。其普通股股本包含1,000股普通股，且其有400股已发行的可转换优先股（一比一）。其还发行了150份认股权证，每份认股权证可以5元的行权价格认购子公司的普通股。子公司每股普通股的平均市价为10元。优先股股利为每股1元。除股利外，不存在其他公司间交易或抵销。此例中税款的影响忽略不计。

子公司的每股收益

基本 EPS $\frac{6,000-400}{1,000}=5.6$ 元

其通过以下计算得出：将子公司的利润扣除计入留存收益的优先股股利，然后除以子公司的普通股股数。

稀释 EPS $\frac{6,000}{1,000+75+400}=4.07$ 元

其为子公司的利润（优先股股利未被扣除，因为其在优先股转换时将得以节省）除以普通股股数加上优先股按一比一转股时所将发行的普通股股数以及行使认股权证时将以零对价发行的普通股股数之和，具体计算如下：

认股权证的款项 150×5元=750元。

可能按公允价值发行的普通股股数 750元÷10元=75

将以零对价发行的普通股股数 150－75=75

合并每股收益

基本 EPS $\frac{100,000+4,680}{10,000}=10.47$ 元

合并利润表中的利润为不包含子公司经营成果前归属于普通股股东的利

before taking account of the subsidiary's results that are included in the consolidated financial statements, of C100,000, plus the share of the subsidiary's profits calculated as:

6,000 − 400 = 5,600 × 800 ÷ 1,000 = 4,480 + 200 (share of preference dividend) = 4,680

$$\text{Diluted EPS} \quad \frac{100,000 + 3,256 + 41 + 814}{10,000} = \text{C}10.41$$

The earnings figure comprises:

(a) The profit of parent entity attributable to ordinary shares (excluding dividends from subsidiary) of C100,000.

(b) The share of subsidiary's profit calculated as (800 shares × 4.07) = C3,256. (C4.07 being the diluted EPS of the subsidiary).

(c) The parent's proportionate interest in the subsidiary's earnings attributable to the warrants calculated as (75 shares × 4.07) × 20 ÷ 150 = C40.7.

(d) The parent's proportionate interest in the subsidiary's earnings attributable to the convertible preference shares calculated as (200 shares × 4.07) = C814.

14.136 The example above discloses the effect on the group diluted EPS of options in a subsidiary that are convertible into shares of the subsidiary.

14.137 The standard also covers the situation where securities of the reporting entity are issued that are convertible into ordinary shares of a subsidiary, joint venture or associate. In such a situation, the securities are assumed to be converted and the profit or loss attributable to ordinary equity holders of the reporting entity is adjusted, in the normal way, for any changes in dividends, interest or other changes that would result from conversion. The profit or loss is also adjusted for any changes in the reporting entity's share of results of the subsidiary, joint venture or associate that would result from the change in the number of shares in the subsidiary, joint venture or associate held by the reporting entity as a result of conversion. The denominator (number of shares and potential ordinary shares) of the diluted EPS calculation is not adjusted because the number

润 100,000 元加上母公司享有的子公司利润的份额，具体计算过程如下：

$6,000 - 400 = 5,600 \times 800 \div 1,000 = 4,480 + 200$（优先股股利份额）$= 4,680$

$$\text{稀释 EPS} \quad \frac{100,000 + 3,256 + 41 + 814}{10,000} = 10.41 \text{ 元}$$

利润的数值包括：

（a）归属于普通股的母公司利润（不包括从子公司获得的股利）100,000 元。

（b）子公司利润的份额计算为（800 股 ×4.07）=3,256 元。（4.07 元为子公司的稀释 EPS）。

（c）子公司利润中归属于认股权证且由母公司享有的权益计算为（75 股 ×4.07）×20 ÷ 150 = 40.7 元。

（d）子公司利润中的归属于可转换优先股且由母公司享有的权益计算为（200 股 ×4.07）=814 元。

14.136　上述示例披露了可转换为子公司股份的子公司发行的期权对集团稀释 EPS 的影响。

14.137　准则也涵盖了报告主体所发行的证券可转换为子公司、合营企业或联营企业的普通股的情况。在此类情况下，假设证券将被转换，且归属于报告主体普通股股东的损益以正常方式就股利、利息的变化或转换所将导致的其他变化进行调整。该损益也就转换将导致报告主体所持子公司、合营企业或联营企业股数的变化，所将导致报告主体在子公司、合营企业或联营企业经营成果中所占份额的任何变化进行调整。稀释 EPS 计算中的分母（股份和潜在普通股的数量）不作调整，因为报告主体自身的股数在转换后不会发生变化。[IAS 33 第 A12 段]。

of shares of the reporting entity itself would not change following conversion. [IAS 33 para A12].

Employee share and incentive plans

14.138 Many companies have in place share options and other share award schemes to remunerate officers and other employees. Under some schemes, share options or share purchase rights are granted solely on the basis that the employees continue to render service for a specified period of time, that is, the award does not specify a performance condition for vesting. In other schemes, vesting of the shares depends on both the employee's rendering service to the employer for a specified period of time and the achievement of a specified performance target, for example, attaining a specified growth rate in return on assets or a specified earnings target.

14.139 IAS 33 states that employee share options with fixed or determinable terms and non-vested ordinary shares are treated as options in calculating diluted EPS, even though they may be contingent on vesting. They are treated as outstanding on the grant date. Performance-related employee share options are treated as contingently issuable shares (see para 14.145 below) because their issue is contingent on satisfying specified conditions in addition to the passage of time. [IAS 33 para 48].

14.140 As noted above, performance-related share options are treated as contingently issuable shares and these are dealt with from paragraph 14.145 below. All other awards that do not specify a performance criteria should be regarded as options for the purposes of computing diluted EPS. They should be considered to be outstanding as of the grant date for purposes of computing diluted EPS even though their exercise may be contingent upon vesting. They should be included in the diluted EPS computation even if the employee may not receive (or be able to sell) the stock until some future date. Accordingly, all shares to be issued should be included in computing diluted EPS if the effect is dilutive. The dilutive effect should be computed using the treasury stock method described in paragraph 14.117 above. If the share awards were granted during the period, the shares issuable must be weighted to reflect the portion of the period during which the awards were

职工股份和激励计划

14.138　许多公司均设有股份期权及其他股份奖励计划用于奖赏管理人员及其他职工。在有些计划中，股份期权或股份购买权的授予仅基于职工将继续提供指定期限的服务，即该项奖励并未规定行权所需的业绩条件。在其他计划中，股份的可行权条件取决于职工向雇主提供指定期限的服务并达到指定业绩目标，例如，达到指定的资产回报增长率或指定的收益目标。

14.139　IAS 33 指出，在计算稀释 EPS 时，带有固定或可确定条款的职工股份期权和未达到可行权条件的普通股作为期权进行处理，即使其可能取决于是否满足可行权条件。上述期权在授予日即视为已发行在外。与业绩相关的职工股份期权作为或有可发行股份处理（参见下文第 14.145 段），因为除时间的推移外，其发行还取决于是否满足指定的条件。[IAS 33 第 48 段]。

14.140　如上所述，与业绩相关的股份期权作为或有可发行股份处理，并从下文第 14.145 段起对此予以论述。所有其他未指定业绩标准的奖励均应在计算稀释 EPS 时视为期权予以处理。即使其行使与否可能取决于是否满足可行权条件，但在计算稀释 EPS 时，上述期权在授予日即视为已发行在外。即使职工在某一未来日期前可能不会取得（或能够出售）股票，也将其纳入稀释 EPS 的计算。相应地，如果股份发行产生稀释作用，则将发行的所有股份均应纳入稀释 EPS 的计算。稀释作用应采用上文第 14.117 段中所述的库存股法予以计算。如果股份奖励在当期被授予，则可发行的股份必须考虑时间权数来反映奖励发行在外的期间。[IAS 33 第 38 段]。

outstanding. [IAS 33 para 38].

14.141 For share options and other share-based payment arrangements to which IFRS 2 applies, the assumed exercise price should include the fair value (as calculated on the date the options were granted) of any goods or services to be supplied to the entity in the future under the share option or other share-based payment arrangement. [IAS 33 para 47A]. Therefore, in applying the treasury stock method described in paragraph 14.117 above, the assumed exercise price, for the purpose of determining the incremental number of shares issued for nil consideration, would comprise the amount, if any, the employee must pay upon exercise and the balance of any amounts calculated under IFRS 2 that has not yet been charged to the income statement. The assumed proceeds should not include cost attributable to past service. Neither should any adjustments be made to the numerator in respect of the IFRS 2 charge to the income statement as the charge represents the cost of issuing potential ordinary shares that would not be saved on conversion. The treatment of employee share options that are not related to performance is illustrated in the following example (ignoring tax).

Example

Share option scheme not related to performance

Company A has in place an employee share option scheme that awards share options to employees on the basis of period of service with the company.

The provisions of the scheme are as follows at the 20X0 year end.

Date of grant	1 January 20X0
Market price of option at grant date	C2.10
Exercise price of option	C2.50
Date of vesting	31 December 20X2
Number of shares under option	1 million

Applying IFRS 2, the income statement is charged with 70c per option in each of the three years 20X0 - 20X2 (that is, C2.10/3).

14.141　对于适用 IFRS 2 的股份期权及其他以股份为基础的支付安排，假设行权价格应包含根据股份期权或其他以股份为基础的支付安排将向主体提供的任何商品或服务的公允价值（在期权授予日的计算结果）。[IAS 33 第 47A 段]。因此，应用上文第 14.117 段中所述的库存股法时，为确定零对价发行股份的增量数，假设行权价格应包含职工在行权时所须支付的金额（如有），以及根据 IFRS 2 计算的尚未计入利润表的任何金额的余额。假设行权的款项不应包括归属于以前服务的成本。根据 IFRS 2 计入利润表的金额代表不会因转股而节省的发行潜在普通股的成本，因此不应对分子作出任何的调整。与业绩无关的职工股份期权的处理在下列示例中进行说明（税款忽略不计）。

示例

与业绩无关的股份期权计划

A 公司设有一项职工股份期权计划，以在公司的服务期限为基础授予职工股份期权。

20X0 年年末该计划的条款如下。

授予日	20X0 年 1 月 1 日
授予日期权的市场价格	2.10 元
期权行权价格	2.50 元
可行权日	20X2 年 12 月 31 日
期权项下的股数	1,000,000

根据 IFRS 2，在 20X0 年至 20X2 年的三年中每年在利润表中对每份期权确认 0.7 元（即 2.10 元/3）。

Profit for year 20X0 (after compensation expense)	C1, 200, 000		
Weighted average number of ordinary shares outstanding	5 million		
Average market price of an ordinary share during the year	C5. 00		
Assumed proceeds per option	C3. 90 (being the exercise price of C2. 50 and IFRS 2 expense attributable to future service, not yet recognised, of C1. 40). Next year C3. 20 (being C2. 50 + 70c).		
Computation of earnings per share	**per share**	**earnings**	**shares**
Profit for year 20X0		C1, 200, 000	
Weighted average shares outstanding for 20X0			5, 000, 000
Basic earnings per share	24. 0c		
Number of shares under option			1, 000, 000
Number of shares that would have been issued at fair value: (1 million × C3. 90)/C5. 00			(780, 000)
Diluted earnings per share	23. 0c	C1, 200, 000	5, 220, 000

[The next paragraph is 14. 143.]

14. 143 Sometimes shares to satisfy the company's obligations under share award schemes have already been purchased by an ESOP trust and are held by the trust as pre – funding for options or other performance – related shares. The trust's holding in the company's shares is treated as treasury shares and deducted from equity. [IAS 32 para 33]. Accordingly, the rules relating to treasury shares would apply

20X0 年利润（扣除报酬费用后）	1,200,000 元		
发行在外普通股的加权平均数	5,000,000		
本年每股普通股的平均市价	5.00 元		
每份期权的假设行权款项	3.90 元（即行权价格 2.50 元加上根据 IFRS 2 计算的归属于未来服务且尚未确认的费用 1.40 元）。 下一年为 3.20 元（即 2.50 元 +0.70 元）。		
每股收益的计算	***每股***	***收益***	***股份***
20X0 年利润		1,200,000 元	
20X0 年发行在外股份的加权平均数			5,000,000
基本每股收益	0.24 元		
期权项下的股数			1,000,000
应以公允价值发行的股份数量：（1,000,000 × 3.90 元）/5.00 元			(780,000)
稀释每股收益	0.23 元	1,200,000 元	5,220,000

[下一段为第 14.143 段。]

14.143 有时用于履行股份奖励计划项下公司义务的股份已由一家 ESOP 信托购买，并由该信托持有并作为对期权或其他业绩相关股份的预先融资。该信托持有的公司股份作为库存股处理并从权益中扣除。[IAS 32 第 33 段]。相应地，如上文第 14.75 段中所述，根据与库存股相关的规定，这些非可行权股份不应纳入基本 EPS 和稀释 EPS 的计算。相反地，稀释 EPS 的计算应以与上

and those non – vesting shares should be excluded from both basic and diluted EPS as discussed in paragraph 14. 75 above. Instead, the calculation of diluted EPS should include non – performance – related shares in the same way as options as set out from paragraph 14. 140 above and performance – related shares in the same way as contingently issuable shares as discussed from paragraph 14. 145 below.

14. 144 If share based awards are payable in ordinary shares or in cash at the election of either the entity or the employee, the determination of whether such awards are potential ordinary shares should be made in the same way as discussed in paragraph 14. 163.

Contingently issuable ordinary share

14. 145 It is not uncommon for acquisition agreements to include a clause under which the purchaser of an acquired entity is required to make an additional consideration payment in the form of ordinary shares in future. The value of such shares may either be known precisely at the time of the acquisition, or may be contingent upon the future performance or future evaluation of the acquired entity. In the first instance, the acquirer has an obligation to issue ordinary shares in future, but the obligation is simply deferred (deferred consideration). In the second instance an obligation may or may not arise depending on whether or not certain earnings conditions are met (contingent consideration). In any event, the need to issue ordinary shares in future could lead to dilution of EPS. The standard refers to these as 'contingently issuable ordinary shares'. [IAS 33 para 52]. Contingently issuable ordinary shares are defined as "*ordinary shares issuable for little or no cash or other consideration upon the satisfaction of specified conditions in a contingent share agreement*" (see also para 14. 77 above). [IAS 33 para 5].

14. 146 The way in which diluted EPS should be calculated to take account of contingently issuable shares is described below:

- Contingently issuable shares are considered outstanding and included in the calculation of diluted EPS as if the conditions of the contingency are deemed to have been met, based on the information available, at the end of reporting period. In effect this means that the diluted EPS computation includes those shares that would be issued under the terms of the contingency, based on the

文第 14. 140 段中所列示期权的相同的方式包含非业绩相关股份，并以与下文第 14. 145 段中所述的或有可发行股份相同的方式包含与业绩相关股份。

14. 144　如果以股份为基础的奖励将由主体或职工选择以普通股还是现金支付，则应以与第 14. 163 段中所述的相同的方式确定此类奖励是否属于潜在普通股。

或有可发行普通股

14. 145　购买方须以发行普通股的方式在未来作出额外的对价支付的条款在收购协议中并不罕见。此类股份的价值可能在购买时已准确获知，也可能视被购买主体的未来业绩或未来评价而定。在第一种情况下，购买方有义务在未来发行普通股，只是该义务被递延（递延对价）。在第二种情况下，义务可能产生也可能不产生，具体取决于是否满足某些收益条件（或有对价）。任何情况下，在未来需要发行普通股均可能导致 EPS 的稀释。准则将这些股份称为“或有可发行普通股”。［IAS 33 第 52 段］。或有可发行普通股被定义为“*满足或有股份协议中的指定条件时，可以极少或零现金或其他对价发行的普通股*”（另请参见上文第 14. 77 段）。［IAS 33 第 5 段］。

14. 146　将或有可发行股份考虑在内计算稀释 EPS 的方式描述如下：

- 如果或有条件根据报告期期末的已知信息被认为已经满足，则或有可发行股份被当做发行在外，并包括在稀释 EPS 的计算中。实际上，这意味着稀释 EPS 的计算包括那些假设报告期期末是或有期期末，根据当前条件，按照或有条款可能已发行的股份。例如，盈利能力支付安排中，对假设该安排在资产负债表日已终止而应该发行的股份数量进行的估计（参见

current status of conditions, as if the end of the reporting period was the end of the contingency period. An example would be an estimate of the number of shares that would have been issued under an earn – out if that agreement had terminated at the balance sheet date (see further para 14. 148). Ordinary shares issuable under such contingent share agreements are included in the diluted EPS calculation as of the beginning of the period or as of the date of the contingent share agreement, if later. Restatement is not permitted if the conditions are not met when the actual contingency period expires. [IAS 33 para 52].

- Where the conditions relating to the issue have been met (the events occurred) by the end of the period, the relevant shares are included in the computation of both basic and diluted EPS. In effect, this will be when issuing the shares is no longer contingent and when there are no circumstances under which the shares would not be issued. [IAS 33 para 52].

14. 147 The criteria under which additional shares are issuable under contingent consideration agreements are many and varied, although in practice most involve either future levels of earnings or the future share price of the issuing company or a mixture of both. It should be noted, however, that such contingently issuable shares should be included in the diluted EPS calculation only if the effect is dilutive.

14. 148 Where the number of contingently issuable shares depends upon the level of earnings, the diluted EPS computation should include those shares to the extent that they would be issuable under the agreement based on the current amount of earnings. However, earnings conditions in earn out agreements come in various forms. Sometimes the terms may specify that further shares will be issued if the average profit earned over a period is a specific amount. Sometimes the maintenance of current earnings levels, or the attainment of specified increased level of earnings of the acquired entity for a specified number of years may be the condition. Other earnings conditions may specify the issue of shares when a minimum earnings target is reached, increasing rateably until the maximum earnings target is reached, with a cap on the maximum number of shares that could be issued.

14. 149 IAS 33 deals specifically with one such type of arrangement, where the achievement or maintenance of a specified level of earnings is the condition and that amount has been achieved at the end of the period, but must be maintained for

第 14. 148 段）。这些或有股份协议下可发行的普通股应从期初，或者或有股份协议签订日（若晚于期初）开始包括在稀释 EPS 的计算中。或有期间期满之时，若条件未满足，亦不允许重述。[IAS 33 第 52 段]。

■ 在报告期期末发行条件满足（即事件已经发生）的情况下，相关股份则既要包括在基本 EPS 的计算中，也要包括在稀释 EPS 的计算中。实际上，上述情况也就是当发行股份不再是或有事项以及没有情形导致股份不可以发行之时。[IAS 33 第 52 段]。

14. 147　或有对价协议项下可发行额外股份的标准众多且各不相同，尽管实务中大多数涉及股份发行公司的未来收益水平或未来股价，或者兼而有之。然而值得注意的是，此类或有可发行股份仅在具有稀释性时才应纳入稀释 EPS 的计算。

14. 148　当或有可发行股份的数量取决于收益水平时，稀释 EPS 的计算即应包括基于当前收益金额将发行的股份。然而，盈利能力支付协议中的收益条件有多种不同的形式。有时条款可能指明，如果一段时期内所赚取的平均利润达到某一特定金额，则将发行额外的股份。有时，维持被收购主体当前的收益水平，或者在指定的数年间实现指定收益水平的上升，也可能是条件。其他的收益条件可能指明在达到最低收益目标时发行股份，且按比例增加，直至达到最高收益目标并同时限定了所能发行的股份的上限。

14. 149　IAS 33 特别阐述了一项此类安排，即条件为实现或维持指定的收益水平，且于期末时已达到该条件，但必须持续一段时间。在此类情况下，如果额外普通股具有稀释性，则应包括在稀释 EPS 中。因为出于计算稀释 EPS

a further period. In such a case the additional ordinary shares are included if dilutive in the *diluted* EPS, because the end of the period is *assumed* to be the end of the contingency period for the purpose of diluted EPS and the level of profit has been achieved at the end of the period. However, the shares are not included in *basic* EPS until the end of the *actual* contingency period, that is, the end of the further period for which the level of earnings must be maintained. This is because there may be losses in that further period that could mean that the contingent condition will not be met at the end of the actual contingency period. [IAS 33 para 53].

14.150 Whatever the earnings criteria, the guiding principle is that the current level of earnings should be used to determine the number of shares that could be issued under the terms, assuming that the contingency period ended on the balance sheet date. They should be included in the diluted EPS calculation only if dilution results. If in the subsequent period, or until the end of the agreement, there is a decline in earnings such that the contingent shares no longer need to be issued, previous period's diluted EPS should not be restated. Hence, basic EPS should not include any contingently issuable shares, because all the necessary conditions have not been satisfied, but the shares would be included in calculating the diluted figure. The following examples illustrate the application of the above principle.

Example 1

Average earnings condition

On 1 January 20X4, company A acquired the whole of the issued share capital of company B. The total consideration payable in respect of the acquisition comprises initial consideration and deferred contingent consideration. Under the terms of the deferred contingent consideration, company A is required to issue 100,000 shares if company B's profit for the year averages C100,000 over a three year period. Any additional shares will be issued on 1 January 20X7 after the end of the three year contingency period. Company B's profit for the year ended 31 December 20X4 amounted to C120,000.

Given that the terms stipulate the achievement of C100,000 of average profit for the three year period, it would appear at first sight that the contingency condition at the balance sheet date has been met as the profit for the year ended 31 December 20X4 exceeds C100,000. This is not the case as it

的目的，期末被假设为或有期间的期末，且该期末已实现利润水平。然而，基本 EPS 不包括该等股份，直至实际或有期间的期末，即必须维持收益水平的后续期间的期末。这是因为在后续期间可能存在亏损，这可能意味着实际或有期间期末或有条件不会得以满足。[IAS 33 第53段]。

14.150 无论收益标准如何，指导原则均为假设或有期间于资产负债表日结束，根据当前收益水平确定根据条款所能发行的股份数量。仅当产生稀释效果时，才应将这些股份纳入稀释 EPS 的计算中。如果在后续期间或直至协议结束时，收益出现下降以致不再需要发行或有股份，前期的稀释 EPS 不应被重述。因此，基本 EPS 不应包括任何或有可发行股份，因为所有必要条件并未满足，但在计算稀释数值时将包括这些股份。下列示例说明了如何应用上述原则。

示例 1

平均收益条件

20X4 年 1 月 1 日，A 公司购买了 B 公司全部已发行股本。此次收购应付对价总额包含初始对价和递延或有对价。根据递延或有对价的条款，如果在三年期内 B 公司的年均利润达到 100,000 元，则 A 公司须发行 100,000股股份。任何额外股份均将于三年或有期间结束后的 20X7 年 1 月 1 日发行。B 公司截至 20X4 年 12 月 31 日止年度的利润共计 120,000 元。

鉴于上述条款规定三年期内平均利润应达到 100,000 元，初看起来资产负债表日或有条件已满足，因为截至 20X4 年 12 月 31 日止年度的利润超出 100,000 元。但情况并非如此，因为其假设公司将于截至 20X6 年 12 月 31 日的未来两年中每年至少赚取 90,000 元。准则并不允许以这一方式

assumes that the company will earn at least C90, 000 for each of the next two years ended 31 December 20X6. Projecting future earnings levels in this way is not permitted under the standard because as stated in paragraph 14. 101 above, the standard takes a historical approach and not a predictive or forward – looking approach in measuring dilution. The provisions relating to contingently issuable shares in the standard are quite specific and do not allow an entity to consider the probability of a contingent issue occurring.

The correct analysis is to measure whether performance achieved in the current period is deemed to be that achieved over the whole of the contingency period as if the end of the reporting period was the end of the contingency period. On this basis, an average over a period has the same effect as if it were expressed as a cumulative amount over the period. So in this situation, the contingency condition should be expressed in terms of a cumulative target of C300, 000 over the three year period. Since the profit for the year ended 31 December 20X4 is only C120, 000, which is less than C300, 000, the contingency condition is not met at the balance sheet and no additional shares would be brought into the diluted EPS computation.

Similarly, if the profit for the year ended 31 December 20X5 were to increase to C150, 000 again the contingency condition is not met in that year, because the cumulative earnings to date amounts to C270, 000. So no additional shares would be included in that year. In the final year ended 31 December 20X6 when the contingency period comes to an end, the company will know for certain whether the contingency conditions have been met or not. If the condition is met in that year, the company will include 100, 000 shares in both basic and diluted EPS.

Example 2

Attainment of a specified increased level of earnings

The facts are the same as in the previous example except that the deferred contingent consideration agreement provides for the issue of 1, 000 shares for each C1, 000 of total profit in excess of C250, 000 over the three years ending 20X6. Using the above principles, the company did not earn C250, 000 for the year ended 31 December 20X4. Again projecting future earnings levels (C120, 000

预测未来收益水平，因为正如上文第 14.101 段中所述，在计量稀释性时，准则采用了历史方法而非预测性或前瞻性的方法。本准则中与或有可发行股份相关的规定相当具体，且不允许主体考虑或有发行发生的可能性。

正确的分析是假设报告期末即或有期间期末，应衡量当期实现的业绩是否可以被视为整个或有期间实现的业绩。据此，一个期间内的平均数与其被示为该期间的累计金额有相同的效果。所以在这一情况下，或有条件应被示为三年期内达到 300,000 元的累计目标。由于截至 20X4 年 12 月 31 日止年度的利润仅为 120,000 元，少于 300,000 元，因而在资产负债表中或有条件未被满足，则无额外的股份将被纳入稀释 EPS 的计算。

类似地，如果截至 20X5 年 12 月 31 日止年度的利润将增至 150,000 元，则或有条件在该年度仍未得以满足，因为截至当日的累计收益为 270,000 元。因此当年不会计入任何额外股份。在截至 20X6 年 12 月 31 日的最后一年即或有期间结束的年度，公司将确切了解是否已满足或有条件。如果条件在该年度得以满足，则公司将把 100,000 股股份计入基本 EPS 和稀释 EPS。

示例 2

达到指定的收益增加水平

事实与前一示例相同，除了递延或有对价协议规定在截至 20X6 年底的三年中，总利润超出 250,000 元后每超出 1,000 元则发行 1,000 股股份。

运用上述原则得出，公司在截至 20X4 年 12 月 31 日止年度并未赚得 250,000 元。预测未来收益水平（120,000 元乘以 3 年 =360,000 元）并

for 3 years = C360, 000) and including 110, 000 ((C360, 000 – C250, 000)/ C1, 000 × 1, 000) contingent shares in the diluted EPS calculation is not permitted by the standard.

For the year ended 31 December 20X5, the cumulative amount earned to that date is C270, 000. As this amount exceeds C250, 000, the contingency condition is met in that year and the company will include 20, 000 contingently issuable shares in the diluted EPS calculation for that year. For the year ended 31 December 20X6, the cumulative amount earned to that date would be known and the actual number of shares issued would be included in both basic and diluted EPS. If the actual number of shares amounts to say 50, 000 shares, prior year's diluted EPS, which was based on 20, 000 contingent shares, should not be restated.

14.151 Similar considerations apply when computing diluted EPS for interim reports. If at 30 June 20X5, the cumulative amount earned to that date was C245, 000 (C120, 000 to 31 December 20X4 + C125, 000 to 30 June 20X5), the contingency provision is not met. Therefore, no contingently issuable shares would be included in calculating the diluted EPS for the half year, even though at the time of preparing the interim report it is apparent that 20, 000 shares will be included in the year end diluted EPS calculation.

14.152 IAS 33 also gives specific guidance for the situation where the number of shares issuable in the future depends on the market price of the shares at the future date. It states that the computation of diluted EPS should reflect the number of shares that would be issued based on the current market price at the end of the reporting period if the effect is dilutive. If the condition is based on an average of market prices over some period of time that extends beyond the end of the reporting period, the average for the period that has elapsed at the period end should be used. Because the market price may change in a future period, basic EPS should not include such contingently issuable shares, because all necessary conditions have not been satisfied. [IAS 33 para 54].

14.153 Where the number of contingently issuable ordinary shares depends on both future earnings and the future market price of ordinary shares, the number of ordinary shares included in the diluted EPS calculation is based on both conditions. Unless both conditions are deemed to be met (using the guidance in the previous paragraphs) the

将 110,000（（360,000 元 - 250,000 元）/1,000 元 × 1,000）股或有股份纳入稀释 EPS 的计算同样不为准则所允许。

截至 20X5 年 12 月 31 日止年度，截至该日所赚取的累计金额为 270,000 元。由于这一金额超出 250,000 元，因而或有条件在该年得以满足，则公司将把 20,000 股或有可发行股份纳入该年稀释 EPS 的计算。截至 20X6 年 12 月 31 日止的年度，截至该日所赚取的累计金额应已知晓，则所发行股份的实际数量将被纳入基本 EPS 和稀释 EPS。如果实际股份数量达到例如 50,000 股，则基于 20,000 股或有股份的前一年度的稀释 EPS 不应被重述。

14.151　计算用于中期报告的稀释 EPS 时，类似的考虑也适用。如果在 20X5 年 6 月 30 日，截至该日所赚取的累计金额为 245,000 元（截至 20X4 年 12 月 31 日的 120,000 元 + 截至 20X5 年 6 月 30 日的 125,000 元），则或有股份发行条件未得以满足。因此，在计算上述半年的稀释 EPS 时不应纳入或有可发行股份，即使在编制中期报告时，显而易见 20,000 股股份将被纳入年末稀释 EPS 的计算。

14.152　IAS 33 还针对未来可发行股份的数量取决于股份在未来日期的市场价格的情况给出了具体指引。其指出，如果其效应是稀释性的，则稀释 EPS 的计算应反映基于报告期末当前市场价格将发行的股份的数量。如果发行条件是基于超过报告期末之外的一段时间内的市场平均价格，则使用截至报告期末已逝去时间段内的平均价格。由于市场价格在未来期间可能发生变化，而且并非所有必要条件均已满足，因而基本 EPS 不应包括此类或有可发行股份。[IAS 33 第 54 段]。

14.153　当或有可发行普通股的股数同时取决于未来收益及普通股未来的市场价格时，包括在稀释 EPS 计算中的普通股股数应基于两方面条件。除非这两方面条件均被视为已满足（使用前述段落给出的指引），否则该等或有可发行股份不包括在稀释 EPS 的计算中。[IAS 33 第 55 段]。

contingently issuable shares are not included in the diluted EPS. [IAS 33 para 55].

14. 154 In some deferred consideration agreements, the value of the deferred consideration is known, but the number of shares to be issued when the deferred consideration falls due is not known. IAS 33 does not specifically consider this situation. However, we consider that the number of shares to be included in the calculation should be based on the market price at the balance sheet date as if it were the end of the contingency period.

14. 155 IAS 33 also gives guidance for the situation where the contingency is based on a condition other than earnings or market price (for example, opening a certain number of retail stores). It states that the contingent shares should be included in the computation of diluted EPS based on the assumption that the current status (at the period end) of the condition will remain unchanged until the end of the contingency period. So, if during the period only half the required number of new stores that would result in the issue of shares were opened, no contingently issuable shares are included in the diluted EPS computation. [IAS 33 para 56].

14. 156 If the contingency is based on a number of different conditions, we consider that the determination of the number of shares included in diluted EPS should be based on the status of all relevant conditions as they exist at the end of each reporting period. If one of the conditions is not met at the end of the reporting period, no contingently issuable shares should be included in diluted EPS. Though not specifically mentioned in IAS 33 it is implicit in the guidance described in paragraph 14. 153 above.

14. 157 Contingently issuable potential ordinary shares that are not covered by a contingent share agreement, such as contingently issuable convertible instruments, should be included in diluted EPS on the following basis:

- It is first necessary to determine whether the potential ordinary shares may be assumed to be issued on the basis of the conditions specified for their issue under the contingently issuable share provisions discussed from paragraph 14. 145.

- Depending on the type of those potential ordinary shares, they should be reflected in diluted EPS by following the provisions for convertible securities discussed from paragraph 14. 114, the provisions for share options and warrants discussed

14.154　在某些递延对价协议中，递延对价的金额已知，但递延对价到期时将发行的股份的数量未知。IAS 33 未特别考虑这一情形。但是，我们认为，计算中包括的股份的数量应以资产负债表日的市场价格为基础确定，视同资产负债表日为或有期间期末。

14.155　IAS 33 还就或有股份发行基于除收益或市场价格以外的其他条件的情形（例如，一定数量的零售商店的开业）给出了指引。其指出，应假设目前状况（期末时）保持不变直至或有期间期末，并基于该假设确定是否将或有股份包括在稀释 EPS 的计算中。因此，如果在本期仅有引致股份发行要求的新店数量一半的新店开张，则稀释 EPS 的计算不包括或有可发行股份。[IAS 33 第 56 段]。

14.156　如果或有股份发行基于多个不同条件，我们认为，稀释 EPS 应包括的股份数量应以在各报告期末所有相关条件的状况为基础确定。如果某个条件在报告期末未得以满足，则稀释 EPS 不包括或有可发行股份。尽管在 IAS 33 中未特别提及，但上文第 14.153 段中所述的指引中已暗含这一点。

14.157　未包括在或有股份协议中的或有可发行潜在普通股，例如，或有可发行可转换工具，应以下列事项为基础包括在稀释 EPS 中：

- 首先有必要确定的是，按照指定的发行条件，根据自第 14.145 段起讨论的或有可发行股份的规定，是否可以假定该等潜在普通股已获发行。

- 取决于这些潜在普通股的类型，应遵循自第 14.114 段起讨论的可转换证券的规定、自第 14.117 段起讨论的股份期权及认股权证的规定以及自第 14.159 段起讨论的可以普通股或现金结算的合同的规定，将这些潜在普通

from paragraph 14. 117, and the provisions for contracts that may be settled in ordinary shares or cash discussed from paragraph 14. 159.

However, exercise or conversion should not be assumed for purposes of computing diluted EPS, unless exercise or conversion of similar outstanding potential ordinary shares that are not contingently issuable is also assumed. [IAS 33 para 57].

14. 158 An example of contingently issuable potential ordinary shares is given in Table 14. 6. This relates to contingent consideration for an acquisition that is subject to a lawsuit.

Table 14. 6 – Diluted EPS and contingent consideration payable in shares

Altana AG – Annual Report and Accounts – 31 December 2002

Earnings per share

Basic earnings per share are computed by dividing net income by the weighted average number of shares outstanding for the year. Diluted EPS reflects the potential dilution that could occur if securities or other contracts to issue common stock were exercised or converted into common stock. Diluted earnings per share are calculated by adjusting the weighted average number of shares for the effect of the stock option plans as well as the impact of the DAT lawsuit which is payable in the Company's shares (Note 31). No adjustments to net income were necessary for the computation of diluted earnings per share.

The diluted earnings per share were calculated under the assumption that all potential diluting options are exercised.

	2002	2001
Basic earnings per share:		
Net income	**324, 408**	327, 937
Weighted average common shares outstanding	**136, 622, 766**	137, 533, 720
Basic earnings per share in €	**2. 37**	**2. 38**
Diluted weighted average shares:		
Net income	**324, 408**	327, 937
Weighted average shares outstanding	**136, 622, 766**	137, 533, 720
Dilution from stock options	**604, 546**	607, 434
Dilution from DAT lawsuit	**306, 391**	306, 391
Diluted weighted average shares outstanding	**137, 533, 703**	138, 447, 545
Diluted earnings per share in €	**2. 36**	**2. 37**

股反映在稀释 EPS 中。

但是，不能为了计算稀释 EPS 就假定行权或转换，除非同时假设类似的已发行的并非或有可发行的潜在普通股亦被假定行权或转换。[IAS 33 第 57 段]。

14.158 表 14.6 中给出了或有可发行潜在普通股的一个例子。其与面临诉讼的一项收购的或有对价有关。

表 14.6——稀释 EPS 和以股份结算的或有对价

阿尔塔纳股份公司——年度报告及报表——2002 年 12 月 31 日

每股收益

基本每股收益按净收益除以当年已发行股份的加权平均数计算得出。稀释 EPS 反映了当发行普通股的证券或其他合同被行权或转换为普通股时，可能产生的潜在稀释。稀释每股收益的计算应调整加权平均股数，以反映股票期权计划及以本公司股份清偿的 DAT 诉讼（附注 31）的影响。稀释每股收益的计算无需对净收益作出调整。

稀释每股收益的计算乃假设所有潜在稀释性期权均已行使。

	2002 年	2001 年
基本每股收益：		
净收益	**324, 408**	327, 937
已发行普通股的加权平均数	**136, 622, 766**	137, 533, 720
基本每股收益（欧元）	**2. 37**	**2. 38**
稀释加权平均股份：		
净收益	**324, 408**	327, 937
已发行股份的加权平均数	**136, 622, 766**	137, 533, 720
股票期权形成的稀释	**604, 546**	607, 434
DAT 诉讼案件形成的稀释	**306, 391**	306, 391
稀释加权平均股份	**137, 533, 703**	138, 447, 545
稀释每股收益（欧元）	**2. 36**	**2. 37**

31 Litigation

Deutsch – Atlantische Telegraphen AG

In 1988, a group of minority shareholders of DAT brought a legal action against the Company in connection with an exchange offer made to these minority shareholders.

After consideration of the case, both the Landesgericht Köln and the Oberlandesgericht Düsseldorf stated that the 1.3 or 1.4 shares offered to the former shareholders was fair consideration. However, in 1999 the Federal Supreme Court of Germany overturned this ruling stating that the fair value should be determined based on a higher market value for DAT shares.

On March 12, 2001, the German Federal Court of Justice (Bundesgerichtshof, BGH) ruled that the exchange ratio must be based on the average market price of the shares to be exchanged during the three months preceding the approval by majority shareholders of DAT to sell its shares to the Company. The BGH referred the appeal back to a lower court (Landgericht Köln).

The expected settlement is recorded as contingent consideration based on the Company's best estimate of the exchange of 3.45 ALTANA shares for one DAT share. However, since all of the assets of DAT were either sold or written off in connection with the Company's restructuring plan in 1995, the additional consideration was expensed immediately as an impairment expense. As of December 31, 2002, consideration expected to be settled by the Company by issuance of shares has been measured at €13.8 million based on the Company's share price at December 31, 2002. The portion of the settlement expected to be paid in cash is €2.3 million. The estimated total settlement of € 16.1 million is recorded as an accrual. The final settlement is subject to change based on the final exchange ratio and the market value of ALTANA's stock on the date of the settlement (Note 32).

In 2001, the addition of the accrual was recorded in other operating expenses. In 2002 the reduction of the accrual (€3.4 million) due to the decrease in the ALTANA's share price at the balance sheet date was recorded in other operating income.

32 Subsequent events (extract)

The management board and the supervisory board of ALTANA AG authorized the issuance of the financial statements as of March 17, 2003.

On January 15, 2003, the federal court decided that the consideration of the former DAT shareholders (Note 31) should be based on a conversion ratio of 3.45 shares of ALTANA for one share of DAT. The Company has appealed against that ruling.

31. 诉讼

Deutsch – Atlantische Telegraphen AG 公司

1988 年，DAT 的一些小股东向本公司提起了一项法律诉讼，该法律诉讼与本公司向这些小股东作出的交换要约有关。

在对该案件进行考虑后，Landesgericht Köln 和 Oberlandesgericht Düsseldorf 均表示，向前股东提供的 1.3 或 1.4 股股份乃公允对价。但是，1999 年德国联邦最高法院推翻了这一裁决，声称应基于更高的市场价值确定 DAT 股份的公允价值。

2001 年 3 月 12 日，德国联邦法院（Bundesgerichtshof，BGH）裁定，换股比例应以 DAT 多数股东批准向本公司出售其股份前的三个月内拟交换股份的平均市价为基础。BGH 将该上诉发回下级法院（Landgericht Köln）重审。

预期发生的偿付按照本公司对于换股比例的最佳估计，即 3.45 股阿尔塔纳股份换 1 股 DAT 股份，确认为或有对价。但是，由于本公司 1995 年的重组计划，DAT 的所有资产均被出售或核销，因而额外对价立即作为减值费用被费用化。截至 2002 年 12 月 31 日，基于本公司 2002 年 12 月 31 日的股价，预期以本公司发行股份来结算的对价估算为 1,380 万欧元。预期以现金支付的部分为 230 万欧元。估计的总偿付款 1,610 万欧元确认为预计负债。最终的偿付金额可能由于最终的换股比例及结算日阿尔塔纳股票的市场价值而变化（附注 32）。

2001 年，预计负债的增加记入其他经营费用。2002 年，预计负债由于资产负债表日阿尔塔纳股价的下降而减少（340 万欧元），记入其他经营收益。

32. 期后事项（摘录）

阿尔塔纳股份公司的管理委员会和监事会于 2003 年 3 月 17 日批准发布本财务报表。

2003 年 1 月 15 日，联邦法院判定 DAT 前股东的对价（附注 31）应基于 3.45 股阿尔塔纳股份换取 1 股 DAT 股份的交换比例。本公司已对此判决提出上诉。

Contracts that may be settled in ordinary shares or cash

14. 159 IAS 33 deals specifically with contracts that may be settled in ordinary shares or cash. The rules differ depending on whether the option is held by the entity (the issuer) or by the holder of the contract, as set out in the following paragraphs.

14. 160 If an entity has issued a contract that may be settled in ordinary shares or in cash at the *entity's option* (but not at the holder's option), IAS 33 lays down the following rules:

- The entity should presume that the contract will be settled in shares, and the resulting potential ordinary shares should be included in diluted EPS if the effect is dilutive.
- When such a contract is presented for accounting purposes as an asset or a liability, or when it has both an equity and a liability component under IAS 32, the entity should adjust the numerator (profit or loss attributable to ordinary equity holders) for any changes in the profit or loss that would have resulted during the period if the contract had been classified wholly as an equity instrument. This is similar to the adjustments required in paragraph 33 of IAS 33 (see para 14. 102 above).

[IAS 33 paras 58, 59].

14. 161 An example of such a contract is a deferred or contingent consideration agreement where the entity has the unrestricted right to settle the consideration in the form of ordinary shares or cash. At the date of acquisition it may not be possible for the entity to determine how the deferred consideration will be settled. It should, therefore, be presumed that the contract will be settled in shares, the more dilutive method, and the resulting potential ordinary shares included in diluted EPS in accordance with the standard's relevant provisions. An example is given in Table 14. 7. Another example given in the standard is a debt instrument that, on maturity gives the entity the unrestricted right to settle the liability in cash or in ordinary shares. [IAS 33 para 61].

可用普通股或现金结算的合同

14.159 IAS 33 特别阐述了可用普通股或现金结算的合同。其视选择权由主体（发行人）还是由合同持有者持有而有所不同，如同下列段落中所示。

14.160 如果主体发行该主体可以选择（并非由合同持有人选择）用普通股或现金结算的合同，IAS 33 制定了下列原则：

- 该主体应假定该合同将会用股份结算，且若其效果具有稀释性，则由此产生的潜在普通股应包括在稀释 EPS 中。

- 如果基于会计目的，把此类合同作为一项资产或负债列报，或者根据 IAS 32 既有权益的成分又有负债的成分，则主体应就如果把该合同全部归类为权益工具情况下可能引致的损益的变化调整分子（归属于普通股股东的损益）。此调整与 IAS 33 第 33 段要求的调整类似（参见上文第 14.102 段）。

[IAS 33 第 58、59 段]。

14.161 此类合同的一个例子是递延或或有对价协议。根据该递延或或有对价协议，主体拥有自主决定以普通股或现金结算对价的权利。于购买日，主体可能尚无法确定递延对价的结算方式。因此，应假定合同将会用股份这一更具稀释性的方法结算，相应由此带来的潜在普通股按照准则的相关规定包括在稀释 EPS 中。表 14.7 给出了一个例子。准则中给出的另一个例子是一种债务工具，这种债务工具赋予主体到期时可自主决定使用现金或普通股结算负债的选择权。[IAS 33 第 61 段]。

Table 14.7 – Diluted EPS, contract that can be settled in shares or cash at entity's option

Informa PLC – Interim report – 30 June 2005

9 Earnings per share

Basic

The basic earnings per share calculation is based on a profit on ordinary activities after taxation of £48, 769, 000 (2004 profit: £15, 115, 000 six months and £69, 836, 000 twelve months). This profit (2004: six months profit and twelve months profit) on ordinary activities after taxation is divided by the weighted average number of shares in issue (less those non – vested shares held by employee share ownership trusts) which is 299, 335, 000 (2004: 193, 647, 000 six months and 244, 928, 000 twelve months).

Diluted

The diluted earnings per share calculation is based on the basic earnings per share calculation above except that the weighted average number of shares includes all potentially dilutive options granted by the Balance Sheet date as if those options had been exercised on the first day of the accounting period or the date of the grant, if later, giving a weighted average of 300, 900, 000 (2004: 195, 557, 000 six months and 246, 713, 000 twelve months). In accordance with IAS 33 the weighted average number of shares includes the estimated maximum number of shares payable to the vendors of Routledge Publishing Holdings Limited assuming that there are no claims for compensation by the Group that will reduce this deferred consideration and assuming that the Company does not exercise its option to pay the balance of deferred consideration in cash. The deferred consideration shares are also assumed for the purposes of this calculation to have been issued on 1 January 2005 at the closing mid – market share price on 30 June 2005 of 379p making 335, 000 (2004: 314, 000 six months and 336, 000 twelve months) ordinary shares potentially issued.

The table below sets out the adjustment in respect of diluted potential ordinary shares:

	6 months 2005	6 months 2004	12 months 2004
Weighted average number of shares used in basic earnings per share calculation	299, 334, 804	193, 646, 662	244, 927, 883
Effect of dilutive share options	1, 230, 032	1, 597, 198	1, 449, 594
Shares potentially to be issued or allotted	334, 734	313, 624	335, 629
Weighted average number of shares used in diluted earnings per share calculation	300, 899, 570	195, 557, 484	246, 713, 106

表 14.7——稀释 EPS，主体可以选择用股份或现金结算的合同

英富曼集团——中期报告——2005 年 6 月 30 日

9. 每股收益

基本每股收益

基本每股收益的计算是基于日常经营形成的税后利润 48,769,000 英镑（2004 年利润：6 个月为 15,115,000 英镑，12 个月为 69,836,000 英镑）。将该日常经营形成的税后利润（2004 年：6 个月利润和 12 个月利润）除以已发行股份的加权平均数（减去职工参股信托所持有的非授予的股份）299,335,000 股（2004 年：6 个月为 193,647,000 股，12 个月为 244,928,000 股）。

稀释每股收益

稀释每股收益的计算以上述基本每股收益的计算为基础，不同之处是加权平均股数包括资产负债表日之前已授予的所有潜在稀释性期权，即，视同这些期权在会计期间首日或授予日（若授予日晚于会计期间首日）已行权，据此得出加权平均股数 300,900,000 股（2004 年：6 个月为 195,557,000 股，12 个月为 246,713,000 股）。根据 IAS 33，加权平均股数包括预计向 Routledge 出版控股有限公司的卖方支付的最大股数，即假设并不存在本集团提出补偿要求从而减少递延对价的情况，并假设公司不行使用以现金支付递延对价的选择权。基于计算目的，同时假设递延对价股份已于 2005 年 1 月 1 日按照 2005 年 6 月 30 日收盘中位股价 379 便士发行，即 335,000 股（2004 年：6 个月为 314,000 股，12 个月为 336,000 股）普通股已潜在发行。

下表列示了就稀释潜在普通股所作的调整：

	6 个月 2005 年	6 个月 2004 年	12 个月 2004 年
基本每股收益计算所使用的加权平均股数	299,334,804	193,646,662	244,927,883
稀释性股票期权的影响	1,230,032	1,597,198	1,449,594
潜在发行或配售的股份	334,734	313,624	335,629
稀释每股收益计算所使用的加权平均股数	300,899,570	195,557,484	246,713,106

14. 161. 1 The standard includes an example of the calculation of diluted EPS where the entity has in issue a convertible bond that may be settled in ordinary shares or cash at the issuer's option. The example illustrates also the adjustments that may have to be made to the numerator under the second bullet point in paragraph 14. 160 above. The example below is based on the example in the standard.

Example

An entity issues 1, 000 convertible bonds at the beginning of 20X5. The bonds have a three-year term and are issued at par with a face value of C1, 000 per bond, giving total proceeds of C1, 000, 000. Interest is payable annually in arrears at a nominal annual interest rate of 4%. Each bond is convertible at any time up to maturity into 150 common shares. The entity has an option to settle the principal amount of the convertible bonds in ordinary shares or in cash.

When the bonds are issued, the prevailing market interest rate for similar debt without a conversion option is 9%. At the issue date, the market price of one common share is C3. Income tax is ignored.

	C
Profit 20X5	1, 000, 000
Ordinary shares outstanding	1, 200, 000
Convertible bonds outstanding	
Liability component	873, 434[1]
Equity component	126, 566
Proceeds of the bond issue	1, 000, 000

Note 1: Present value of the principal and interest discounted at 9% – C1, 000, 000 payable at the end of three years; C40, 000 payable annually in arrears for three years.

The liability and equity components would be determined in accordance with IAS 32. These amounts would be recognised as the initial carrying amounts of

14.161.1 准则包括一个计算稀释 EPS 的案例。在该案例中，主体发行了可由发行人选择用普通股或现金结算的可转换债券。该案例还说明了按照上文第 14.160 段第二点对于分子需要作出的调整。下列示例乃基于准则中的上述案例。

示例

某主体于 20X5 年年初发行了 1,000 份可转换债券。债券期限为三年，按每份面值 1,000 元发行，取得资金共计 1,000,000 元。按年名义利率 4% 按年支付利息。每份债券在到期前的任何时间内均可转换为 150 股普通股。主体拥有用普通股或现金清偿可转换债券本金的选择权。

债券发行时，没有转换选择权的同类债务的通行市场利率为 9%。发行日普通股的市价为 3 元。不考虑所得税。

	元
20X5 年利润	1,000,000
已发行普通股	1,200,000
已发行可转换债券	
负债部分	873,434[1]
权益部分	126,566
债券发行取得的资金	1,000,000

注 1：代表按 9% 利率折现后的本金和利息——三年后的年末要支付 1,000,000 元，三年内每年要支付 40,000 元的现值。

负债部分和权益部分将按照 IAS 32 确定。这些金额在资产负债表中被确认为负债部分和权益部分的初始账面金额。分配至发行人转换选择权的

the liability and equity components presented on the balance sheet. The amount assigned to the issuer conversion option equity element is a permanent addition to equity and is not adjusted.

Basic earnings per share 20X5:

$$\frac{C1,000,000}{1,200,000} = C0.83 \text{ per ordinary share}$$

Diluted earnings per share 20X5:

It is presumed that the issuer will settle the contract by the issue of ordinary shares; the dilutive effect is calculated in accordance with paragraph 14.158.

$$\frac{C1,000,000 + C78,609(a)}{1,200,000 + 150,000(b)} = C0.80 \text{ per ordinary share}$$

(a) The initial carrying amount is adjusted for the accretion of the liability using the effective interest rate – that is, C78,609 (C873,434 × 9%).

(b) 150,000 ordinary shares = 150 ordinary shares × 1,000 convertible bonds

[IAS 33 Example 8].

14.162 For contracts that may be settled in ordinary shares or cash at the *holder's option*, the more dilutive of cash settlement and share settlement should be used in calculating diluted EPS. [IAS 33 para 60]. An example might be an incentive scheme where annual bonuses may be payable in either shares or cash at the election of the employee. In that situation it should be presumed that the contract will be settled by the more dilutive method. Another example given in the standard is a written put option that gives the holder the choice of settling in ordinary shares or cash. [IAS 33 para 61].

14.163 Whilst the standard does not specifically cover the point if a contract may be settled in cash or shares at either the issuer's or the holder's option, the more restrictive of the above rules, that is those where only the issuer has an option should be applied. In practice the rules in the standard recognise that it is likely that only one party will have the option as otherwise there could be a conflict.

[The next paragraph is 14.166.]

权益部分的金额是对权益的永久性加项，不调整。

20X5 年基本每股收益：

$$\frac{1,000,000\text{ 元}}{1,200,000} = \text{每股普通股 } 0.83\text{ 元}$$

20X5 年稀释每股收益：

假定发行人会以发行普通股的方式结算该合同；稀释效应按照第 14.158 段计算。

$$\frac{1,000,000\text{ 元} + 78,609\text{ 元(a)}}{1,200,000 + 150,000\text{(b)}} = \text{每股普通股 } 0.80\text{ 元}$$

(a) 针对按照实际利率计算的负债增加，即 78,609 元（873,434 元 × 9%），对原账面利润进行调整。

(b) 150,000 股普通股 ＝ 150 股普通股 × 1,000 份可转换债券

[IAS 33 例 8]。

14.162 对于那些持有人可以选择用普通股或现金结算的合同，计算稀释 EPS 时，应使用现金结算和股份结算这两者中稀释性较大的一种。[IAS 33 第 60 段]。一个例子是职工可以选择用股份或现金结算的年终奖金激励计划。在这一情况下，应假定合同将按照稀释性较大的方式进行结算。准则给出的另一个例子是签出看跌期权，它给予持有者以普通股或现金结算的选择权。[IAS 33 第 61 段]。

14.163 虽然该准则并未特别说明可由发行人或持有者选择以现金或股份结算的合同的处理方法，但应采用上述原则中更具限制性的原则，即仅发行者拥有选择权时适用的原则。实务中，该准则中的原则认为很可能仅一方拥有选择权，否则可能存在冲突。

[下一段为第 14.166 段。]

Purchased options

14.166 The standard notes that contracts such as purchased put options and purchased call options held by an entity over its own ordinary shares are not included in the calculation of diluted EPS. This is because their inclusion would be anti-dilutive. A put option (defined by IAS 33 as a contract that gives the holder the right to sell ordinary shares at a specified price for a given period) would be exercised only if the option exercise price were higher than the market price and a call option would be exercised only if the option exercise price were lower than the market price. [IAS 33 para 62]. In both instances, the options' effect would be anti-dilutive under the treasury stock method (see para 14.118 above) and the reverse treasury stock method (see para 14.167 below).

Written put options

14.167 The standard also deals with written put options. Contracts that require the entity to repurchase its own shares, such as written put options and forward purchase contracts are reflected in diluted EPS if their effect is dilutive. If the contracts are 'in the money' during the period, that is, if the exercise or settlement price is above the average market price for the period, their dilutive effects should be calculated using the 'reverse treasury stock' method. Under that method:

- It should be assumed that at the beginning of the accounting period sufficient ordinary shares will be issued at the average market price for the period to raise the necessary proceeds to satisfy the contracts.
- It should be assumed that the proceeds from this issue are used to satisfy the contract to buy back ordinary shares.
- The incremental ordinary shares, that is, the difference between the number of shares assumed to be issued and the number of shares received (bought back) on satisfying the contract will be included in the calculation of diluted EPS.

[IAS 33 Para 63].

购入期权

14.166 该准则指出，主体持有的针对其自身普通股的合同，诸如购入看跌期权及购入看涨期权，不包括在稀释 EPS 的计算中。这是因为将其包括在内具有反稀释性。看跌期权（IAS 33 将其定义为赋予持有者在给定期间内以规定价格卖出普通股权利的合同）只有在期权行权价格高于市场价格时才会被行权，而看涨期权只有在期权行权价格低于市场价格时才会被行权。[IAS 33 第 62 段]。在两种情况下，按照库存股法（参见上文第 14.118 段）和反向库存股法（参见下文第 14.167 段），期权的作用均是反稀释性的。

签出看跌期权

14.167 该准则还涉及签出看跌期权。要求主体回购其自身股份的合同，如签出看跌期权和远期购入合同，若具有稀释性，则包括在稀释 EPS 的计算中。如果这些合同在当期为价内期权，即行权价或结算价高于当期平均市场价，则应采用“反向库存股”法计算其稀释作用。根据该方法：

- 应假定在会计期间期初按照该期间的平均市价发行足量的普通股，以筹集必要的资金履行该合同。
- 应假定通过该发行获得的资金被用于履行该合同，即回购普通股。
- 增量普通股，即假定发行股份的数量与因履行合同而取得（回购）的股份数量之间的差额，将包括在稀释 EPS 的计算中。

[IAS 33 第 63 段]。

Example

Assume an entity has outstanding 160 written put options on 160 of its ordinary shares with an exercise price of C10 per option. The put obligation is, therefore, C1,600. The average market price of the entity's ordinary shares is C8 for the period. In calculating diluted EPS the entity assumes that it issues 200 ordinary shares at C8 per share to raise the proceeds necessary to satisfy the put option. The difference between the 200 ordinary shares assumed to be issued and the 160 ordinary shares that would have been received on exercise of the option, that is 40 shares is added to the denominator (number of shares) in calculating the diluted EPS. No adjustments are made to the numerator (profit attributable to ordinary shareholders) as the shares are deemed issued for nil proceeds. [IAS 33 para A10].

Restatement of EPS data

14.168 Diluted EPS of any prior period presented should not be restated for changes in the assumptions used (such as for contingently issuable shares) or for the conversion of potential ordinary shares (such as convertible debt) outstanding at the end of the previous period. [IAS 33 para 65]. This is because these factors are already taken into account in calculating the basic and, where applicable, the diluted EPS for the current period. However, in some circumstances, prior period's EPS data should be restated. These circumstances include certain post balance sheet changes in capital (see para 14.169) and prior period adjustments (see para 14.171).

Post balance sheet changes in capital

14.169 As noted in paragraph 14.80 above, the weighted average number of ordinary shares outstanding for all periods presented (and, therefore, both basic and diluted EPS for all periods presented) should be restated for bonus issues, share splits, share consolidations and other similar events occurring during the period that change the number of shares in issue without a corresponding change in

示例

假定某主体发行了160份针对其160股普通股的签出看跌期权，行权价格为每份期权10元。该签出看跌期权的义务为1,600元。当期该主体普通股的平均市价为8元。在计算稀释EPS时，该主体假定以每股8元发行200股普通股，以筹集履行签出看跌期权需要的资金。假定发行的200股普通股与期权行权时获得的160股普通股之间的差额，即40股，应在计算稀释EPS时加到分母（股份数）中。由于这些股份被视为零对价发行，无需对分子（归属于普通股股东的利润）作出调整。[IAS 33第A10段]。

EPS的重述

14.168　如果计算稀释EPS使用的假设发生变化（例如或有可发行股份），或者前期期末已发行的潜在普通股转换成为普通股（例如可转换债券），以前任何期间列报的稀释EPS均不应重述。[IAS 33第65段]。这是因为在计算当期基本EPS以及稀释EPS（如适用）时，这些因素已被考虑在内。但在有些情况下，以前期间的EPS应被予以重述。这些情况包括某些资产负债表日后资本变动（参见第14.169段）及前期调整（参见第14.171段）。

资产负债表日后资本变动

14.169　正如上文第14.80段中所述，各列报期间已发行的普通股加权平均数（相应所有列报期间的基本EPS和稀释EPS）均应根据当期发生的、改变已发行股份数量而主体资源无相应变化的事项（派送红股、拆股、并股及其他类似事件）进行重述。[IAS 33第26段]。此外，若此类事项发生在资产负债表日之后、财务报表被批准报出之前，则当期以及前期的基本EPS和稀释

the resources of the entity. [IAS 33 para 26]. In addition, if such events occur after the balance sheet date, but before the financial statements are approved for issue, the basic and diluted EPS figures for the current period and for prior periods should be presented on the basis of the new number of shares. [IAS 33 para 64]. Where the EPS figures reflect such post balance sheet date changes, this fact should be disclosed (see further para 14.181 below).

14.170 Other post balance sheet changes in capital should not be adjusted for, but disclosure is required of ordinary share transactions or potential ordinary share transactions that would have changed significantly the number of ordinary shares or potential ordinary shares outstanding at the end of the period if they had occurred before the end of the period (see further para 14.182).

Prior period adjustments

14.171 EPS for all periods presented should be adjusted for the effects of errors and adjustments resulting from changes in accounting policies accounted for retrospectively in accordance with IAS 8. [IAS 33 para 64]. That is, the EPS figure for the prior period should be restated as if the restated profit or loss had been reported originally in the prior period or periods.

14.172 When a change in accounting policy: has an effect on the current period or any prior period; would have such an effect except that it is impracticable to determine the amount of the adjustment; or might have an effect on future periods, an entity should disclose for the current period and each prior period presented, to the extent practicable, the amount of the adjustment for basic and diluted earnings per share. Similarly, for the retrospective correction of material prior period errors, an entity should disclose for each prior period presented, to the extent practicable, the amount of the correction for basic and diluted earnings per share. [IAS 8 paras 28(f)(ii), 29(c)(ii), 49(b)(ii)]. Table 14.8 is an example of disclosure.

EPS 均应以新的股份数量为基础列报。[IAS 33 第 64 段]。若 EPS 反映此类资产负债表日后变化，该事实应予以披露（参见下文第 14.181 段）。

14.170　不应就资产负债表日后发生的其他资本变化作出调整，但对于那些如果在期末之前发生会大幅改变期末已发行普通股或潜在普通股数量的普通股交易或潜在普通股交易，应予以披露（参见下文第 14.182 段）。

前期调整

14.171　根据 IAS 8，对于进行追溯调整的会计差错及会计政策变更，所有列报期间的 EPS 均应就其影响进行调整。[IAS 33 第 64 段]。即，前期 EPS 应予以重述，就如同重述后的损益在前一期间或以前各期已被列报一样。

14.172　若会计政策变更影响当期或任何前期，则存在此类影响，除非无法确定调整金额，或会计政策的变更是对未来期间产生影响。在这种情况下，主体应在可行的范围内，就当期及各列报前期，披露对基本每股收益和稀释每股收益作出的调整。类似地，对于重大前期差错的追溯更正，主体应在可行的范围内，就各列报前期，披露对基本每股收益和稀释每股收益作出的更正。[IAS 8 第 28（f）（ii）、29（c）（ii）、49（b）（ii）段]。表 14.8 为一个披露相关的例子。

Table 14.8 – Effect of changes in accounting policy on EPS

China Mobile Limited – Annual Report and Accounts – 31 December 2009

2 Changes in accounting policies (extract)

(ii) IFRIC/HK(IFRIC) Interpretation 13, *Customer loyalty programmes*

The Group has launched a Reward Program to its customers, which provides customers the option of electing to receive free telecommunications services or other gifts. The level of point reward earned by customers under the Reward Program varies depending on the customers' services consumption, years in services and payment history.

In prior years, the Group accounted for the obligation to provide free or discounted services or goods offered to the customers under the Reward Program using the incremental costs method. The estimated incremental cost to provide free or discounted services or goods was recognized as expenses and accrued as a current liability when customers were entitled to bonus points. When customers redeemed awards or their entitlements expired, the incremental cost liability was reduced accordingly to reflect the outstanding obligations.

With effect from 1 January 2009, as a result of adoption of IFRIC/HK(IFRIC) Interpretation 13, the point reward is accounted for as a separately identifiable component of the sales transactions in which the points are granted. The consideration received in relation to the sales transactions is allocated to points reward by reference to the estimated fair value of the points as revenue and is deferred until such reward is redeemed by the customers or the points expired.

The new accounting policy has been adopted retrospectively and the comparative amounts have been restated.

The effect on the consolidated balance sheet as at 1 January 2008 is an increase in deferred tax assets, an increase in deferred revenue, a decrease in accrued expenses and other payables and a decrease in net assets of RMB676,000,000, RMB6,308,000,000, RMB3,542,000,000 and RMB2,090,000,000, respectively.

The effect on the consolidated balance sheet as at 31 December 2008 is an increase in deferred tax assets, an increase in deferred revenue, a decrease in accrued expenses and other payables and a decrease in net assets of RMB730,000,000, RMB6,841,000,000, RMB3,855,000,000 and RMB2,256,000,000, respectively.

The effect on the Group's consolidated statement of comprehensive income for the year ended 31 December 2008 is an decrease in operating revenue, operating expenses, taxation and profit for the year of RMB533,000,000, RMB313,000,000, RMB54,000,000 and RMB166,000,000, respectively. The effect on the basic earnings per share and diluted earnings per share for the year ended 31 December 2008 is a decrease of RMB0.01 and RMB0.01, respectively.

表 14.8——会计政策变更对 EPS 的影响

中国移动有限公司——年度报告及报表——2009 年 12 月 31 日

2. 会计政策变更（摘录）

（ii）国际财务报告/香港财务报告解释公告第 13 号——*客户忠诚度计划*

本集团向其客户推出积分奖励计划，客户可根据其消费金额、在网年限及以往账单支付记录获得积分奖励，以换取免费电信服务或其他礼品。

本集团以往使用递增成本法计量因积分奖励计划向客户提供免费或折扣服务、礼品的义务。在客户有资格获得积分时，其所对应的免费或折扣服务、礼品所带来的估计递增成本会确认为费用及流动负债。当客户兑换奖励积分或其兑换权期限届满时，相关负债相应予以冲减，以反映尚未完结的义务。

自 2009 年 1 月 1 日起，由于采用了国际财务报告/香港财务报告解释公告第 13 号，本集团将奖励积分视为给予该等积分的销售交易的可辨认组成部分进行会计处理。销售交易收到的对价会根据积分的预计公允价值分摊至奖励积分并作为递延收入，直至客户兑换奖励积分或其兑换权期限届满之时，相关分摊收入方被确认。

本集团已追溯采用新的会计政策，并已重述比较财务报表。

对 2008 年 1 月 1 日的合并资产负债表的影响为：递延所得税资产增加人民币 676,000,000 元、递延收入增加人民币 6,308,000,000 元、预提费用及其他应付款减少人民币 3,542,000,000 元以及净资产减少人民币 2,090,000,000 元。

对 2008 年 12 月 31 日的合并资产负债表的影响为：递延所得税资产增加人民币 730,000,000 元、递延收入增加人民币 6,841,000,000 元、预提费用及其他应付款减少人民币 3,855,000,000 元以及净资产减少人民币 2,256,000,00 元。

对本集团截至 2008 年 12 月 31 日止年度的合并综合收益表的影响为：营业收入、营业费用、所得税费用和利润分别减少人民币 533,000,000 元、人民币 313,000,000 元、人民币 54,000,000 元和人民币 166,000,000 元。对截至 2008 年 12 月 31 日止年度基本每股收益和稀释每股收益的影响为分别减少人民币 0.01 元和人民币 0.01 元。

Presentation and disclosure

Presentation of basic and diluted EPS

14.173 An entity should present both basic and diluted EPS on the face of the statement of comprehensive income or if an entity presents the components of profit or loss in a separate statement, it presents the basic and diluted EPS in that separate statement. The basic and diluted EPS should be presented for profit or loss from continuing operations attributable to the entity's ordinary equity holders and for profit or loss for the period (that is, including both continuing and discontinued operations) attributable to the entity's ordinary equity holders. The basic and diluted EPS should be presented with equal prominence for all periods presented. [IAS 33 paras 66, 67A]. This applies even if the basic and diluted EPS are the same. If they are the same the entity can disclose just one line described as 'Basic and diluted EPS'. [IAS 33 para 67].

14.174 In practice, unless an entity has discontinued operations that it must disclose in accordance with IFRS 5, the EPS from continuing operations is likely to be identical to total EPS. Accordingly, if the basic EPS for continuing and total EPS is the same and the diluted EPS is the same, the entity could disclose the figures as follows:

Basic EPS for profit from continuing operations and for profit for the year	x
Diluted EPS for profit from continuing operations and for profit for the year	y
If the basic and diluted figures are the same the disclosure could be:	
Basic and diluted EPS for profit from continuing operations and for profit for the year	x

14.175 The standard also requires disclosure either on the face of the statement of comprehensive income (or the income statement, if presented separately) or in the

列报和披露

基本 EPS 和稀释 EPS 的列报

14.173　主体应在综合收益表正表中列报基本 EPS 和稀释 EPS，或者如果主体在单独的报表中列报损益要素，则其应在该单独的报表中列报基本 EPS 和稀释 EPS。应针对持续经营所产生的归属于主体普通股股东的损益和归属于主体普通股股东的损益（即包括持续经营和终止经营）列报基本 EPS 和稀释 EPS。对于各列报期间，基本 EPS 和稀释 EPS 的列报应当以同等显著的方式列报。[IAS 33 第 66、67A 段]。即使基本 EPS 与稀释 EPS 相同也应如此列报。如两者相同，则主体可在同一行内列报，即“基本及稀释 EPS”。[IAS 33 第 67 段]。

14.174　在实务中，除非主体存在应按照 IFRS 5 披露的终止经营，否则持续经营 EPS 很可能与 EPS 总额相同。相应地，若持续经营基本 EPS 与基本 EPS 总额相同，而稀释 EPS 也如此，则主体可按以下方式披露相关数字：

年度持续经营基本 EPS 和年度基本 EPS	x
年度持续经营稀释 EPS 和年度稀释 EPS	y
若基本每股收益与稀释每股收益相同，则披露可以是：	
年度持续经营基本及稀释 EPS 和年度基本及稀释 EPS	x

14.175　准则还要求主体在具有终止经营并须按照 IFRS 5 对其进行披露时，在综合收益表（或单独列报的利润表）正表或附注中披露终止经营基本 EPS

notes of basic and diluted EPS for discontinued operations, where an entity has such operations and is required to disclose them in accordance with IFRS 5. [IAS 33 para 68]. Where an entity has such operations, its EPS from continuing operations will not be the same as its total EPS and so disclosure of three basic and three diluted EPS figures will be required. Assuming that the EPS figures for profit or loss on discontinued operations are disclosed on the face of the statement of comprehensive income the disclosure might be as follows:

	20X5	20X4
Earnings per ordinary share:		
Profit from continuing operations	x	x
Profit from discontinued operations	x	x
Profit for the period	x	x
Diluted earnings per share:		
Profit from continuing operations	x	x
Profit from discontinued operations	x	x
Profit for the period	x	x

An example is also given in Table 14. 5 above.

14. 176 Where there is more than one class of ordinary shares in issue with different rights to share in the profit for the period, basic and diluted EPS figures must be calculated and disclosed for each such class of ordinary shares. [IAS 33 para 66]. The way in which such calculations should be performed is considered from paragraph 14. 57 above.

14. 177 If a company incurs a loss or the amount it earns for the ordinary equity holders is a negative figure, basic and diluted EPS should be determined in accordance with the rules set out in the standard and shown as a loss per share. [IAS 33 para 69]. Where the diluted loss per share is the same as the basic loss per share, because the company has incurred a loss from continuing operations and

和稀释 EPS。[IAS 33 第 68 段]。在主体具有此类经营时，持续经营 EPS 与 EPS 总额不同，因而须披露三项基本 EPS 和三项稀释 EPS。假设终止经营 EPS 在综合收益表正表中予以披露，则可按以下方式作出披露：

	20X5 年	20X4 年
普通股每股收益：		
持续经营产生的利润	x	x
终止经营产生的利润	x	x
当期利润	x	x
稀释每股收益：		
持续经营产生的利润	x	x
终止经营产生的利润	x	x
当期利润	x	x

上文表 14.5 中也给出一个例子。

14.176 如果有不同类别的对当期利润具有不同分享权的普通股发行在外，应针对每一类普通股计算和披露基本 EPS 和稀释 EPS。[IAS 33 第 66 段]。相关计算方式在上文第 14.57 段中进行论述。

14.177 如果一家公司发生亏损或其为普通股股东赚取的金额为负值，则基本 EPS 和稀释 EPS 应按照准则中所列示的规定确定并显示为每股亏损。[IAS 33 第 69 段]。如果公司在持续经营中发生亏损，由于公司所有现有潜在普通股的影响是减少持续经营亏损，其不具稀释性，因此稀释每股亏损等于基本每股亏损，在这种情况下，主体可在同一行中对这些进行披露。下表 14.9 中

all the company's existing potential ordinary shares are not dilutive as they decrease the loss from continuing operations, the entity can disclose these in one line. An example is given in Table 14.9 below. The example illustrates the basic and diluted EPS figures for the loss attributable to ordinary equity holders only and does not illustrate the disclosure for continuing or discontinued operations.

Table 14.9 – Basic and diluted loss per share

Elan Corporation plc – Annual Report and Accounts – 31 December 2010

Consolidated Income Statement

For the Year Ended 31 December 2010 (extract)

	Notes	**2010**	**2009**
Basic and diluted net loss per Ordinary Share	14	$ (0.55)	$ (0.32)
Weighted-average shares outstanding (in millions)	14	584.9	506.8

14. Net Loss Per Share

Basic loss per share is computed by dividing the net loss for the period attributable to ordinary shareholders by the weighted-average number of Ordinary Shares outstanding during the period. Diluted net loss per share is computed by dividing the net loss for the period, by the weighted-average number of Ordinary Shares outstanding and, when dilutive, adjusted for the effect of all potentially dilutive shares, including share options and RSUs.

The following table sets forth the computation for basic and diluted net loss per share for the years ended 31 December:

	2010	**2009**
Numerator (amounts in $m):		
Basic and diluted net loss	(322.6)	(162.3)
Denominator (amounts in millions):		
Denominator for basic and diluted-weighted-average number of Ordinary Shares outstanding	584.9	506.8
Basic and diluted earnings per share:		
Basic and diluted net loss per share	$ (0.55)	$ (0.32)

给出了一个例子。该案例仅说明归属于普通股股东的亏损形成的基本和稀释每股亏损，而未说明持续经营或终止经营的相关披露。

表 14.9——基本和稀释每股亏损

Elan Corporation plc 公司——年度报告及报表——2010 年 12 月 31 日

合并利润表

截至 2010 年 12 月 31 日止年度（摘录）

	附注	2010 年	2009 年
普通股基本及稀释每股净亏损	14	（0.55）美元	（0.32）美元
已发行股份的加权平均数（单位：百万）	14	584.9	506.8

14. 每股净亏损

基本每股亏损通过归属于普通股股东的当期净亏损除以当期已发行普通股的加权平均数计算得出。稀释每股净亏损通过当期净亏损除以已发行普通股的加权平均数计算得出，其中已发行普通股的加权平均数应针对所有潜在稀释性股份，在其具有稀释性时，就其影响进行调整。潜在稀释性股份包括股份期权和受限股票单位。

下表列示了截至 12 月 31 日止年度基本及稀释每股净亏损的计算：

	2010 年	2009 年
分子（金额以百万美元为单位）：		
基本及稀释净亏损	（322.6）	（162.3）
分母（金额以百万为单位）：		
已发行普通股的基本及稀释加权平均数	584.9	506.8
基本及稀释每股收益：		
基本及稀释每股净亏损	（0.55）美元	（0.32）美元

Con.

For the years ended 31 December 2010 and 2009, there were no differences in the weighted-average number of Ordinary Shares used for basic and diluted net loss per Ordinary Share as the effect of all potentially dilutive Ordinary Shares outstanding was anti-dilutive. As at 31 December 2010, there were 22.9 million (2009: 21.3 million) share options and RSUs outstanding that could potentially have a dilutive impact in the future but were anti-dilutive in 2010 and 2009.

Additional disclosures

14.178 The following additional information should be given for both basic and diluted EPS:

- The amounts used as the numerators in calculating the basic and diluted EPS figures. These amounts should also be reconciled with the profit or loss for the period. The reconciliation should include the individual effect of each class of instrument that affects EPS, that is, it should describe and list the adjustments arising from each of the types of potential ordinary share that has affected the basic earnings figure.

- The weighted average number of ordinary shares used as the denominator in calculating the basic and diluted EPS figures. The denominators used in the basic and diluted EPS should also be reconciled to each other. This reconciliation should include the individual effect of each class of instrument that affects EPS, that is, it should list and describe the effects of each of the types of dilutive potential ordinary shares that has affected the basic weighted average number.

[IAS 33 para 70(a)(b)].

14.179 An example of how a company can give the above information in a concise manner is shown in the table below. The example illustrates the basic and diluted EPS figures for the profit attributable to ordinary equity holders only and does not illustrate the disclosure for continuing or discontinued operations.

续表

截至2010年12月31日止年度和截至2009年12月31日止年度，用于计算普通股基本及稀释每股净亏损的普通股加权平均数是相同的，原因是所有已发行潜在稀释性普通股的作用均为反稀释性的。于2010年12月31日，有2,290万（2009年：2,130万）期权和受限股票单位已发行，该等期权和受限股票单位在未来可能具有潜在稀释影响，但在2010年和2009年具有反稀释性。

额外披露

14.178　应就基本EPS和稀释EPS提供下列额外信息：

- 计算基本和稀释EPS时用作分子的金额以及该等金额与当期损益之间的调节。该调节应包括影响EPS的各类工具的个别影响，即，应描述和列示影响基本收益的各类潜在普通股导致的调整。

- 计算基本和稀释EPS时用作分母的加权平均普通股股数。基本和稀释EPS使用的分母也应互相调节。该等调整应包括影响EPS的各类工具的个别影响，即，应列示和描述影响基本加权平均数的各类稀释性潜在普通股的影响。

[IAS 33第70（a）（b）段]。

14.179　下表列示了一个以简明的方式提供上述信息的例子。该案例仅说明归属于普通股股东的利润形成的基本及稀释EPS，而未说明持续经营或终止经营的披露。

Example

	Year ended 31 December 20X5		
		Number of	Per-share
	Earnings	**shares**	**amount**
Profit for the year	6, 525, 000		
Less: preference dividends	75, 000		
Basic EPS:			
Earnings available to ordinary shareholders	6, 450, 000	2, 500, 000	C2. 58
Effect of dilutive securities:			
Options		45, 000	
Convertible preferred stock	35, 000	255, 000	
6% convertible debentures	60, 000	60, 000	
Diluted EPS:			
Adjusted earnings	6, 545, 000	2, 860, 000	C2. 29

A further example is given in Table 14. 4 above.

14. 180 The standard also requires disclosure of instruments, including contingently issuable shares, that could dilute EPS in the future, but that were not included in the computation of diluted EPS in the period (or periods) presented, because they were anti-dilutive in that period (or those periods). [IAS 33 para 70(c)].

14. 181 As stated in paragraph 14. 80, basic and diluted EPS for all periods presented should be restated for bonus issues, share splits, share consolidations and similar events occurring during the period that change the number of shares in issue without a corresponding change in the resources of the entity. If these events occur after the balance sheet date, but before the financial statements are approved for issue, the EPS figures for the current period, and those of any prior periods, should be based on the new number of shares issued (see para 14. 169). As a result, the number of shares used in the EPS calculation will not be consistent with that shown in the balance sheet. Therefore, disclosure should be made to that effect. [IAS 33 para 64]. An example of a share split that occurred in the year is Table 14. 10 (only the figures for basic EPS are reproduced in the table).

示例

	截至 20X5 年 12 月 31 日止年度		
	收益	**股份数目**	**每股金额**
本年利润	6,525,000		
减:优先股股利	75,000		
基本 EPS:			
普通股股东可获得的收益	6,450,000	2,500,000	2.58 元
稀释性证券的影响:			
期权		45,000	
可转换优先股	35,000	255,000	
利率为 6% 的可转换债券	60,000	60,000	
稀释 EPS:			
经调整收益	6,545,000	2,860,000	2.29 元

进一步的示例在上文表 14.4 中给出。

14.180　准则还要求披露未来可能稀释 EPS、但由于在列报当期（或各期）具有反稀释性而未包括在该期间（或该等期间）稀释 EPS 计算中的工具，包括或有可发行股份。[IAS 33 第 70(c) 段]。

14.181　正如第 14.80 段中所述，各列报期间的基本及稀释 EPS 均应就当期发生的、改变已发行股份数量而主体资源无相应变化的事项（派送红股、拆股、并股及其他类似事件）进行重述。如果这些事项发生在资产负债表日之后、财务报表被批准报出前，则当期和过往各期的 EPS 均应以新的已发行股份数量为基础（参见第 14.169 段）。因此，计算 EPS 使用的股份数量与资产负债表中所列示的股份数量不一致。财务报表应就此作出披露。[IAS 33 第 64 段]。表 14.10 是一个当年发生拆股的例子（表中仅列示了基本 EPS）。

Table 14.10 – EPS adjusted for share split in the year

STADA Arzneimittel AG – Report and Accounts – 31 December 2004

2.18. Earnings per share (extract)

Earnings per share	2004	Previous year
Net income distributable to shareholders of STADA Arzneimittel AG in € 000s	48,484	43,869
Average number of shares	53,348,910[1,2]	43,327,286[1,2]
Earnings per share in €	0.91[2]	1.01[2]

Basic earnings per share are calculated according to IAS 33.10 by dividing net income distributable to the shareholders of STADA Arzneimittel AG by the average number of shares outstanding, less treasury stock.

[1] Please refer to the notes on shareholders' equity (see note 3.12) regarding the change in the number of shares.

[2] Pursuant to IAS 33.20 in conjunction with IAS 33.22, a capital increase from existing funds changes the average number of shares without any concomitant change in the level of resources. The number of common shares in issue prior to the capital increase is adjusted in accordance with the proportional change in the number of outstanding common shares after the share issue as if the event (the de facto 1:1 stock split) had occurred at the beginning of the period under review. For the purposes of historical comparison, the historical figure for the average number of shares in each fiscal year ending prior to the conversion date will be doubled to adjust for the stock split when calculating the earnings per share.

3.12. Share capital (extract)

As of the balance sheet date, share capital consisted of 53,390,820 common shares, each with an arithmetical par value of €2.60 (prior year: 26,695,290).

The increase in the number of shares in 2004 is almost entirely due to the de facto 1:1 stock split that took place in the year under review and only to a very small extent due to the increase in shares resulting from the initial exercise of options from STADA warrants 2000/2015. STADA executed the de facto 1:1 stock split resolved by the Annual Shareholders' Meeting on June 15, 2004 after close of trading on Friday, July 30, 2004, once the capital measure had been entered into the commercial register.

表 14.10——就当年拆股作出调整的 EPS

德国史达德制药公司—— 报告及报表——2004 年 12 月 31 日

2.18. 每股收益（摘录）

每股收益	2004 年	前一年度
可向史达德制药公司股东分配的净收益（单位：千欧元）	48,484	43,869
平均股数	53,348,910[1,2]	43,327,286[1,2]
每股收益（单位：欧元）	0.91[2]	1.01[2]

基本每股收益乃根据 IAS 33.10 计算，即可向史达德制药公司股东分配的净收益除以已发行股份的平均数减库存股。

[1] 股份数量的变化请参考关于股东权益的附注（见附注 3.12）。

[2] 根据 IAS 33.20 和 IAS 33.22，来自现有资金的资本增加改变了平均股份数量而主体的资源无相应变化。资本增加前的已发行普通股股数，按照股份发行后已发行普通股股数按比例进行调整，如同该事项（实际按 1∶1 拆股）在审核期初即已发生。出于历史数据可比目的，在计算每股收益时，转换日前结束的各财政年度平均股份数量予以翻倍，以反映拆股作出的调整。

3.12. 股本（摘录）

于资产负债表日，股本由 53,390,820 股普通股构成，每股算术上的面值为 2.60 欧元（上年：26,695,290 股）。

于 2004 年，股份数目的增加几乎全部来自审核年度实际按照 1∶1 进行的拆股，仅很小比例来自史达德 2000/2015 认股权证的初始行权。史达德于 2004 年 6 月 30 日周五交易结束后，一经资本计量录入商业登记簿后，即执行 2004 年 6 月 15 日年度股东大会审批的实际按 1∶1 进行的拆股。

Con.

STADA shareholders received one bonus share for every registered bearer share of restricted transferability they already held (ISIN DE0007251803, WKN 725180). The Company's share capital thereby increased to € 138,816,132.00. As a total of 26,695,410 bonus shares were issued, the number of STADA shares also doubled, arithmetically reducing its share price by half. This capital measure therefore constitutes a de facto 1:1 stock split. The bonus shares created by this capital increase from the Company's own funds were automatically credited to STADA shareholders' custody accounts with a value date of August 2, 2004. Shareholders holding their own shares were requested to effect the credit of the bonus shares to which they were entitled via a bank by submitting profit participation certificate no. 11 as proof of entitlement. The text of the official notification to shareholders was also published on STADA's website, www.stada.de.

14.182 Entities are required to disclose details of all material ordinary share transactions or potential ordinary share transactions entered into after the reporting period, other than those described in the preceding paragraph. Such transactions should be disclosed where they would have significantly changed the number of ordinary or potential ordinary shares outstanding at the end of the reporting period if the transactions had occurred before the end of the reporting period. [IAS 33 para 70(d)]. EPS for the period is not adjusted for such post balance sheet transactions, because they do not affect the amount of capital used to produce the profit or loss for the period. Such transactions include:

- Issue of shares for cash.
- Issue of shares where the proceeds are used to repay debt or preference shares outstanding at the balance sheet date.
- Redemption of ordinary shares.
- Conversion of potential ordinary shares outstanding at the balance sheet date into ordinary shares.
- Issue of warrants, options or convertible securities.
- Achievement of conditions that would result in the issue of contingently issuable shares.

续表

对于史达德股东持有的转让受限的不记名股票(ISIN DE0007251803, WKN 725180),每股登记在册的不记名股票可获得一股红股。由此本公司的股本增至138,816,132.00欧元。由于共计发行了26,695,410股红股,史达德股份的数量翻了一倍,并在算术上将其股价降低一半。这一资本计量构成了实际按1:1进行的拆股。本公司自有资金形成的资本增加所产生的红股自动记入史达德股东的托管账户,交割日为2004年8月2日。持有自有股份的股东被要求提交利润分配参与证明第11号作为权利证据,通过银行实现其有权获得的上述红股。致股东的官方通知的文本已在史达德的网站www.stada.de上公布。

14.182 除前段所述的交易外，主体须披露报告日后进行的所有重要普通股交易或潜在普通股交易。对于那些如果发生在报告期末前，就会显著地改变报告期末已发行普通股或潜在普通股数量的此类交易，则予以披露。[IAS 33第70（d）段]。当期EPS不因此类资产负债表日后交易而进行调整，因为该类交易不影响用于产生当期损益的资本金额。此类交易包括：

- 发行股份以获取现金。
- 发行股份，所得资金用于偿还债务或资产负债表日已发行的优先股。
- 赎回普通股。
- 资产负债表日已发行的潜在普通股转换为普通股。
- 发行认股权证、期权或可转换证券。
- 或有可发行股份的发行条件得以满足。

[IAS 33 para 71].

14. 183 Most of these transactions would fall to be disclosed anyway as material non-adjusting post balance sheet events under IAS 10, 'Events after the balance sheet date'. An example of disclosure is Table 14. 11.

Table 14. 11 – Disclosure of post balance sheet changes in capital

Swisscom AG – Annual Report and Accounts – 31 December 2004

41 Post balance sheet events (extract)

Approval by the Board of Directors

Swisscom Board of Directors approved these consolidated financial statements on March 7, 2005.

Dividend

At the General Meeting of Shareholders on April 26, 2005, a dividend of CHF 14 per share, amounting to a total income distribution of CHF 861 million, is to be proposed for 2004. In these financial statements this dividend payable is not disclosed as a liability. It is accounted for as a dividend contribution against shareholders' equity in 2005. The dividends declared at the 2004 General Meeting of Shareholders in respect of 2003 was CHF 861 million (previous year: CHF 794 million).

Share buy-back

In 2005 the Board of Directors decided to launch a share buy – back scheme in the amount of around CHF 2 billion in order to distribute the entire equity free cash flow.

Convertible bond of the Swiss Confederation on Swisscom shares

About one third of the convertible bonds of the Swiss Confederation related to Swisscom shares, which mature at the end of February 2005, were exercised by the maturity date. According to the Swiss Confederation authorities, of the 2. 67 million shares included in the convertible bond, around 915, 000 shares were converted. As a result of the conversion the share of the Confederation in Swisscom fell from 62. 7% to 61. 4%. On April 26, 2005 the Board of Directors applied to the Shareholders' Meeting for a capital reduction. Taking this into account the share of Confederation in Swisscom is now 66. 1%.

14. 184 The standard also encourages companies to disclose the terms and conditions of financial instruments and other contracts generating potential ordinary

［IAS 33 第 71 段］。

14.183　大部分此类交易无论如何均须根据 IAS 10 作为重大资产负债表日后非调整事项予以披露。表 14.11 是一个披露的例子。

表 14.11——资产负债表日后资本变动的披露

瑞士电信公司——年度报告及报表——2004 年 12 月 31 日

41. 资产负债表日后事项（摘录）

董事会审批

瑞士电信的董事会于 2005 年 3 月 7 日批准该等合并财务报表。

股利

2005 年 4 月 26 日的股东大会将提议 2004 年度股利为每股 14 瑞士法郎，合计分派收益 861 百万瑞士法郎。本财务报表未将该应付股利披露为负债。其在 2005 年作为冲减股东权益的股利支付进行会计处理。2004 年度股东大会宣告的 2003 年度股利为 861 百万瑞士法郎（上年：794 百万瑞士法郎）。

股份回购

2005 年，董事会决定启动一项金额约 20 亿瑞士法郎的股份回购计划，旨在分派全部的股权自由现金流。

针对瑞士电信股份的瑞士联邦可转换债券

瑞士联邦持有的与瑞士电信股份相关的可转换债券（于 2005 年 2 月底到期），已有约三分之一于到期日前被行使。据瑞士联邦当局透露，可转换债券包含的 267 万股股份中，约有 915,000 股已被转换。转换的结果是，瑞士联邦在瑞士电信中的份额从 62.7% 降至 61.4%。2005 年 4 月 26 日，董事会向股东大会申请减少资本。考虑到这一点，瑞士联邦在瑞士电信中的份额目前为 66.1%。

14.184　对于 IAS 32 或 IFRS 7 未要求披露，但可产生潜在普通股的金融工具及其他合同，准则鼓励公司披露其条款和条件。此类披露可帮助报表使用者

shares if disclosure is not already required by IAS 32 or IFRS 7. Such disclosure may help users to understand the extent to which these instruments are dilutive and, if so, the effect they have on the disclosed diluted EPS data. Disclosure of the terms and conditions are particularly relevant for those anti-dilutive securities that are not included in the computation of diluted EPS. [IAS 33 para 72].

Volatility of published EPS

14.185 The EPS figure, which is based on the profits available to ordinary equity holders, is an 'all inclusive' figure and may be volatile. This is because profits or losses of a period may be affected by certain unusual (exceptional) items, such as: profits or losses on the sale or termination of an operation; reorganisation costs; and profits and losses on the disposal of fixed assets. As a result, the presence or absence of such items will affect the EPS figure from one period to another. The requirement to disclose EPS figures for continuing and discontinued operations goes some way to explaining the volatility caused by disposing of operations. However, many companies prefer also to report an adjusted EPS that removes profits and losses of an unusual nature that do not relate to the entity's trading activities. An adjusted EPS is also popular with analysts.

[The next paragraph is 14.187.]

Additional earnings per share

14.187 IAS 33 recognises that there may be instances where a company would wish to disclose additional EPS figures calculated on a level of earnings other than one required by the standard. It, therefore, permits companies to disclose an additional EPS using a reported component of the statement of comprehensive income other than profit or loss for the period, profit or loss for continuing operations and profit or loss for discontinued operations attributable to ordinary equity holders. Such EPS data should, however, be calculated using the weighted average number of ordinary shares determined in accordance with the standard. This means that the weighted average number of ordinary shares used in the calculation of this additional EPS should be the same as the number used in the

了解这些工具的稀释性，及如果具有稀释性，对所披露稀释 EPS 的影响。上述条款和条件的披露与未纳入稀释 EPS 计算的具有反稀释性的证券尤为相关。[IAS 33 第 72 段]。

已公布 EPS 的波动

14.185　基于普通股股东可获得的利润计算的 EPS 是一个总括性的数字，容易发生波动。这是由于一定期间的损益可能受到某些非正常（例外）项目的影响，例如，出售或终止一项经营的损益、重组成本以及固定资产处置损益。相应地，此类项目的存在与否会影响各期的 EPS。披露持续经营和终止经营 EPS 的要求，对于解释处置某经营所引起的波动有所帮助。然而，许多公司更喜欢同时列报经调整的 EPS，其剔除了与主体经营活动无关的非正常性质的损益。经调整的 EPS 也受到分析师的欢迎。

[下一段为第 14.187 段。]

额外每股收益

14.187　IAS 33 确认公司可能希望披露按照某一收益水平（不同于准则要求的收益）计算的额外 EPS。因此，除归属于普通股股东的当期损益、持续经营损益和终止经营损益外，准则允许公司使用综合收益表的一个报表数字计算额外 EPS 并予以披露。但该 EPS 的计算应使用按照准则确定的普通股加权平均数。这意味着用于计算该额外 EPS 的普通股加权平均数应与计算准则要求的基本及稀释 EPS 所使用的数字相同。主体应说明分子，即利润表数值的确定基础，包括每股收益金额是税前还是税后的。此外，如果所使用的利润表数字并非综合收益表（或利润表，如已列报）中单独列报的项目，则应提供所使用的数字与综合收益表中单独列报的项目之间的调节。额外基本每股收益与额外稀释每股收益金额应在财务报表附注中同等地予以列报。应于附

basic and diluted EPS figures required by the standard. Entities should indicate the basis on which the numerator, that is, the income statement figure, is determined, including whether amounts per share are before or after tax. In addition, if a component of the income statement is used that is not reported as a line item in the statement of comprehensive income (or income statement if presented), a reconciliation should be provided between the component used and a line item that is reported in the statement of comprehensive income. Additional basic and diluted per share amounts should be disclosed with equal prominence and should be presented in the notes to the financial statements. The requirement that such figures should be presented in the notes means that they should not be shown on the face of the income statement as has often been the practice in the past, before the 2003 revision to IAS 33. [IAS 33 paras 73, 73A].

14.188 In November 2005 the Committee of European Securities Regulators (CESR) issued a recommendation on disclosure of alternative performance measures (APMs), which were defined as including 'operating earnings', 'cash earnings', 'earnings before one-time charges', 'EBITDA – earnings before interest, taxes, depreciation, and amortisation' and similar terms denoting adjustments to line items of income statement, balance sheet or cash flow statement. Thus, for example, they would include additional EPS figures. The recommendation included the following points:

- Under the IAS Framework, there are four qualitative characteristics that make the information provided in financial statements useful to users: understandability, relevance, reliability and comparability. CESR believes that issuers should always follow these principles for preparation and presentation of financial information including the preparation of alternative performance measures.

- Issuers should define the terminology used and the basis of calculation adopted (that is, defining the components included in an alternative performance measure). Clear disclosure is key to the understandability of any alternative performance measure and its relevance. Where relevant, investors should be made aware of the fact that alternative performance measures are not prepared in accordance with the accounting standards applied to audited financial statements. Alternative performance measures should be given meaningful names reflecting

注中列报该等数字的要求意味着该等数字不应列示于利润表正表中，而在2003年IAS 33被修订之前，在利润表正表中列示该等数字是过去常见的做法。[IAS 33第73、73A段]。

14.188 2005年11月，欧洲证券监管委员会（“CESR”）发布了一项关于披露可选业绩指标（“APMs”）的建议；APMs被定义为包括“经营收益”、“现金收益”、“扣除一次性费用之前的收益”、“EBITDA——扣除利息、税项、折旧和摊销之前的盈利”以及类似的意味着需调整利润表、资产负债表或现金流量表项目的条目。因此，例如，其应该包括额外EPS。建议包括以下几点：

- 在IAS的框架下，使财务报表中提供的信息对使用者有用的四项质量特征为：可理解性、相关性、可靠性和可比性。CESR认为，在编制与列报包括可选业绩指标在内的财务信息时，报表发布者应始终遵循这些原则。

- 报表发布者应定义使用的术语以及采用的计算基础（即，定义可选业绩指标中包括的组成部分）。清晰的披露对于任何可选业绩指标的可理解性及其相关性颇为关键。如果相关，应使投资者意识到可选业绩指标并非按照已审财务报表采用的会计准则编制这一事实。可选业绩指标应冠以能够反映其编制基础的有意义的名称，从而避免提供误导性的信息。

their basis of preparation in order to avoid misleading messages.

- Where possible, issuers should present alternative performance measures only in combination with defined measures (for example GAAP measures). Furthermore, issuers should explain the differences between both measures. This might be through a reconciliation of figures to provide investors with enough information to fully understand the company's results and financial position.
- Comparatives should be provided for any alternative performance measure presented.
- Alternative performance measures should be presented consistently over time.
- To ensure that investors are not misled, alternative performance measures should not be presented with greater prominence than defined GAAP measures. Where alternative performance measures are derived from audited financial statements and resemble defined performance measures, but do not actually have the characteristics of the defined measures (such characteristics include being audited, based on an identified reporting framework, consistent and comparable with performance measures of other enterprises), CESR recommends that defined measures should be given greater prominence than the alternative performance measures.
- Issuers may internally use alternative performance measures for measuring and controlling the company's profitability and financial position. Generally, issuers explain this as the reason for presenting alternative performance measures to investors. CESR expects issuers to give an explanation of the internal use of alternative performance measures in order to make investors understand the relevance of this information. This explanation is useful only when presented in direct relation to the alternative performance measures.

[CESR Recommendation on Alternative Performance Measures].

14.189 In practice, most of these recommendations would normally be observed under IFRS in any case. For example, a requirement for consistency of presentation is contained in IAS 1 and it would normally be logical to explain the reason for presenting additional EPS numbers. The recommendation for a

■ 如有可能，报告发布者应结合已定义的指标（例如公认会计惯例的指标）列报可选业绩指标。此外，报告发布者还应说明两种指标之间的差异。这可通过数字之间的调节来完成，从而向投资者提供足够的信息以完全了解公司的经营成果和财务状况。

■ 应对列报的任何可选业绩指标提供比较数据。

■ 不同期间可选业绩指标应列报一致。

■ 为确保投资者不被误导，可选业绩指标的列报不应较已定义的公认会计惯例指标更为显著。当可选业绩指标源于已审财务报表并与已定义的业绩指标相似，但实际上不具有这些已定义指标的特征（此类特征包括经审计、基于某确定的报告框架、与其他企业的业绩指标一致并具有可比性）时，CESR 建议已定义的指标应较可选业绩指标更为显著。

■ 报告发布者可能会内部使用可选业绩指标来衡量和控制公司的利润和财务状况。通常，报告发布者将此作为向投资者列报可选业绩指标的原因。CESR 期望报告发布者说明可选业绩指标的内部使用情况，以使投资者了解该信息的相关性。该说明只有在其被列示为与可选业绩指标直接相关时才有用。

[CESR 关于可选业绩指标的建议]。

14.189　在实务中，大部分该等建议都能在 IFRS 中找到。例如，列报一致性的要求包含在 IAS 1 中，且通常列报额外 EPS 的原因是符合逻辑的。对调节表的建议在很大程度上为 IAS 33 的要求所涵盖，即如果使用的利润组成部分未在利润表中列报，则应调节至利润表项目。

reconciliation is to a large extent covered by the IAS 33 requirement that if components of profit are used that are not reported in the income statement there should be a reconciliation to a line item in the income statement.

14. 190 Where a company has disclosed an EPS that is additional to the ones required by IAS 33, the requirements stated in paragraph 14. 187 above should be followed. An example where a company has followed the standard's requirements where an additional EPS is presented (as explained in para 14. 187) is shown in Table 14. 12 below. In this example there are no discontinued operations and basic and diluted continuing and total EPS figures are the same.

Table 14. 12 – Disclosure of additional EPS figures

Sappi Limited – Annual Report and Accounts – 2 October 2011

7. (Loss) earnings per share and headline (loss) earnings per share

Basic (loss) earnings per share (EPS)

EPS is based on the group's (loss) profit for the year divided by the weighted average number of shares in issue during the year under review.

	2011			2010			2009		
	Loss US $ million	**Shares millions**	**Loss per share US cents**	Profit US $ million	Shares millions	Earnings per share US cents	Loss US $ million	Shares millions	Loss per share US cents
Basic EPS calculation	**(232)**	**519. 9**	**(45)**	66	516. 7	13	(177)	482. 6	(37)
Share options and performance shares under Sappi Limited Share Trust	–	–	–	–	3. 9	–	–	–	–
Share options granted under the Broad-based Black Economic Empowerment transaction	–	–	–	–	0. 2	–	–	–	–
Diluted EPS calculation	(232)	519. 9	(45)	66	520. 8	13	(177)	482. 6	(37)

The diluted EPS calculations are based on Sappi Limited's daily average share price of ZAR33. 66 (2010: ZAR31. 86; 2009: ZAR30. 12) and exclude the effect of certain share options granted under the Sappi Share Incentive Scheme as well as share options granted under the Broad-based Black Economic Empowerment transaction as they would be anti-dilutive.

14.190　当公司在 IAS 33 的要求之外披露了额外 EPS 时，应遵循上文第 14.187 段所述的要求。下表 14.12 列示了某公司列报额外 EPS 时遵循准则要求（如第 14.187 段中所解释）的例子。此例中不存在终止经营，且基本 EPS、稀释 EPS 与 EPS 总额的金额相同。

表 14.12——额外 EPS 的披露

Sappi 有限公司——年度报告及报表——2011 年 10 月 2 日

7. 基本每股(亏损)/收益和主营每股(亏损)/收益

基本每股(亏损)/收益("EPS")

EPS 按照本集团当年(亏损)/利润除以审核年度已发行股份的加权平均数计算。

	2011			2010			2009		
	亏损(百万美元)	**股份(百万)**	**每股亏损(美分)**	利润(百万美元)	股份(百万)	每股收益(美分)	亏损(百万美元)	股份(百万)	每股亏损(美分)
基本 EPS 的计算	**(232)**	**519.9**	**(45)**	66	516.7	13	(177)	482.6	(37)
Sappi 有限公司 股份信托(Sappi Limited Share Trust)项下的股份期权和业绩股	–	–	–	–	3.9	–	–	–	–
广泛黑人经济权利交易(Broad-based Black Economic Empowerment transaction)中授予的股份期权	–	–	–	–	0.2	–	–	–	–
稀释 EPS 的计算	(232)	519.9	(45)	66	520.8	13	(177)	482.6	(37)

稀释 EPS 的计算是基于 Sappi 有限公司日平均股价 31.86 兰特(2010 年：31.86 兰特；2009 年：30.12 兰特)且不包括 Sappi 股份激励计划下授予的某些股份期权以及广泛黑人经济权利交易(Broad-based Black Economic Empowerment transaction)中授予的股份期权的影响，因为该等股份期权具有反稀释性。

Con.

There are 12.0 million (2010: 10.6 million; 2009: 15.6 million) share options that could potentially dilute EPS in the future that are not included in the diluted weighted average number of shares calculation as they are anti-dilutive.

Headline (loss) earnings per share[2]

Headline (loss) earnings per share is based on the group's headline (loss) earnings divided by the weighted average number of shares in issue during the year. This is a JSE Limited listings required measure.

Reconciliation between attributable (loss) earnings to ordinary shareholders and headline (loss) earnings:

	2011			2010			2009		
	Gross	**Tax**	**Net**	Gross	Tax	Net	Gross	Tax	Net
Attributable earnings (loss) to ordinary shareholders	**(221)**	**11**	**(232)**	86	20	66	(218)	(41)	(177)
Profit on sale and write-off of property, plant and equipment	**(1)**	–	**(1)**	(4)	–	(4)	(1)	–	(1)
(Impairment reversals) impairment of plant and equipment	**167**	**17**	**150**	10	–	(10)	(79)	–	(79)
Headline earnings (loss)	**(55)**	**28**	**(83)**	72	20	52	(140)	(41)	(99)
Basic weighted average number of ordinary shares in issue (millions)			**519.9**			516.7			482.6
Headline earnings (loss) per share (US cents)			**(16)**			10			(21)
Diluted weighted average number of shares (millions)			**519.9**			520.8			482.6
Diluted headline earnings (loss) per share (US cents			**(16)**			10			(21)

(1) In the 2009 financial year, Sappi conducted a renounceable rights offer of 286,886,270 new ordinary shares of ZAR1.00 each to qualifying Sappi shareholders.

(2) Headline earnings – as defined in circular 3/2009 issued by the South African Institute of Chartered Accountants, separates from earnings all separately identifiable remeasurements. It is not necessarily a measure of sustainable earnings.

14.190.1 Under the IAS 32 amendments, certain puttable financial instruments that would otherwise be presented as liabilities are presented as equity (see chapter 7 of IFRS Manual of Accounting-Financial Instruments for further details). The IAS 32 amendment does not extend to IAS 33, so these puttable financial instruments do not meet the definition of ordinary shares for EPS purposes. Entities can, however, elect to provide EPS figures for these instruments, similar to the

续表

存在 12 百万(2010 年:10.6 百万;2009 年:15.6 百万)份在未来可能对 EPS 产生潜在稀释作用的股份期权,且其因具有反稀释性而未被包括在稀释加权平均股数的计算中。

主营每股(亏损)收益(2)

主营每股(亏损)收益按照本集团的主营(亏损)收益除以当年已发行股份的加权平均数得出。这是在约翰内斯堡证券交易所有限公司上市所需的计量指标。

归属于普通股股东的(亏损)/收益与主营(亏损)/收益之间的调节表:

	2011			2010			2009		
	总额	**税项**	**净额**	总额	税项	净额	总额	税项	净额
归属于普通股股东的收益(亏损)	**(221)**	**11**	**(232)**	86	20	66	(218)	(41)	(177)
出售和报废不动产、工厂和设备的利润	**(1)**	**–**	**(1)**	(4)	–	(4)	(1)	–	(1)
(转回)计提工厂和设备的减值	**167**	**17**	**150**	10	–	(10)	(79)	–	(79)
主营收益(亏损)	**(55)**	**28**	**(83)**	72	20	52	(140)	(41)	(99)
已发行普通股的基本加权平均数(百万)			**519.9**			516.7			482.6
主营每股收益(亏损)(美分)			**(16)**			10			(21)
稀释加权平均股数(百万)			**519.9**			520.8			482.6
稀释主营每股收益(亏损)(美分)			**(16)**			10			(21)

(1)2009 年财务年度,Sappi 实施可弃权配股,以每股1 兰特向符合条件的Sappi 股东发行286, 886, 270 新普通股。

(2)主营收益——由南非特许会计师协会所发布的2009 年3 号通知所定义,其将所有可单独识别的计量与收益分开。其未必是可持续收益的计量指标。

14.190.1 根据对 IAS 32 的修改,某些本列报为负债的可售出金融工具被列报为权益(进一步的详情,参见《国际财务报告准则实务指引——金融工具系列》第七章)。IAS 32 的修改并未延伸至 IAS 33,因而这些可售出金融工具就 EPS 而言并不符合普通股的定义。然而,类似于第 14.57 段起段落中所述的其他参与性工具的披露,主体可选择就这些工具提供 EPS。

disclosures for other participating instruments as explained in 14. 57 onwards.

14. 191 Directors should carefully consider what profit measure to choose when calculating additional EPS figures and what information they would wish those figures to convey. This is because whatever profit measure is chosen it must be used consistently (see para 14. 189 above). It is not possible to choose a profit measure to present a particular aspect of a company's performance in one year, because performance at that level is good, and then to ignore that measure in the following year when performance at that level is not so good.

[The next paragraph is 14. 200.]

Financial statistics in the historical summary

14. 200 Entities often publish a historical summary, usually covering at least five years. IAS 33 does not deal specifically with adjustments to historical summaries, but the following guidance is relevant in such situations. In order to present a fair comparison of EPS figures published in such a summary, the basic EPS figure will need to be adjusted for subsequent changes in capital as set out below:

- Where a capitalisation issue or share split has taken place during a financial year, all previously published EPS figures should be adjusted by the bonus factor as explained in paragraph 14. 80 above.
- Where a rights issue at less than full market has taken place during a financial year, all previously published EPS figures should be adjusted by the reciprocal of the bonus element inherent in the rights issue as explained from paragraph 14. 85 above.

Where there is more than one capitalisation or rights issue during the year, both these factors will operate cumulatively. The cumulative effect of all the above events should be taken into account. The resultant figures should be described as restated EPS and should be set out separately from the other financial data that is not so adjusted.

14. 201 Where there has been a bonus or rights issue in the period covered by the summary, the ordinary dividend actually paid in those periods should be set out in

14.191　董事们应仔细考虑计算额外 EPS 时选择何种利润计量指标及其希望通过这些数据传递何种信息。这是因为无论选择何种利润计量指标，均须一致地运用（参见上文第 14.189 段）。不能由于某年公司在某特定方面的业绩较好，在该年选择某利润计量指标列报该特定方面的业绩，而在下一年该层面的业绩不再良好时不再使用该指标。

[下一段为第 14.200 段。]

历史汇总数据中的财务统计数据

14.200　主体经常会公布历史汇总数据，通常涵盖至少 5 个年度。IAS 33 并未特别涉及对历史汇总数据所作的调整，但下列指引与此类情形相关。为在此类汇总中反映对所公布 EPS 的公允比较，基本 EPS 需就资本的期后变化作出如下调整：

- 若某财务年度内发生了资本化发行或拆股，则如上文第 14.80 段中所述，以前公布的所有 EPS 均应就分红要素作出调整。
- 若某财务年度内按照低于市场价格的股价配股，则如上文第 14.85 段中所述，以前公布的所有 EPS 均应根据配股所固有的分红要素的倒数进行调整。

若当年发生多次资本化发行或配股，则这些因素会累积作用。所有上述事项的累积影响均应被考虑。得出的数字应被描述为经重述的 EPS，并应与未作此类调整的其他财务数据分开列报。

14.201　如果汇总数据涵盖的期间内派送红股或配股，则该等期间实际支付的普通股股利应以每股若干元的形式列报，并针对重述 EPS 时使用的相同因

the form of C per share and similarly adjusted by the same factors used in restating EPS. This adjustment is necessary to ensure that the ordinary dividends and EPS data are comparable. The adjusted dividend per share should be described as restated. In practice, the adjusted EPS and the adjusted dividend per share are normally presented next to each other.

14. 202 Sometimes companies also disclose a dividend cover, which is the number of times a dividend is covered by current earnings. Some companies even disclose price/earnings ratios, high and low share prices or market capitalisation.

14. 203 An example of disclosure in a historical summary is Table 14. 13. This example includes adjustment of earlier years for a bonus issue (see para 14. 200 above).

14. 204 IFRS 1 requires at least one year of comparative information prepared under IFRS in an entity's first IFRS financial statements. [IFRS 1 para 36]. The IFRS does not require earlier years in a historical summary (that is, the years before the current and previous year) to comply with IFRS. However, those earlier years, if not presented in compliance with IFRS, must be clearly labelled as not being prepared under IFRS. In addition the nature of the main adjustments that would make those earlier years comply with IFRS should be disclosed. An entity need not quantify those adjustments. [IFRS 1 para 37]. IFRS 1's requirements are considered in detail in chapter 3.

14. 205 In Table 14. 13, Huhtamaki Oyj, presents the latest two years of the historical summary in accordance with IFRS and earlier years in accordance with Finnish GAAP, but gives the 2002 figures for the year of transition to IFRS under both Finnish GAAP and IFRS. Elsewhere in the financial statements it includes a detailed description of the differences between accounting policies applied under Finnish GAAP and IFRS (not reproduced in Table 14. 13).

Table 14. 13 – EPS in historical summaries

Huhtamaki Oyj – Annual Report and Accounts – 31 December 2003

Per share data

Comparison figures (1999 – 2001) adjusted for the 3:1 bonus issue in August 2002

素作出类似调整。该调整对于确保该普通股股利和 EPS 的可比性是必要的。经调整的每股股利应被描述为经重述。实务中，经调整的 EPS 和经调整的每股股利通常彼此相邻列报。

14.202　公司有时也会披露股利保障倍数，即当前收益涵盖股利的倍数。有些公司甚至会披露市盈率、高低股价或资本市值。

14.203　表 14.13 是一个历史数据汇总披露的示例。该例包括因派发红股而对早些年度作出的调整（参见上文第 14.200 段）。

14.204　IFRS 1 要求在主体的首份 IFRS 财务报表中应披露至少一个年度的根据 IFRS 编制的比较信息。[IFRS 1 第 36 段]。IFRS 不要求历史数据汇总中早些年度（即当年和上年之前的年度）的数据遵循 IFRS。但是，如果该等早些年度的数据未遵循 IFRS 列报，则必须清楚标明并非根据 IFRS 编制。此外，使该等早些年度遵循 IFRS 而需要作出的主要调整的性质应被予以披露。主体无需量化这些调整。[IFRS 1 第 37 段]。IFRS 1 的要求在第三章中予以详细论述。

14.205　表 14.13 中，Huhtamaki Oyj 公司按照 IFRS 列报了历史数据汇总中最近两年的数据，按芬兰 GAAP 列报了早些年度的数据，但对于转换至 IFRS 的年度 2002 年，同时列示了芬兰 GAAP 和 IFRS 的数据。在财务报表中的其他地方，其详细介绍了芬兰 GAAP 下和 IFRS 下应用的会计政策之间的差异（未在表 14.13 中复制）。

表 14.13——历史数据汇总中的 EPS

Huhtamaki Oyj 公司——年度报告及报表——2003 年 12 月 31 日

每股数据

针对 2002 年 8 月按 3:1 派发红股进行调整后的比较数据（1999 年—2001 年）

Con.

		FAS				IFRS	
		1999	2000	2001	2002	2002	2003
Earnings per share	EUR	0.60	0.65	0.74	0.88	0.86	0.38
Earnings per share (diluted)						0.86	0.38
Dividend, nominal	EUR	0.26	0.28	0.31	0.38	0.38	0.38[1]
Dividend/earnings per share	%	43.3	43.1	41.9	43.2	44.2	100.0[1]
Dividend yield	%	3.1	3.9	3.5	4.0	4.0	4.1[1]
Shareholders' equity per share	EUR	7.61	8.20	8.64	8.79	8.26	7.85
Share price at December 31	EUR	8.40	7.10	8.88	9.55	9.55	9.35
Average number of shares adjusted for share issue		111,856,128	125,903,852	117,117,696	100,769,970	100,769,970	96,292,220
Number of shares adjusted for share issue at year end		125,903,852	125,903,852	101,215,792	97,547,792	97,547,792	96,161,703
P/E ratio		14.0	10.9	12.0	10.9	11.1	24.6
Market capitalization at December 31 EUR million		1,057.6	893.9	898.3	931.6	931.6	899.1

[1] 2003: Board's proposal.

续表

		芬兰会计准则 1999 年	（"FAS"） 2000 年	2001 年	2002 年	IFRS 2002 年	2003 年
EPS	欧元	0. 60	0. 65	0. 74	0. 88	0. 86	0. 38
EPS（稀释的）						0. 86	0. 38
名义股利	欧元	0. 26	0. 28	0. 31	0. 38	0. 38	0. 38[1]
股利支付率	%	43. 3	43. 1	41. 9	43. 2	44. 2	100. 0[1]
股利收益率	%	3. 1	3. 9	3. 5	4. 0	4. 0	4. 1[1]
每股股东权益	欧元	7. 61	8. 20	8. 64	8. 79	8. 26	7. 85
12 月 31 日股价	欧元	8. 40	7. 10	8. 88	9. 55	9. 55	9. 35
就股份发行进行调整后的平均股数		111, 856, 128	125, 903, 852	117, 117, 696	100, 769, 970	100, 769, 970	96, 292, 220
就股份发行进行调整后的年末股数		125, 903, 852	125, 903, 852	101, 215, 792	97, 547, 792	97, 547, 792	96, 161, 703
市盈率		14. 0	10. 9	12. 0	10. 9	11. 1	24. 6
12 月 31 日资本市值（百万欧元）		1, 057. 6	893. 9	898. 3	931. 6	931. 6	899. 1

[1] 2003 年：董事会提议。

PwC Assurance Service Contacts
联系普华永道审计业务部

北京 Beijing
梁伟坚 Thomas Leung
电话 Tel：+86（10）6533 2838
电子邮件 Email：thomas. w. leung@ cn. pwc. com

上海 Shanghai
李丹 Daniel Li
电话 Tel：+86（21）2323 3388
电子邮件 Email：daniel. li@ cn. pwc. com

重庆 Chongqing
李松波 Bobby Lee
电话 Tel：+86（23）6393 7388
电子邮件 Email：bobby. lee@ cn. pwc. com

深圳 Shenzhen
张展豪 Albert Cheung
电话 Tel：+86（755）8261 8833
电子邮件 Email：albert. cheung@ cn. pwc. com

大连 Dalian
关兆文 Dorman Kwan
电话 Tel：+86（411）8379 1666
电子邮件 Email：dorman. kwan@ cn. pwc. com

苏州 Suzhou
汪超 Arthur Wang
电话 Tel：+86（512）6273 1998
电子邮件 Email：arthur. wang@ cn. pwc. com

广州 Guangzhou
何国辉 Timothy Ho
电话 Tel：+86（20）3819 2888
电子邮件 Email：timothy. kf. ho@ hk. pwc. com

天津 Tianjin
郑广安 Kwong On Cheng
电话 Tel：+86（22）2318 3003
电子邮件 Email：kwong. on. cheng@ cn. pwc. com

青岛 Qingdao
张国俊 Kevin Zhang
电话 Tel：+86（532）8089 1818
电子邮件 Email：kevin. zhang@ cn. pwc. com

西安 Xi'an
叶骏 Joe Ye
电话 Tel：+86（29）8720 3998
电子邮件 Email：joe. ye@ cn. pwc. com

PwC Accounting Consulting Services Contacts
联系普华永道会计专业咨询服务

金以文 Yvonne Kam
电话 Tel：+86（21）2323 3267
电子邮件 Email：yvonne. kam@ cn. pwc. com

陈保郎 Baolang Chen
电话 Tel：+86（21）2323 2555
电子邮件 Email：baolang. chen@ cn. pwc. com

方毅贤 Ian Farrar
电话 Tel：+852 2289 2313
电子邮件 Email：ian. p. farrar@ hk. pwc. com

陈燕华 Tracy Chen
电话 Tel：+86（21）2323 3070
电子邮件 Email：tracy. yh. chen@ cn. pwc. com

许心莹 Samying Huie
电话 Tel：+86（10）6533 2965
电子邮件 Email：samying. s. huie@ cn. pwc. com

苏虹 Shelley So
电话 Tel：+852 2289 2955
电子邮件 Email：shelley. so@ hk. pwc. com

沈洁 Jie Shen
电话 Tel：+86（21）2323 3659
电子邮件 Email：jie. shen@ cn. pwc. com

白鸿安 Hendry Pai
电话 Tel：+86（10）6533 7760
电子邮件 Email：hendry. pai@ cn. pwc. com

陈嘉怡 Clarry Chan
电话 Tel：+852 2289 2169
电子邮件 Email：clarry. chan@ hk. pwc. com

吴慧莹 Monica Ng
电话 Tel：+852 2289 1218
电子邮件 Email：monica. wy. ng@ hk. pwc. com

阮慧瑶 Elza Yuen
电话 Tel：+852 2289 2314
电子邮件 Email：elza. yuen@ hk. pwc. com

梁少宝 Dorothy Leung
电话 Tel：+852 2289 2151
电子邮件 Email：dorothy. sp. leung@ hk. pwc. com

戴奈尔 Nigel Dealy
电话 Tel：+852 2289 1221
电子邮件 Email：nigel. dd. dealy@ hk. pwc. com

孙宇辉 Yuhui Sun
电话 Tel：+86（10）6533 7331
电子邮件 Email：yuhui. sun@ cn. pwc. com

For further help，please contact：
如需更多帮助，请联系：

北京 Beijing
中国北京市
朝阳区东三环中路 7 号
北京财富中心写字楼 A 座 26 楼
邮政编码 100020
26/F Office Tower A
Beijing Fortune Plaza
7 Dongsanhuan Zhong Road
Chaoyang District
Beijing 100020，PRC
电话 Tel：+86（10）6533 8888
传真 Fax：+86（10）6533 8800

大连 Dalian
中国大连市西岗区中山路 147 号
森茂大厦 8 楼
邮政编码 116011
8/F Senmao Building
147 Zhongshan Road
Xigang District
Dalian 116011，PRC
电话 Tel：+86（411）8379 1888
传真 Fax：+86（411）8379 1800

重庆 Chongqing
中国重庆市渝中区邹容路 68 号
大都会商厦 19 楼 1905 室
邮政编码 400010
Room 1905
19/F Metropolitan Tower
68 Zou Rong Road
Chongqing 400010，PRC
电话 Tel：+86（23）6393 7888
传真 Fax：+86（23）6393 7200

广州 Guangzhou
中国广州市天河区珠江新城
珠江西路 10 号
普华永道中心 18 楼
邮政编码 510623
18/F PwC Center
10 Zhujiang Xi Road
Pearl River New City
Tianhe District
Guangzhou 510623，PRC
电话 Tel：+86（20）3819 2000
传真 Fax：+86（20）3819 2100

杭州 Hangzhou
中国杭州市下城区环城北路 208 号
坤和中心 3205 室
邮政编码 310006
Room 3205, Canhigh Center
208 Huancheng Road North
Xiacheng District
Hangzhou 310006, PRC
电话：+86（571）2807 6388
传真：+86（571）2807 6300

宁波 Ningbo
中国宁波市江东区民安东路 268 号
宁波国际金融服务中心 E 座 1203 室
邮政编码 315040
Room 1203, Tower E
Ningbo International Financial Center
268 Min An Road East
Jiangdong District
Ningbo 315040, PRC
电话 Tel：+86（574）8187 1788
传真 Fax：+86（574）8187 1700

香港 Hong Kong
中国香港中环太子大厦 22 楼
22/F Prince's Building
Central
Hong Kong, PRC
电话 Tel：+852 2289 8888
传真 Fax：+852 2810 9888

青岛 Qingdao
中国青岛市市南区延安三路 234 号
海航万邦中心 1 号楼 37 楼
邮政编码 266071
37/F Tower One, HNA IMC Center
234 Yanan Third Road, Shinan District
Qingdao 266071, PRC
电话 Tel：+86（532）8089 1888
传真 Fax：+86（532）8089 1800

澳门 Macau
中国澳门苏亚利斯博士大马路 323 号
中国银行大厦 29 楼
29/F Bank of China Building
323 Avenida Doutor Mario Soares
Macau, PRC
电话 Tel：+853 8799 5111
传真 Fax：+853 8799 5222

上海 Shanghai
中国上海市黄浦区湖滨路 202 号
企业天地 2 号楼
普华永道中心 11 楼
邮政编码 200021
11/F PwC Center
2 Corporate Avenue
202 Hu Bin Road
Huangpu District
Shanghai 200021, PRC
电话 Tel：+86（21）2323 8888
传真 Fax：+86（21）2323 8800

南京 Nanjing
中国南京市鼓楼区中央路 201 号
南京国际广场南塔 12A 层 01 室
邮政编码 210009
Room 12A01, South Tower
Nanjing International Center
201 Zhongyang Road
Gulou District
Nanjing 210009, PRC
电话 Tel：+86（25）6608 6288
传真 Fax：+86（25）6608 6210

深圳 Shenzhen
中国深圳市罗湖区深南东路 5016 号
京基 100 – A 座 34 楼
邮政编码 518001
34/F Tower A, Kingkey 100
5016 Shennan East Road
Luohu District
Shenzhen 518001, PRC
电话 Tel：+86（755）8261 8888
传真 Fax：+86（755）8261 8800

新加坡 Singapore
新加坡 048424 邮区
PWC 大厦
克罗士街 8 号 17 楼
8 Cross Street # 17 – 00
PWC Building
Singapore 048424
电话 Tel：+65 6236 3388
传真 Fax：+65 6236 3300

天津 Tianjin
中国天津市和平区
南京路 189 号
津汇广场 2 座 36 楼
邮政编码 300051
36/F The Exchange Tower Two
189 Nanjing Road
Heping District
Tianjin 300051, PRC
电话 Tel：+86（22）2318 3333
传真 Fax：+86（22）2318 3300

苏州 Suzhou
中国苏州市苏州工业园区
旺墩路 188 号建屋大厦 1501 室
邮政编码 215028
Room 1501, Genway Tower
188 Wang Dun Road
Suzhou Industrial Park
Suzhou 215028, PRC
电话 Tel：+86（512）6273 1888
传真 Fax：+86（512）6273 1800

厦门 Xiamen
中国厦门市思明区鹭江道 8 号
国际银行大厦 11 楼 B 室
邮政编码 361001
Unit B, 11/F
International Plaza
8 Lujiang Road
Siming District
Xiamen 361001, PRC
电话 Tel：+86（592）210 7888
传真 Fax：+86（592）210 8800

台湾 Taiwan
中国台北市信义区 110
基隆路一段 333 号 27 楼
International Trade Building
27F, 333 Keelung Road, Section 1
Taipei 110, Taiwan
电话 Tel：+886 2 2729 6666
传真 Fax：+886 2 2757 6371

西安 Xi'an
中国西安市南关正街 88 号
长安国际中心 D 座 7 楼
邮政编码 710068
7/F, D Block, Chang'an Metropolis Center
88 Nanguan Street
Xi'an 710068, PRC
电话 Tel：+86（29）8469 2688
传真 Fax：+86（29）8469 2600

如欲了解更多资讯，敬请登陆公司网站：
For more information, please visit our websites at：
pwccn. com
pwchk. com

图书在版编目（CIP）数据

国际财务报告准则实务指引．第14章，每股收益/沈洁等译．—北京：中国财政经济出版社，2013.6

（普华永道国际财务报告准则实务指引系列）

ISBN 978-7-5095-4448-8

Ⅰ.①国… Ⅱ.①沈… Ⅲ.①会计准则-世界-汉、英 Ⅳ.①F233.1

中国版本图书馆CIP数据核字（2013）第078632号

责任编辑：蔡丽兰　　　　责任校对：胡永立

中国财政经济出版社出版

URL：http：//www.cfeph.cn

E-mail：cfeph@cfeph.cn

社址：北京市海淀区阜成路甲28号　邮政编码：100142

营销中心电话：88190406　北京财经书店电话：64033436　84041336

北京富生印刷厂印刷　　各地新华书店经销

787×1092毫米　16开　15.75印张　264 000字

2013年12月第1版　2013年12月北京第1次印刷

定价：40.00元

ISBN 978-7-5095-4448-8/F·3602

（图书出现印装问题，本社负责调换）

本社质量投诉电话：010-88190744

反盗版举报热线：88190492　88190446